Antichrist Chronicles

Unveiling the Rise of Earth's Final Führer

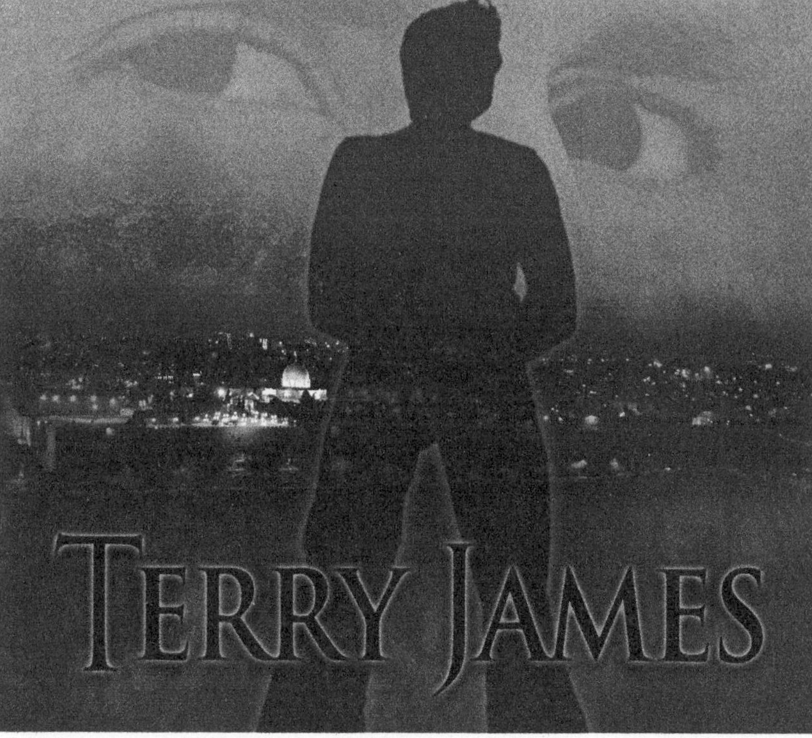

Defender
Crane

ANTICHRIST CHRONICLES

Unveiling the Rise of Earth's Final Führer

Defender

Crane, MO 65633

Printed in the United States of America.

ISBN: 978-0-9904974-1-7

A CIP catalog record of this book is available from the Library of Congress.

Cover illustration and design by Daniel Wright: www.createdwright.com.

All Scripture quotations are from the Holy Bible, Authorized King James Version.

Dedication

To my longtime friend Gail Blackburn, whose shared love for our Lord and Bible prophecy over the years has meant so much to me.

Acknowledgments

Thanks again to my Margaret, as always, for her love, patience, and understanding in matters involving the writing process.

Love and thanks to Angie Peters, the best editor in the world, for always making things just right when I more often than not hand them to her in less than presentable condition.

To Dana, much love and thanks for never failing to come up with exactly the needed research, often in almost miraculous ways and with astounding timeliness.

Thanks to Tom Horn and the terrific professionals within his publishing household. His expertise, acumen, and great friendship are much appreciated.

To Todd, my close associate and even closer friend at www.raptureready.com—the Net's number-one Bible prophecy site, which he founded in 1987—my love and appreciation.

Many thanks to my good friend, Gary Stearman, host of *Prophecy in the News*, for his writing of the foreword to *Antichrist Chronicles*—and for his many years of bringing us all deeper understanding of God's prophetic Word.

To the Lord Jesus Christ, in whose mighty hand I'm eternally held—deepest love and thankfulness.

My profound thanks and appreciation to you, the reader, without whom the writing of books would be pointless!

Foreword
By Gary Stearman

Students of Bible prophecy have followed Terry James' writing for many years. He has established himself as a keen commentator on the times in which we live. His thoughts and observations are formed around a deep faith in the Lord Jesus Christ and a literal, historical and grammatical belief in the Word of God. In simple terms, he believes that it means what it says. And on that basis, he has traced the rise and fall of prophetic events for many years.

Often, someone will begin a sentence with, "Do you remember…?" Then they'll recount an event that hasn't crossed your mind for a long, long time. With interest and delight, you'll recall a long-buried memory that adds perspective to your mental landscape. That's the treasure you'll find in Terry's recollections.

Many of us whose Bible study goes back for decades have watched trends rise to the level of fads and have heard panicked warnings that the end is upon us. We've been repeatedly warned that we are about to go through the Great Tribulation. Sometimes, apparent "facts" push us to jump the gun. Still, patient waiting is the key to the effective study of prophecy.

We remember the time when a thought caught fire as Christians recalled Israel's wars, especially the Six-Day War of 1967, with its brief retaking of the Temple Mount, and the Yom Kippur War of 1973. An explosive awareness grew, with many saying that Israel's fortieth year would mark the catching-away of the church. And then, Israel's modern march through the wilderness would finally bring Israel's people into full possession of the land. With the departure of the body of Christ in the Rapture, Israel's leaders would surge forth to victory in the Kingdom Age. The excitement was palpable.

Then came the year 1988, forty years after Israeli statehood. There arose factions whose belief reached certainty that the Rapture was only days away. Disappointment followed as the year came and went uneventfully...without a Rapture. In the natural course of things, there followed a long period of eschatological introspection.

After that, Israel became increasingly involved with the Arabic tribal uprisings of the Intifada. As the world forged onward, toward the turn of the millennium, the siege of the Promised Land grew more and more severe. Prophecy watchers noted each assault against Israel with renewed interest, and increasing dejection.

The twentieth century faded in a combination of gloom and a note of panic as the year 2000 approached. We all remember the infamous specter of Y2K. It arose to haunt the world with the images of crashing airliners, metropolitan darkness, and ice-cold paralysis.

Many saw the turn of the millennium as the harbinger of calamity, as computers failed, electrical grids collapsed, and economic systems crashed. But then...nothing happened. The world sailed peacefully into the twenty-first century before the big storms broke out.

The big one—9/11—in 2001 began the long descent into universal "security." The Transportation Security Administration (TSA) was built out of the ashes of the World Trade Center. Security is control, and control is a function of intelligence—or why not just use the word that's on all lips these days: "surveillance."

The past decade has been utterly amazing. When the angel said to Daniel, "But thou, O Daniel, shut up the words, and seal the book, even to the time of the end: many shall run to and fro, and knowledge shall be increased" (Daniel 12:4), he was making a statement that we have hardly begun to understand. Events are spinning out of control at computer speed, measured in terabytes and microseconds. Knowledge isn't just increasing, it is exploding!

Return in your mind to, let's say, the year 1983 in Israel. That year, both Ariel Sharon and Menachem Begin resigned from power. Two hundred and sixteen marines were killed in the infamous Beirut bombing, and five thousand PLO prisoners were traded for six Israeli soldiers. Hostility exploded. It's still exploding.

Around that time, back in the United States, basic cable television was beginning to be up and running, bringing dozens of channels instead of the three or four local ones into our homes. Giant, room-filling computers were just beginning to be replaced by personal computers (PCs, as they were called) and Macs, those friendly little boxes with their familiar Apple logos.

Back in those days, if you had told a friend that by the year 2014, virtually everyone would be carrying a tiny computer, combined with both still and movie cameras, a telephone, and World Wide Web connection with a global positioning system, electronic mail, and a texting device—well, quite simply, he wouldn't have believed you. In fact, he might have been shocked to discover that people would be willing to pay large sums of money to do this.

Of course, we call them c-phones or cell phones. In our pockets, they provide continuous connection, constant tracking, and universal surveillance by the "friendly" governments of the world.

Let's say that the friend with whom you shared this futuristic information was a Bible-believing Christian. Thinking about this situation for a moment, he would probably have felt a chill at the realization that it would be impossible to go anywhere without being electronically tracked and photographed. Global positioning...GPS?! What was then a device in the hands of the military would soon fall into the grasp of every teenager in the world.

If you went on to mention escalating spiritual apostasy, coupled with things like DNA identification, genetic modification, and the rise of artificial intelligence, he would probably say, "I don't want to live there."

This is our world, in a period of rising Christian persecution. The prophetic implications are staggering. All these years later, the geopolitics of the Middle East are beginning to drive the armies of the world. Russia,

Iran, Turkey, Syria, Jordan, Saudi Arabia, Egypt, Ethiopia, and Libya are precisely juxtaposed around national Israel, just as described in the Bible thousands of years ago. They are militant, most of them unified in their intention to obliterate the Jews.

Students of the Bible are amazed these days, mostly because we're still here. Christians who know their Bible prophecy are well aware that Jesus linked His return with the days of His resurrection. It's been about two thousand years—two days. Now, we're entering the third day, the millennium in which He said He would return.

A short while ago, there was great excitement about the coming of the year 2012. It would be hard to count the number of books that spoke of the Mayan long-count calendar prophecies. Who can forget the dire predictions? Many said that its 5,125-year calculation would bring humanity to the auspicious (or deadly) date of December 21, 2012. Great change and even catastrophe were prophesied.

To name just one of many such speculations, a major motion picture, appropriately entitled *2012,* foretold violent changes in solar radiation, with x-ray flares and electrical disruptions that wreak havoc upon earth. Somehow, the Mayans had known that earth's orbit would align with our galactic center at that time, making the prophecy virtually universal in scope. Or so we were told.

But 2012 came and went. Nothing changed. Or did it? Some said that the famous "Prophecy of the Popes" was fulfilled with the resignation of Pope Benedict and election of Pope Francis I on March 13, 2013.

There was also the re-election of Barak Obama in November, 2012. The U.S. economy shuddered once again, echoing the convulsions already taking place in Europe. In the months that have followed, one could sense a great, worldwide shaking. Socioeconomic, political, and military movements raged around the world.

In the same period, Iran effectively became a nuclear power, with only limited resistance from the declining Western governments. Predictably, the Iranians steadfastly pledged to annihilate both Israel and the United States. But as they progressively armed Israel's enemies and forged closer alliances with Russia, no one in power seemed to be listening to them.

The gigantic military stabilization that once kept the forces of Islam in check is slowly pulling away. Israel's friends are fewer and weaker, allowing the siege of Jerusalem, just as described in Zechariah's prophecy. Meanwhile, America has announced its intention to drastically reduce its military forces.

And so it goes. Christians now speak to each other in expectant terms, saying, "These are the days. How can we make sense of them?"

With that question, we find a source of perspective. Terry looks at all these things through the lens of Christian hope and comfort.

Beginning in the opening days of 2012, he helps us remember what we were all thinking, as we return to the ideas that would blossom into reality. Looking back, our lives were radically changed.

As we follow his day-by-day observations, things past leap to life once again, bringing new insights and drawing us to deeper conclusions. He is a great commentator whose apt remarks bring us back to faith with a solidly Christian point of view.

The things we thought we had forgotten arise in ways that help us make some sense of the dramatic landscape...the common sense that we all thought had completely disappeared.

Now, spend some time with a Christian friend. Relax, reminisce, enjoy, and renew your faith.

Gary Stearman
March 1, 2014
Oklahoma City, Oklahoma

JANUARY 2012

January 2, 2012
2012: The Dreaded Year Has Arrived

Fear of the year 2012 has been simmering for a couple of years at least. World issues and events have caused those fears to boil and bubble to the top of the cauldron, but then the ominous broth would settle to simmer again for a while, until the next eruption of conjecture about what 2012 means. I wrote the following more than a year ago about this impending number that has now burst to the top of our calendars.

2012: The End?

Ominous sounds of the approaching year 2012 rumble in the ears of this generation. The thunder comes from constant media-mantra meanderings about the end of days as foretold by the Mayan calendar hundreds of years ago. Is this generation looking the end of the world squarely in the face on December 21, 2012?

Suddenly, it is as if those of the news and entertainment world have forgotten that prophecy is, at best, fodder for fun-poking, and now have a date that they believe is genuinely filled with foreboding. They often snicker at Bible prophecy and those who bring it into public discourse; however, they aren't snickering at the foretellings left us by the long-since extinct Mayans. Something of catastrophic nature, they are fearfully conjecturing, might be about to change life forever on planet earth.

But, with news and entertainment producer types, you never know. Could it be they are seeing in the 2012 "prophecies" a chance for numerous remunerative documentaries and films

> that appeal to the always-lucrative fright flicks, thus the genuine tone of reverential fear for the Mayan holy men and their prognostications?

Since the time of publication of that article, most all have become aware of the tremendous amount of ink, cyberspace, and documentary film that has been devoted to the Mayans and all that is wrapped up in the fears that they were indeed onto something with regard to the end of the world as we know it. December 21, 2012, will—the direst of predictions continue to project—bring some calamitous things upon this old planet.

In reviewing Dr. Mark Hitchcock's book, *2012: The Bible and the End of the World*, I wrote the following, which lightly encapsulates the 2012 Mayan matter:

> One senses the fear building: "The end is near!" A mental image of the little bearded man in a long robe holding a placard affixed to a wooden stake with those words in broad red letters comes to mind. Only, it isn't a cartoon we are facing, but the end of the world as we've known it. Planet earth is about to—because of powerful astral alignment dynamics—most likely suffer instant pole reversals, thus horrific tectonic plate shifts. This will cause the catastrophic end for most, perhaps all, human life. This is the fear of proponents of ancient Mayan calendar predictions.
>
> The year 2012 is but some twenty-seven months away, and the hype is on. December 21 at 11:11 p.m. Universal Time of that year will...well, we don't really know. But, it will—according to pundits from scientists, astrologers, and religionists to new agers, fiction writers, and documentarians—be very bad indeed for inhabitants of the earth.
>
> The drumbeat for the astonishing prophetic capabilities of those ancient shamans hasn't let up since that time twenty-seven months ago. The hyperbolists laud the Mayan holy men as if they were not the savages they were, but as if they were from the gods

that were, of course, the ancient astronauts, as those who hold to such sophist-history put forth for our consumption.

I presented in my article what one website praising the Mayans had to say:

> The Mayan civilization was extremely advanced in mathematics, engineering, and astronomy. They also had an incredible understanding of time and space. Various calendars were in use to track time in linear progressions within cycles. The "Great Cycle" of the "Long Count" calendar equates to 5,125.36 years. The current Great Cycle is due to be completed on the winter solstice of 2012, December 21. So, it has been interpreted that on this day, the Great Cycle ends, time ends, so the earth must end as well.[1]

As I wrote in that article all of those months previous, the Mayans completely disappeared as a civilization hundreds of years ago. What, really, did they know? They apparently didn't foresee the end of their own people well before the December 21, 2012, date with destiny their shamans claimed would be calamitous to themselves as well as to the rest of the world.

Mayan predictions aside, there are harbingers of apocalyptic things on the horizon of human history. "Something wicked this way comes," to quote from Shakespeare's *Macbeth*. Todd Strandberg and I are looking to install a regular feature for this portentous year of 2012, counting down to the doomsday prediction by the Mayans. But, remember, we are Rapture Ready, so it will be a feature unlike any other in analyzing that dreaded, approaching date, December 21, 2012. Stay tuned...

January 9, 2012
Gog's "Evil Thought"

One can sense the dark, coalescing thoughts that are going on within the 2012 presidential election cabals. No, I'm not talking about the

U.S. presidential-election, smoke-filled, back-room wheeling and dealing. Rather, I refer to the intrigues no doubt presently taking place in the political chambers of Moscow. A very interesting Russian politician we all know about sits snugly ensconced within the seat of power at the Kremlin, despite the façade he and his fellows present that he is candidate for the Russian presidency. Mysterious doings revolve around this self-promoting, sixty-year-old former KGB officer with his ongoing macho performances, both actual and of questionable credibility.

We remember his photo ops on the shores of the Black Sea and other places where he proudly displayed his six-pack abs. Then, there is the story where he singlehandedly dove into the depths of some body of water, then came up with hands full of treasure—treasure that no one, not even professional marine salvage crews, had been previously able to find.

Vladimir Putin, although officially in a secondary position within the Russian governmental system because of constitutional restrictions regarding succession, nonetheless moves ahead, paying scant attention to the fact that he has not yet been elected once again to the nation's top post. There is little observable opposition to his power brokering and manipulations, either officially or unofficially. It is as if his is a predestined leadership imperative for his most prophetically significant nation.

One billionaire Russian accuses Putin of trying to reprise a system at least somewhat similar to the Soviet Union, and is opposing Putin's campaign for the Russian presidency, but isn't making much headway. One wonders just how long such opposition will be allowed, when considering the recent track records of those who opposed ol' Vlad. Many of these are in gulag—or are no longer among the living.

A couple of recent news items piqued my interest regarding this man who so dominates the headlines coming out of the country that many of us who observe prophetic movement believe will be the nation that will lead the Gog-Magog attack of Ezekiel 38–39. Putin's thinking about Russia's future differs from the Soviet model in some significant ways, according to one of those articles. At the same time, I find Putin's emphasis on economy particularly fascinating. His thought is not necessarily on taking over nations surrounding Russia, but in sucking those nations into an inescapable fiscal orbit. The news story explains:

> Vladimir Putin has a vision for a Soviet Union—like he hopes will become a new Moscow-led global powerhouse. But, his planned Eurasian Union won't be grounded in ideology: This time it's about trade. The concept of regional economic integration may be losing some of its allure in Europe, where a debt crisis is threatening the existence of the eurozone. But some countries across the former Soviet Union, still struggling economically 20 years after becoming independent, are embracing Putin's grand ambition....
>
> In anticipation of a new six-year term as president, Putin has made forming a Eurasian Union by 2015 a foreign policy priority. He is promoting the union as necessary for Russia and its neighbors to compete in the modern global economy. His broader goal is to restore some of Moscow's economic and political clout across former Soviet space and thus strengthen Russia's position in the world.[2]

Mr. Putin's thought, obviously, is to convince those he hopes to lure within his orbit that great economic gain is a possibility in such a coalition as he will put together once he is president of Russia. This kind of thinking, of course, might just be the nucleus around which could be built a much more ambitious and volatile plan of action. Might that plan include a future invasion to the south, as outlined in the Ezekiel 38–39 prophecy?

Certainly, that prophecy indicates an ambitious and volatile plan of action following the Magog coalition leader's "evil thought" of Ezekiel 38:10–12. Until relatively recently, Israel has had little prospect for great wealth of the sort indicated in this prophecy that would entice such a thought or action by enemies to the north. Oh, there has long been talk of great mineral wealth in the Dead Sea, which is within the territory of the tiny nation of Israel today. Yet there seems to be little interest of Israel's enemies in those very uncertain riches. But, such wealth as would be sufficiently enticing to provoke that future "Gog" to think to attack Israel has appeared on the prophetic horizon.

The second news item that caught my attention explains further:

> As the liquid oil supply curve continues to drop on an international level, oil prices will only rise dramatically, necessitating the development of unconventional oil productions, IEI CEO Relik Shafir told *The Jerusalem Post* at a meeting in Tel Aviv on Monday. Creating oil from shale—a dark sedimentary rock containing hydrocarbons—is one such unconventional method, and resources are particularly robust in Israel, Jordan, North America, Russia, Mongolia, China and Australia, according to Shafir....
>
> "Our vision is to allow Israel energy independence," Shafir said. "This is the vision that brought Harold Vinegar to Israel to make aliya, and the vision of the company."
>
> In Israel's case, the largest source of shale is in the Shfela basin region outside Jerusalem, where the hydrocarbons are located between 200 and 400 meters below the surface, beneath an impermeable layer of rock.[3]

While the tables of world oil reserves continue to drop dramatically, will the genius that God has placed within the progeny of Abraham, Isaac, and Jacob leap to the forefront of petroleum technology and produce the "spoil" that will provoke Gog to bring his coalition down over the mountains of Israel? This is a developing story to which every watchman of Bible prophecy should pay attention.

January 16, 2012
Nuclear Iran: To Be or Not To Be?

Iran continues to resist and/or ignore all attempts by the United Nations and the international community to warn that nation to back off its nuclear development program. The threat implicit in that bombastic government's attempts to join the world's nuclear club has been the fodder of supposition, conjecture, and postulation for years now. It seems that predictions of Iran having a nuclear weapon about to be a reality have been offered for a near time frame every week I can remember for the past twenty-four months or so.

It is almost as if Iranian President Mahmoud Ahmadinejad is getting a thrill of some perverse sort out of tweaking the world—and particularly the U.S. and Israel—with his sly threats. Of course, his threats have been of the straightforward sort, too. He has threatened to wipe Israel from the map many times in public speaking forums. He has threatened to shut down oil shipments through the Straits of Hormuz. But, as of late, he has taken to playing slyly worded games of threatening, like a junior high school prankster forewarning of high jinks being planned for his classmates.

For example, he and his bully-pal of Venezuela have been noticed off in a corner whispering to each other and grinning knowingly while casting mischievous glances at the rest of us.

Ahmadinejad shared jokes about his country's nuclear project with one of his closest foreign allies, Venezuelan President Hugo Chavez, during a visit to Chavez's nation.

> "One of the targets that Yankee imperialism has in its sights is Iran, which is why we are showing our solidarity," said Mr. Chavez during a joint press conference with the Iranian president in Caracas. Scorning western fears of Iran's nuclear ambitions, Mr. Chavez added: "That hill will open up and a big atomic bomb will come out."
>
> Mr. Ahmadinejad responded by praising his host as the "champion in the war on imperialism."[4]

So, the question comes to mind: With this nation at the heart of what was ancient Persia playing mind games for so long, but having not yet achieved—apparently—the actual objective of producing an atomic weapon, exactly what is Iran's future with regard to becoming a nuclear military power?

Certainly, by all rationale one can muster, it appears that it is just a matter of time—perhaps days—until the announcement will be made, and, as Venezuela's dictator says, "That hill will open up and a big atomic bomb will come out."

Like so much else in this stage-setting era for end-times Bible prophecy to unfold, God's staying hand can be sensed slowing, preventing Iran's progress in producing that "big bomb." We continue to wonder over why, for example, the world's economic structure hasn't completely imploded. The situation is unsustainable, untenable, to put it mildly. Yet there continues to be an air of normalcy—although the term "normalcy" certainly can be defined differently than, say, a decade ago.

Of course, when thinking on Iran, we who consider Bible prophecy as the guiding light for things to come believe we must put all of what is happening within the context of the Gog-Magog prophecy of Ezekiel chapters 38 and 39. This is because Persia is one of the chief allies mentioned to come down with the Gog-Magog force to "take great spoil" from the land of Israel. What the Iran of the prophetic day that attack takes place will look like is the question. Will Iran be a nation with nukes or not?

It seems safe to say that whether Iran is or isn't a nuclear-weapons bearer at the time of that future attack, any such weapon doesn't seem scheduled to be used against Israel.

Whether through God's staying hand or by the attack plan's designer, Gog, Israel apparently will not suffer catastrophic damage in the Gog-Magog attack. There will be carnage from the damage the Lord will do to the attackers, that's for sure. But, Israel will apparently be preserved throughout the assault.

Will nuclear weapons be used at the time? The prophetic Word says "fire" will fall on "the coastlands." This indicates the possibility of nuclear weaponry. But the term "coastlands" doesn't indicate an interior nation like Israel, even though Israel does have some coastal area along the Mediterranean.

So, Ahmadinejad's consistent threat to wipe Israel off the map with a nuclear strike just isn't going to happen. Neither is Iran or any other nation on the planet going to wipe Israel off the map by any means whatsoever. Israel is destined to be the head of nations as Christ rules and reigns over all of God's creation, and King David rules in his supernatural body over God's chosen nation atop Mt. Zion in the City of David.

How all of this nuclear weapons program stuff plays out will be most interesting to watch over the course of the days, weeks, and months just ahead.

January 23, 2012
Big Brother's Noose Tightens: Part 1

It is always with reticence that I write about government intrusion into our lives. This is because so much wild-eyed speculation is thrown around in cyberspace that one must be alert to what is and isn't true in this incendiary area of concern. We get an endless parade of alerts that FEMA (Federal Emergency Management Agency) camps are almost ready to begin herding Christians, in particular, into the American version of Nazi-style concentration camps. The reports never cease of things such as the claim that gigantic, coffin-like containers are stacked and ready for mass burials at such a time when citizen resistance will be met with deadly force to put down rioting throughout the homeland.

The very term "homeland security" evokes thoughts of 1930s Germany and the rise to power of Adolf Hitler and his genocidal Nazi maniacs. Janet Napolitano, director of Homeland Security, is referred to caustically in some circles as "Big Sis," a takeoff on George Orwell's sinister symbol of tyranny, Big Brother. It is a matter concerning which she is said to recently have expressed her considerable irritation.

No matter how one chooses to frame in words the growing hold the federal government progressively exerts on our lives, it is essential that we look seriously at the problem while there remains freedom to do so. I dislike triteness, but the trite is true in this case: Where there is smoke, there is fire. There is a lot of smoke clouding our future with regard to whether Americans will remain a free people.

The most immediate news that sparked this writing is the report so close to the doings of Hitler's rise to power as to be chilling. At the same time, the news item seems so low key at first glance as to be innocuous. But, after that first glance, it becomes so blatant that even the strangest of bedfellows are joined in resistance to the intrusion.

> Children in the Long Island, New York, area have been strapped with monitors to keep a running check on their health. The program is the results of the school administrators' desire to know about the condition of the kids' problems with obesity. The action was apparently taken without the parents' knowledge in many cases.
>
> Reports are that this will soon become a full-scale program to monitor the children's physical activities around the clock. The devices are like wristwatches, and count heartbeats, monitor body movement during daily activities, and even measure sleep habits, according to the story. It is all an attempt to get a handle on what the powers that be consider a growing obesity problem, according to those doing the monitoring.
>
> The information is displayed on a color-coded screen and gets transmitted to a password-protected Web site that students and educators can access.... The monitors are distributed by Polar Electro, of Lake Success, LI, the US division of a Finland firm.[5]

The devices have been put on children in public school systems around the U.S. on a limited scale thus far, without the knowledge of many of the parents whose children are involved. This is apparently being done on a test basis, with the intention of making it a part of monitoring the health of students to assess possible future health risks. Considering the government-controlled health system voted in before 2010 by Congress and signed by President Barack Obama, we can only imagine where use of this kind of information might lead.

The matter is of sufficient concern that even an entity traditionally sycophantic toward any liberal government program is expressing concern. Jay Stanley of the American Civil Liberties Union said, "When you get into monitoring people's biological vital signs, that's a pretty intrusive measurement. There are key privacy interests at play."[6] Stanley said that at the very least, parents must have a say in how long the data will be stored and who will have access to it—and schools must obtain parents' consent. "A program like this should only be voluntary. Nobody should be forced to reveal biological indicators," Stanley added.[7]

The Hitler Youth Corps comes to mind when thinking on this and other of today's government power grabs to control the structure of the American family and the day-to-day rearing of our children.

When Congress—and the president—decided in 1963 to try to kick God out of the American public school system, a flood of insanity gushed in to fill the void. It hasn't stopped gushing. We have reared generations of children who are becoming ever more alienated from the family model the God of heaven instituted. Government has become the keeper of our children. The results are not greater freedom, but an increasingly restrictive way of life in what was once called "the land of the free." Big Brother's noose of enslavement, like that Hitler perpetrated those many decades ago, might be on America's horizon.

Next, we will look at how other signals of impending government control are threatening the American way of life.

The cure for what ails this or any nation, of course, is found in the most notable of scriptural prescriptions found in God's Holy Word. It is an R_x that speaks directly to all born-again children of God today—the church:

> If my people, which are called by my name,
> shall humble themselves, and pray, and seek my face,
> and turn from their wicked ways, then will I hear from heaven,
> and will forgive their sin, and will heal their land.
>
> 2 Chronicles 7:14

January 30, 2012
Big Brother's Noose Tightens: Part 2

A cursory glance would seem to indicate that the decision last week by Congress to flush the anti-piracy legislation into the sewer reserved for liberty-robbing legislation accomplished the preservation of Internet freedom. The following excerpt from one news story sets the seeming defeat of the threatening legislation.

> Lawmakers stopped anti-piracy legislation in its tracks on Friday, delivering a stunning win for Internet companies that staged an unprecedented online protest this week to kill the previously fast-moving bills. Senate Democratic leader Harry Reid said he would postpone a critical vote that had been scheduled for January 24 [2012] "in light of recent events." Lamar Smith, the Republican chairman of the House of Representatives' Judiciary Committee, followed suit, saying his panel would delay action on similar legislation until there is wider agreement on the issue.[8]

The Obama administration displayed a moment of atypical behavior, quickly jumping on the bandwagon against the very legislation to govern Internet they had been championing.

> White House officials weighed in on Saturday, saying in a blog post that they had concerns about legislation that could make businesses on the Internet vulnerable to litigation and harm legal activity and free speech.
>
> Then on Wednesday, protests blanketed the Internet, turning Wikipedia and other popular websites dark for 24 hours. Google, Facebook, Twitter and others protested the proposed legislation but did not shut down.
>
> The protest had quick results: several sponsors of the legislation, including senators Roy Blunt, Chuck Grassley, Orrin Hatch, John Boozman and Marco Rubio [withdrew their support].[9]

To put it bluntly, so many people within cyberspace communities went into fits of rage that it threw Big Brother into shock. The Harry Reids who are bent on controlling every aspect of our lives from cradle to grave instantly pulled back their meddling fingers that had just been bitten by the entities that the government was intent on collaring.

But, notice the phraseology of Reid's and Smith's decisions to take the legislation off the table. Reid, the Democrat, said he would "postpone" a vote on the matters involved. Smith, the Republican, said he would "delay" action on such legislation until there was agreement—i.e., the hounds of Big Brotherism haven't given up on ways to get into governing the Internet. They are merely backing off for the time being to figure new ways to come at that area of freedom from other angles. And, they are indeed continuing to come at our freedoms from every angle.

Their intrusion is always in the guise of wanting to benevolently secure one area or the other of our lives. In the case of the Internet legislation, PIPA (Protect IP Act) in the Senate and SOPA (Stop Online Piracy Act) in the House solutions were promised to piracy and copyright infringement in America and around the world. Now, the forces are marshaling to come up with new versions that the enforcers are promising will not chill free expression or threaten the economic growth and innovation the Internet provides.

When reading about the backtracking of the would-be Internet masters, I can't help but think on what Bible prophecy tells us will be the cry of the end-times New World Order builders. It is a mantra we have heard time and time again in the Middle East land-for-peace deals these same types have been striving to knit together for a decade or more. They want to build an era of peace and security, with the land God gave Israel as the price for such an arrangement. Even Benjamin Netanyahu, Israel's prime minister, uses the phrase "peace and security."

We know what God's Word says about that humanistic process:

> For when they shall say, Peace and safety;
> then sudden destruction cometh upon them, as travail
> upon a woman with child; and they shall not escape.
>
> 1 Thessalonians 5:3

We have been witness to the results of demand for security. Since September 11, 2001, developments within the U.S. government and other governments of the world have been stunning in terms of prophetic import. The Transportation Security Administration (TSA) has, by itself, demonstrated how easy it is to take liberty from the American citizen. The pat-downs, body scans, and other violations of basic personal rights simply stagger the mind of one who still believes in the U.S. Constitution as a viable, governing document.

More and more federal government intrusion into daily life should cause even the most ardent anticonspiracy skeptics to wonder.

For one example, Tuesday, January 17, 2012, residents of Leesburg, Florida, had their tranquility disrupted when their local Social Security office suddenly became a random Homeland Security checkpoint. Department of Homeland Security (DHS) officers armed with semiautomatic rifles and accompanied by sniffer dogs forced locals to present identifications. At least one DHS officer was stationed at a door to the building with his automatic weapon at the ready, it was reported.

The action was apparently part of something called "Operation Shield," an unannounced drill conducted by the DHS' Federal Protective Service centered on "detecting the presence of unauthorized persons and potentially disruptive or dangerous activities," according to the DHS website.[10]

One report gave the following account:

> Thomas Milligan, district manager for the Social Security Administration office, said staff were not informed their offices were about to be stormed by armed FPS officers. DHS officials refused to answer questions asked by local media and left with no explanation at noon.[11]

The fact that we're seeing our rights eroding at a frightening pace is bad enough. But, it is the staggering implications of what the present ground-laying assaults on our freedoms will likely mean in terms of the fulfillment of Bible prophecy that are especially troubling, but at the same time, quite fascinating. Big Brotherism, in its contemporary stage of metamorphosis, makes the lie that our lives will be more secure if we will just acquiesce to governing by those who know best the centerpiece of their enslaving master plan. The noose that is tightening day by day is the incrementalism being employed in every facet of our lives.

Take heart. God is in control. Although Antichrist's forces can be sensed forming and his noose is tightening, the final page of man's long, brutal history will be written by the finger of Jesus Christ:

> And then shall that wicked be revealed, whom the Lord shall consume with the spirit of his mouth, and shall destroy with the brightness of his coming.
>
> 2 Thessalonians 2:8

FEBRUARY 2012

February 6, 2012
What Kind of Love Is This?

A strange literary brain glitch seems to afflict mainstream news media types these days. I find the disorder asserting its influence even in news briefs found on the front pages of my hometown newspaper. Such is the case as follows.

> Mohammed Shafia, 58; his wife, Tooba Yahya, 42; and their son, Hamed, 21, all originally from Afghanistan, have been found guilty in Canada of first-degree murder in the killings of Shafia's three teenage daughters and another of his wives in a polygamous marriage because they dishonored the family by defying its rules on dress, dating, socializing and Internet use.[12]

The story is front and center, yet a glaring fact is missing. It is as if the reporters are being blocked from finding the cause of the brutal killings that are almost routinely committed these days in the name of religious doctrine. The murders in the above news brief were, for example, reported in the following way by the Associated Press as passed along by Fox News:

> KINGSTON, Ontario—A jury on Sunday found an Afghan father, his wife and their son guilty of killing three teenage sisters and a co-wife in what the judge described as "cold-blooded, shameful murders" resulting from a "twisted concept of honor." The jury took 15 hours to find Mohammad Shafia, 58; his wife Tooba Yahya, 42; and their son Hamed, 21, each guilty of four counts of first-degree murder in a case that shocked and riveted Canadians from coast to coast.[13]

Nowhere is the specific religious affiliation of the murderers mentioned. As a matter of fact, only one religion is mentioned, and that is through the use of the word "Christian" later in the piece. One of the teenagers murdered for her "twisted" concept of honor had condoms in her room and photos of herself wearing short skirts and hugging her Christian boyfriend, according to the story. The story published by Fox actually never mentioned that religious reasons were at the core of the killings.

One might take from the story as presented that the reporting source wants us to infer that the girl was morally loose—as was her Christian boyfriend—and somehow deserved punishment.

What is it about the American media that causes an apparently unwritten rule that the use of the words "Muslim" and "Islam" are taboo in the contemporary journalistic lexicon?

The answer resides within the politically correct minds of those bent on shaping opinion in these dark days of setting the stage for the coming of Antichrist.

More to the point is the question posed by the title of this commentary:

What kind of love is found in Islam, which we are told time and time again is a religion of love, not of hatred and violence?

It is a religion that commands—or at least condones—strapping bombs onto women and children and sending them out to kill as many as possible in the name of the religion's god. When nearly three thousand people are murdered by nineteen adherents of the religion's most fundamental tenets by flying airliners into buildings, the majority of Muslims celebrate in their streets. When every head of state and the governments—all of which are driven by Islamist rage—demand genocide to wipe the people of Israel from the map, good, loving Muslims around the world say nothing or agree that the Jews must go because the Koran demands it.

Killing teenage girls for the sake of Allah and a long-dead prophet of Islam because the youngsters want to assimilate into the culture that surrounds them is a growing crime in North America. Yet the news reports are completely silent about the real source of the beastly activity.

Of course, this shouldn't surprise. Those who write and broadcast the stories are clueless pawns of the "prince of the power of the air":

> Wherein in time past ye walked according to the course of this
> world, according to the prince of the power of the air,
> the spirit that now worketh in the children of disobedience:
>
> Among whom also we all had our conversation in times past in the
> lusts of our flesh, fulfilling the desires of the flesh and of the mind;
> and were by nature the children of wrath, even as others.
>
> Ephesians 2:2–3

Islam is neither a religion of love nor of peace—both of which are rooted in the same source. God's Word tells us about His (the REAL God's) prescription for living in love and peace:

> Be careful for nothing; but in everything by prayer and supplication
> with thanksgiving let your requests be made known unto God.

> And the peace of God, which passeth all understanding,
> shall keep your hearts and minds through Christ Jesus.
> Philippians 4:6–7

February 13, 2012
The Russian Prophetic Dynamic

We move ever deeper into these fleeting, prophetic hours. Each day adds detail and brings more clarity to the end-times portrait painted by, in particular, the prophets Isaiah and Ezekiel. Russia is the brush observably moving across the last-days canvas.

Kremlin hegemony is on the ascent within the former Soviet Union's vast geographical sphere of influence. Vladimir Putin appears to be the power behind the power. Russia's interacting and meshing with two client-states in particular pose fascinating, biblically prophetic points of interest.

The week just past brought one of Bible prophecy's most currently monitored issues into sharper focus. Russia, consistently a matter of such focus because of the generally accepted opinion that it is the chief candidate for the power that will lead the Gog-Magog attack of Ezekiel 38–39, asserted its previously mentioned influence over another of prophecy's most focal nations.

Syria's brutal regime, ruled by Bashar al-Assad, has for the moment replaced Israel as the nation most under the microscope of castigation by the international community. At the center of dispensing that obloquy is the Arab conglomerate led by Saudi Arabia.

The anxiety and anger are engendered by Assad's defying the so-called Arab Spring by murdering more than five thousand of Syria's citizens to this point. It is quite the interesting development. The dictators of the Arab world want the successor to his father, Hafez al-Assad, to abdicate so that the Muslim Brotherhood can see to it that another dictator of their choosing can be installed over the Syrian masses. This is desired, of course, under the guise of wanting to show the United Nations and all points west that democracy is spreading in the dark reaches of the Middle East.

The Western nations' leaderships and the world's mainstream news media seem totally mesmerized by promises of this Islamist democratization—an oxymoron, if ever there was one. The Muslim Brotherhood and all those influenced by Mohammed and Allah want anything but democracy. Egypt is an example to watch. The Brotherhood wants the Egyptian military—who removed Hosni Mubarak as dictator/president—to now get behind someone of the Brotherhood's choosing and install that leader as president/dictator of Egypt. So, Assad is on the wrong side of the equation that is formulated to bring in the Arab Spring. The total, radical Islamization of the Middle East is underway, and Assad's time as tyrant is limited. And, now, Russia finds itself on the wrong side of what is taking place to her south. The vote last week in the U.N. Security Council, in which Russia and China blocked action against the Syrian regime, has opened the proverbial can of worms, particularly for Russian leadership.

> Moscow and Beijing were the only members of the 15-member U.N. Security Council to vote against the resolution backing an Arab League call for Assad to yield power and start a political transition. The double veto prompted unusually undiplomatic Western criticism, which [Sergei] Lavrov said verged on "hysteria."[14]

Kremlin powers that be realize, however, that they must consider a much more serious problem than criticism by the Western leaders. One result of the vote was that protesters burned Russian and Chinese flags outside the Russian embassy in Beirut, Lebanon. That might be the mildest aftereffects Russia will have to endure. And, the Russians were quick to begin cleaning up after themselves in order to assuage the anger that is bound to grow in the Muslim world.

The Russians quickly tried to diplomatically dance around their Security Council vote by undertaking a "mission" to Syria to talk to Bashar al-Assad about his brutal treatment of his people. Some fancy verbal dancing was offered, too:

> President Dmitry Medvedev ordered the mission, the statement said, because Russia "firmly intends to seek the swiftest stabilisation of the situation in Syria on the basis of the swiftest implementation of democratic reforms whose time has come."[15]

The miscalculation made in backing Assad, thus risking enraging the radical Islamists, was, it is thought in some circles, Vladimir Putin's. The once and most likely future Russian president is thought to have decided to shore up Assad, because of the billions of dollars worth of contracts for Russian arms and because Syria has a naval maintenance and supply facility on its Mediterranean coast that is Russia's only military base outside the territory that comprised the former Soviet Union.

Also, Putin's reasons for backing Assad by voting against the Muslim-Brotherhood types' wishes might have been—it is thought—at least partly so he could demonstrate his leadership prowess to the West by preventing it from trying to impose its collective will on the nations within Russia's sphere of influence.

Russia has declared that any attack on the Assad regime will be considered an attack on Russia, and would be met with retaliation that is appropriate.

All of this, of course, the observer of Bible prophecy must consider within the framework of the Isaiah 17:1 prophecy.

The second matter that is the subject of this commentary involves another major player the Bible indicates will be closely associated with the Russian who will be the leader of the Gog-Magog coalition against Israel. In this regard, there are some intriguing aspects to the Russia and Iran relationship, considering the foregoing Russian/Syrian things we have just reviewed.

One element of the association that interests me intensely is the fear the Saudis have for Iranian apocalyptic fanaticism. The Iranian form of Islamist eschatology preaches belief—as often expressed by the likes of Iranian President Mahmoud Ahmadinejad—that Armageddon must come to pass before the Twelfth Imam, whom he considers Islam's messiah, can take over the world. The Iranian president, even his fellow Muslims fear, is intent on starting World War III, if it will summon forth the Mahdi.

Much of the Arab hordes in the regions fear Iran producing a nuclear weapons capability almost as much as do the Israelis. The fear is so great that it is pretty much a confirmed matter that the Saudi royals have given Israel permission to fly over Saudi air space if and when it becomes necessary to take out Iran's nuclear production facilities.

Russia is again on the wrong side of the diplomatic equation regarding the leaders of most of Islam, in that the Russians have so much tied up in military assets and in other ways with a regime that seems near the lunatic fringe, even proclaiming publicly that when they get a nuclear weapon, they will use it against Israel. While the Russians seek to give the impression that they are backing Iran to the hilt in their nuclear program, many back-channel reports tell a different story. It seems there are fears in the Kremlin of an Iran with deliverable nuclear weapons.

> On July 13, 2011, Russia made a proposal for a "step-by-step" approach, according to which, Iran could address questions about its nuclear program and be rewarded with a gradual easing of sanctions.
>
> The Iran Six, comprising Russia, the United States, China, Britain, France and Germany, have been trying since 2003 to convince Iran to halt its uranium enrichment program.
>
> "Just like the West, Russia is worried that Iran can make a nuclear weapon, if necessary," [former Iranian president Akbar] Rafsanjani said.[16]

Now to some thoughts on prophetic application.

It should be clear to any Bible prophecy student who views prophecy as literal that Russia is moving into position for fulfilling its part as given in Ezekiel 38–39. That nation is exactly where it should be, if it is to play its end-times role.

Russia is involved with Syria, the nation that sits at ground zero for fulfillment of one of the most stunning prophecies of catastrophe given in God's Word—the destruction of Damascus in a single hour (Isaiah 17:1).

Russia is front and center in dealing with Iran (ancient Persia), which has the most vocal of all the leaders of Israel's enemies in declaring Israel will be wiped off the map.

At the same time, Russia is playing a middle-man role that seems to be trying to some extent to keep the hot passions of Islam from igniting the Middle East, thus, perhaps, World War III.

Gog, of Gog-Magog infamy, is said to be a demon-spirit that will one day inhabit a Russian leader and be instrumental (used by God) in instigating an "evil thought" to attack Israel. The "prince" of Persia is apparently a fallen angel who is among the most powerful of the luciferic forces. Both demonic entities are doubtless active at this present hour, positioning their wards (humans who will serve them) for playing out their fiendish roles in the final act of human history this side of Christ's return.

It is within reason to ask whether these satanic minions—under Almighty God's control—are plotting not to bring about World War III at this particular time, as so many who consider Bible prophecy fear. Rather, might they perhaps be plotting for a time when diplomacy might have economically and militarily denuded God's chosen nation and the Western powers to the point that the Russian-led coalition will, they will believe, have easy pickings when they finally attack?

Might we learn one day not too distant that, rather than Israel having attacked Iran's nuclear facilities, thus bringing on an escalating war that would engulf the region—if not the whole world—in conflagration, the news will be that the Russians have brokered a deal whereby Iran gives up its nuclear ambitions? Such a scenario certainly more fits the Ezekiel 38–39 Gog-Magog profile than does a nuclear Iran.

Don't get mad at me…it's just food for prophetic thought.

February 20, 2012
Greek Tragedy Now Playing...

The *Iliad* and the *Odyssey* of the unknown Homer—the many tragedies that spun from Aeschylus, Sophocles, Euripides, and other ancient Greek playwrights—are but shadowy scripts of insignificance in the end-times stage lights that illuminate our headlines hourly these days. Gripping reality in the land that gave us the stories of the likes of Oedipus, Agamemnon, Prometheus, and, of course, Zeus, Aphrodite, Hercules, and all that make up the Greek fictional accounts, present movement toward tragedy with a far more bitter ending than any in mythology.

It is not tragedy for the Greeks alone of which I write. The stage is set to bring the whole world to the prophetic destiny laid out in Bible prophecy. When considering the roots of the continent of Europe, most first think of Italy or the center of that great empire, the city of Rome. The other state that most often comes to mind when thinking on where Europe began is Greece and its ancient center, Athens.

Athens, of course, predates Rome in fame—or infamy, depending upon one's view of those empires. But, the thing to keep in mind for prophetic cogitation is that the ancient Roman Empire—which had at its heart great portions of the ancient Greek culture—is foretold to one day be a major power player. This will happen, according to Daniel the prophet, some time before the world leader who will be Antichrist achieves his full, satanic power.

We have given the Scriptures that present the geological location out of which the beast of Revelation 13 will come many times in these commentaries. Prophecy teachers have over the years persistently and consistently put the prophecy in front of us. Here it is again:

> And after threescore and two weeks shall Messiah be cut off,
> but not for himself: and the people of the prince
> that shall come shall destroy the city and the sanctuary;
> and the end thereof shall be with a flood,
> and unto the end of the war desolations are determined.
>
> And he shall confirm the covenant with many for one week:
> and in the midst of the week he shall cause the sacrifice
> and the oblation to cease, and for the overspreading of

abominations he shall make it desolate, even until the
consummation, and that determined
shall be poured upon the desolate.
Daniel 9:26-27

Antichrist, that man of sin and abomination of desolation, will come forth out of the Romans, who destroyed Jerusalem and the Jewish Temple in AD 70. His biological heritage will be of the people of the area that comprised ancient Rome.

Greece, then, because of its tremendous influences on that ancient Roman culture, will be at the center of the revived Roman Empire as it develops for prophetic fulfillment. So, in the news coming out of that nucleus nation that will have to, by its very history, be front and center in the end times, we find another signal of where this generation must stand on God's prophetic timeline.

Greece's present predicament presents a snapshot of how the fate of other nations—particularly the nations of the Western world—will almost certainly play out. It will be a tragedy of the first magnitude! Bottom line is that the Greek populace, used to getting government subsidies and outright handouts at every level, particularly in the public work sector, are going nuts because of austerity measures to bring fiscal stability.

> Tens of thousands of protesters clashed with police before the parliament in Syntagma Square, with buildings set ablaze and more than 80 people injured.
>
> Trade unionists, nationalists, communists, students, retired people were among those denouncing the "EU-IMF blackmail," many of them equipped with gas masks to resist the tear gas used by riot police. German flags were also burnt in protest as what is seen as a Berlin-prescribed austerity package for Greece.[17]

Pundits on nightly news programs are wondering aloud whether, in looking at Greece and the angry protests over government yanking giveaway programs from people used to them, we are witnessing an unrest infection that will eventually spread to the U.S. Their answer should be stunningly obvious, especially for a mainstream news conglomerate that has worked with liberal presidential administrations—and even some moderate administrations—to create a cash-cow government, a political system that buys votes through taxpayer money.

We have already seen the storm fronts of financial turbulence. Remember Wisconsin, when the Democrat state legislators left the state rather than face up to their obligation to vote on cutting state giveaways (a vote the Democrats would have lost)? Remember the ugliness of the protesters—union thugs, mostly—who did an estimated $7 million in damage to the state capitol building?

The "Occupy" protesters haven't been as successful to this point, in jinning up violence of the sort some desire in order to disrupt the domestic tranquility. Ultimately, though, the violence will come—not only to the United States, but to the entire world. It will be not just a Greek tragedy, but a worldwide tragedy—the Tribulation, as given in God's prophetic Word.

Antichrist will bring some degree of order for a time. He will do so by lopping off heads and causing all to take a number and a mark. Ultimately, he will force all to worship him as God. It will take Jesus Christ to bring the curtain down on the final act of that great tragedy.

February 27, 2012
Restraining Sudden Destruction

There is a sense among many at this moment in history that impending disaster presses against the fabric of life on planet earth from every side. This is not mere paranoia pushing against the collective, anxiety-ridden psyche of a world uncertain about its future. The threat is real, and it is in Bible prophecy. A quick scan of issues, events, and anticipated actions testifies to the reality of the threat and validates the angst.

Israel is ground zero for much of the fear pressing upon a world full of dread. The Jewish state is considered the trigger point for possible nuclear conflict in the Middle East—conflict that is sure to spread globally once unleashed. Iran is the antagonist that is the cause of the most immediate threat to regional and world peace—although the world diplomatic community seems intent on making Israel responsible for keeping war from erupting. This is the way it is, despite the fact that the Iranian regime's leaders threaten to wipe Israel off the map.

It is puzzling to many as to why there hasn't been an uncontrollable explosion in the ancient Bible land. Israel's restraint has been remarkable, considering the threat from its neighbors, particularly from Iran and its developing nuclear program. Rumors continue to fly of war-making against that program, thus to eliminate atomic weapons that will almost certainly be unleashed against Israel if allowed to come to fruition.

The world is in absolute economic chaos. Everywhere one looks, untenable fiscal circumstances threaten not only national, but continental and even planetary, economic implosion. Greece is the most recent to require a $170 billion bail-out—done, incidentally, with money that doesn't really exist. Debt forgiveness and other sleight-of-hand chicanery are at the root of the "fix"—a trick similar to the trillions-of-dollars, smoke-and-mirrors maneuvering employed to keep America's financial ship afloat for these months since the current administration began to wrestle with the controls of power.

Like in the case of the Israeli/Iranian threat to world peace, it is dumbfounding to many as to why these economic pressures, pressing in upon the fabric of world stability, haven't ruptured the building bubble and collapsed the global monetary structure. The worldwide terrorism factor—wrapped up in militant, fanatic Islam and the ongoing jihad declared against everyone who refuses to bow to Allah—amazingly hasn't broken through the fabric of the world's relative stability. Tremendous pressure from that quarter is on the rise in a mighty way, however.

No matter at which of Israel's enemy neighbors one looks, there is seen the arising of Islamist insurgency. The Muslim Brotherhood—which, inexplicably, continues to be viewed by mainstream news and the Obama administration as a benign embryo of democracy on the ascent—is spreading its malignant tentacles through the Arab Spring assaults on governments in the region. It seeks to replace present dictatorships with other dictatorships controlled by an oligarchy-like rulership.

Why, many puzzle, has that incendiary movement not torched the combustible Mideast situation, igniting the conflagration the world's diplomatic community fears?

I wrote at the beginning of this commentary that these pressures that represent a cataclysmic threat are in Bible prophecy. The end-of-the-age combination of absolute evil will, God's prophetic Word says, comes much like the antediluvian age of Noah's day, which ended with a great, destructive deluge.

Daniel the prophet put it this way:

> And after threescore and two weeks shall Messiah be cut off,
> but not for himself: and the people of the prince that shall come
> shall destroy the city and the sanctuary;
> and the end thereof shall be with a flood,
> and unto the end of the war desolations are determined.
>
> Daniel 9:26

Jesus' death, burial, and resurrection would, the prophet foretold, set in motion events that will culminate with mankind's final war that will be fought this side of Christ's return. The desolations of that era will be like a flood—i.e., the war of good versus evil will include many troubles, which God's Word outlines for anyone who truly is a watchman in the last days.

Jesus told those watchmen (mentioned in Mark 13:37) that when we see all of these things, including great wars and rumors of war, that we are to know that the end "is not yet" (Matthew 24:6). But we are to be looking up, because He is very near to His time of return (Luke 21:28).

When is the end coming, then? We know from Daniel's prophecy that a flood of issues and events with evil at their core will mark the end. Jesus Himself prophesied that the time of His coming will be like the time of Noah's day and Lot's day in Sodom (read Luke 17:26–30 and Matthew 24:36–42). Things will be moving along relatively as usual for those times.

We must remember that those times were filled with godlessness and great evil, even though people were buying, selling, marrying, and planting. Jesus then said that the same day Noah went into the ark, and the same day that Lot was taken from Sodom, God's judgment fell. He said it will be exactly like in those days at the time He returns.

That first phase of His return will be at the Rapture of His church—not at His Second Advent (Revelation 19:11). We can know that is true, because at the time of His Second Coming at Armageddon, it will not be business as usual. The earth will be almost completely destroyed, and nearly three-fourths of mankind will have been killed by that time.

Prophetic observers of God's Word are witnessing that end-times onslaught of pressures from evil that Daniel called a flood. But, that flood hasn't broken the dam holding it back. This is amazing, even to many who watch and believe in prophetic stage-setting. Why hasn't the Middle East completely exploded in war? Why hasn't the world economy imploded, bringing about worldwide financial collapse? Why have the Muslims been allowed to continue to set up their long-desired, worldwide caliphate, while Israel more and more is viewed as the troublemaker that might be the instigator of war?

Paul the apostle, through inspiration of the Holy Spirit, told us the reason things haven't yet completely come apart—why evil hasn't yet taken over:

> And now ye know what withholdeth that he might be revealed in his time. For the mystery of iniquity doth already work: only he who now letteth will let, until he be taken out of the way.
>
> And then shall that wicked be revealed, whom the Lord shall consume with the spirit of his mouth, and shall destroy with the brightness of his coming:
>
> Even him, whose coming is after the working of Satan with all power and signs and lying wonders,

And with all deceivableness of unrighteousness in them
that perish; because they received not the love of the truth,
that they might be saved.

2 Thessalonians 2:7-10

The King James Version word "withholdeth" in the Greek language is *katecho*. It means to "restrain." So, this prophecy is about the one who will "restrain" evil until he is taken out of the way. The Restrainer is God the Holy Spirit, the third Person of the Holy Trinity. God Himself is restraining the evil, which can't take over the world and be ruled by Antichrist.

How can God be "taken out of the way" so evil and Antichrist can take over for a time? This will happen only when the church—all believers in Christ (the born again) are taken to heaven in the Rapture. The Holy Spirit indwells each and every Christian at present. When the church is taken from the earth, the Holy Spirit will serve a different purpose in God's plan for the consummation of human history. He will no longer restrain the evil thoughts of mankind. He will no longer govern the consciences of those left behind to endure the Tribulation—the final seven years of history before Christ's Second Coming. It is no wonder that Jesus said that time will be the worst that has ever been or ever will be (Matthew 24:21).

It will be hell on earth when the Restrainer no longer holds back evil as He does in this present hour. Jesus says that at the time the Holy Spirit leaves His restraining office, judgment will fall that very day (again, reread Luke 17: 26–30 and Matthew 24:36–42).

That stupendous change for all of mankind can take place at any moment. Here is what Jesus told us further:

Therefore be ye also ready: for in such an hour as ye
think not the Son of man cometh.

Matthew 24:44

MARCH 2012

March 5, 2012
Gog Spirit Surfaces

"Prophetic progression," as Todd Strandberg terms it, continues at a pace that is astonishing. Prophecy might not be being "fulfilled" as most seminary-trained students of eschatology would have it. No one who understands Bible prophecy from the premillennial, pretribulational view, however, denies that things foretold by Jesus and the prophets are being set up on the end-times stage for what looks to be not-too-distant fulfillment.

Even the most reserved among the pretrib seminary scholars sometimes admit that Israel being back in the Promised Land and at the center of worldwide controversy might just possibly be prophecy in the process of being fulfilled. Only slightly less profound than Israel's being at stage center are developments afoot with regard to the area of ancient Persia, now called Iran. Hard on the prophetic coattail of those developments are the tremendous changes that have taken place in Russia and the coming to power of a "really spooky dude," as I've heard him called in one form or the other over recent months and years. I refer, of course, to Vladimir Putin—the just-elected (or would that be reelected) president of Russia.

Putin, as prime minister, recently made the following statement about Israel's feared military action against Iran's nuclear development facilities: "Without a doubt, Russia is concerned about the growing threat of a military strike on this country. If this happens the fallout would be truly catastrophic."[18]

The statement actually seems tempered by diplomatic buffering, considering some of the more bellicose rhetoric coming from the Russian strongman in his ongoing career engineering over the years as he has grabbed for absolute control. Putin's voracious hunger for power on the world stage is seen in his overshadowing the then president Dmitry Medvedev's presence as Russian leader. Just days before winning the Sunday, March 4, election, Putin set future Russian policy in hardened rhetoric, making it clear who was and is boss.

He used a bit of cold war-type bluster—but with nuance that veiled the threat—in flexing his pre-election muscles, as illustrated in this excerpt of his words from a week ago:

> ...Putin again criticized the U.S.-led plans for a NATO missile defense system in Europe, saying it's aimed against Russian nuclear forces.
>
> "The Americans are obsessed with the idea of ensuring absolute invulnerability for themselves, which is utopian and unfeasible from both technological and geopolitical points of view," he said. "An absolute invulnerability for one means an absolute vulnerability for all the others. It's impossible to accept such a prospect."[19]

Putin has come down hard on American diplomatic involvement in backing the Arab Spring agenda, using invective against U.S. State Department moves to try to raise his standing with the Russian electorate. He and his campaign apparatus have been particularly angry sounding about any of the Western alliance's threats to remove Syrian President Bashar al-Assad from power.

Russia has strategically placed missile-carrying ships in waters near Syrian territory, backing with military threat Putin's tough talk about securing the Assad regime. When surveying the overall actions and interactions undertaken by this unusual man who has just assumed the Russian presidency for the second time, one who studies Bible prophecy from a futurist perspective must raise an eyebrow of realization—or at least of suspicion. Ezekiel, chapters 38 and 39, of course, come to the forefront of supposition and postulation. Vladimir Putin's future role in Mideast and world politics must by the very weight and volume of its probabilities be a matter of extreme fascination, not mere curiosity.

The great prophetic book of Revelation presents a hellish angel—a spirit—that will, during the Tribulation, ascend from the bottomless pit. His name is Abaddon, as given in Hebrew, and Apollyon in the Greek language. Daniel the prophet mentioned a powerful angel called "the Prince of Persia" who caused all sorts of troubles to be inflicted upon Daniel's people, the Israelites who were in Babylonian captivity. Ezekiel foretold an evil spirit of the ancient region that is present-day Russia that will at a time near Christ's return inhabit a person who will lead a coalition of armies against God's chosen nation. That evil one is called "Gog."

With so many signals on the prophetic horizon indicating that the Church Age is in the process of being brought to a wind-up, it isn't unreasonable to surmise that the evil being held back by the hand of God might be very near the time of release. Certainly the one called Gog must not be too far below the surface in these troubling, although exciting, days.

March 12, 2012
Chariots of Fire Rumbling?

Many sense foreboding in today's world, despite the fact that we in America go about daily life in more or less normal fashion. Government and media types strive through constant attempts at propagandizing to convince us that the societal/cultural and economic gloom as well as the terroristic threatening that looms just beyond civility are no more than cyclical conditions through which we have passed before. Washington, D.C., wizards of smart, we are to accept, will soon have the sensation of spiraling, out-of-control national descent into the abyss cleared up for us.

Yet a great many among the American populace harbor the dread that the world could be thrown into conflict on a global scale at any moment, if Israel attacks Iran's nuclear facilities. Europe is in the deadly fiscal turbulence that is the economic equivalent of being in one of Saddam Hussein's wood chippers, and might be torn apart because of the economic chaos at any time. America will suffer the loss of the lifestyles to which many have become accustomed, if either of those things eventuates, is the visceral fear in this country today.

The building bubble of financial catastrophe in the U.S. is itself more than enough to assure many that the feeling of gloom and doom of the first order are thoroughly justified. As Glenn Beck has declared, we might awaken one morning and find the nation and world changed beyond repair, with our money and way of life wiped out completely.

Christians who are paying attention—and, I'm sad to say, there seem far too few who are—see the moral rot that long ago infected our nation. There are fewer and fewer who stand against the constant assault by the hedonistic among us. When Christians or others do object to the decline in morality, they are held up as intolerant hate mongers. Indeed, we are in a time in which good is called evil, and evil is called good.

The past week, when a thirty-four-year-old old law student went before the news cameras at a sham hearing—arranged by the Democrat officials who set it up because they didn't want to go through proper congressional procedures—this moral slide came into stark focus for me. The woman, a student at Georgetown Law School, expressed her dismay, and, she said, that of her fellow women law students over not having contraceptives paid for by the school's insurance program. She expressed that they were all under great financial duress because the contraception they needed wasn't, in effect, being provided free, or at least subsidized. The implication was that the government should make such institutions pay for protection from disease and/or pregnancy that might be the result of sexual activity.

Rush Limbaugh got in trouble for saying the rest of us shouldn't have to pay for their sex. The howls from the if-it-feels-good-do-it crowd and from news pundits, under the guise of defending against those who would impose their brand of morality on society, were as loud as some of the strange night sounds from the skies that some have purported to have recorded and put on YouTube.com (more about which we will consider momentarily).

The thing I wish to point out is that the whole ruse with the woman and her dismay was about having sex when and where one wants, married or not. Contraception should have no limitations in its free distribution was the tone and tenor of her message. The only people I heard talking about this issue were Limbaugh and his colleagues on talk radio, and, of course, some on both sides (and a few in the middle) of politics. There were no real outcries from Christians—at least, not organized Christianity—that I personally found speaking out for moral purity. There were no Jerry Falwells decrying the fact that people should take personal responsibility for their own sexuality and its consequences.

So, I come to the place the Christian who truly cares about the critical state of the world finds himself or herself. The thought most often conveyed from those who look at the world crowding in on them—with the walls constraining evil seeming to be about to collapse—is that of being almost alone with impending cataclysm all around. There sometimes seems no hope. The devil's forces are all around and about to win.

The reports I'm sure many have read in Rapture Ready news and from other sources of the strange night sounds coming from around the world sparked the thought of Elias, Elijah's protégé, and the young man who was his companion in his prophet's work. The following excerpt will orient you if you haven't read the news reports on the matter.

> Mysterious sounds have been heard booming from the sky all around the world—in some cases they were so loud they set off car alarms. The unsettling noises were heard recently from Europe to Canada, sounding like groans and powerful horns. In Germany noises coming from the sky were recorded on a video camera and uploaded to YouTube, with car alarms clearly heard going off in the background.[20]

These times that are filled with so many prophetic signals—which are so obvious to the student of Bible prophecy who hold to a pretrib view—evoke thoughts of just how near the Lord is to His time of intervention into the anti-God, hedonistic affairs of mankind. This made me think of, as I said, Elias and the young man who came to the prophet terrified that they were about to be overrun and murdered by the Syrian army.

Here's what Elias did:

And he answered, Fear not: for they that be with us are more than they that be with them.

And Elisha prayed, and said, Lord, I pray thee, open his eyes, that he may see. And the Lord opened the eyes of the young man; and he saw: and, behold, the mountain was full of horses and chariots of fire round about Elisha.

2 Kings 6:16-17

I'm not saying the strange sounds—the groans and horns and violent noises that some say they have recorded and put on YouTube.com—are Elisha's chariots of fire. But the sounds are obviously being heard over much of the planet, and no one has been able to satisfactorily explain what the noise is all about. Another Scripture of timely interest is the following:

For we know that the whole creation groaneth and travaileth in pain together until now.

And not only they, but ourselves also, which have the firstfruits of the Spirit, even we ourselves groan within ourselves, waiting for the adoption, to wit, the redemption of our body.

Romans 8:22-23

One thing sure, my fellow watchmen and watchwomen, we are not alone, while the enemy seems to have the battle in hand. The Lord is—therefore we are—on the very brink of victory!

March 19, 2012
Catholic Kudos

While most all others who claim the Christian model for their faith system remain silent on one of God's most prominent signals of the end of the age, Pope Benedict XVI has not. I never thought I would be saying it, but kudos to the pontiff for speaking out on what many of those I consider the most Bible-centered ministers and ministries won't touch these days.

Speaking out against homosexuality has been rendered akin to racism and use of the "N" word by American media. Government has all but made speaking against the immorality of homosexual activity and the dangers it presents to culture and society a hate crime, in many ways. The results have been phenomenal. I've noticed the deafening silence from even some of the most fundamental evangelicals—that is, those with significant capability of reaching out in a ubiquitous way. In my observation, speaking out against the gay agenda by Christian ministers and organizations whose purpose it is to guard the nation's gates of morality with Bible truth seems to have died with the deaths of men like Adrian Rogers, Jerry Falwell, and D. James Kennedy. There are exceptions to the generalization I've made. John Hagee, for example, is one who thunders against the modern sodomite goings-on.

Most do not want to reopen the can of worms that the powerful homosexual lobby presents. That lobby has managed to close that lid, and the news and entertainment media have placed it high upon the shelf so as to make it out of reach as a topic of criticism. Anyone within Christian circles of any prominence can, if he or she talks against the gay lifestyle or gay marriage, expect the wrath of the entire propaganda conglomerate to come down in the most vicious torrent of invective that can be gathered.

Ol' Pope Benedict XVI has stuck out his aged neck, though, and I, for one, whose personal, Christian belief system is about as far from the Catholic system as Protestantism gets, give this pope a high five for expressing God's unchanging view of marriage and sexuality. The following news item frames the issue and the pope's stance:

> Pope Benedict on Friday denounced the "powerful political and cultural currents" seeking to legalize gay marriage in the United States, where Maryland has just become the eighth state to allow it. The pope's latest comments in opposition to homosexual mar-

riage came in an address to bishops from several Midwestern states on a regular visit to the Vatican.

"Sexual differences cannot be dismissed as irrelevant to the definition of marriage," he said. He added that the traditional family and marriage had to be "defended from every possible misrepresentation of their true nature" because, he said, whatever injured families injured society.

"In this regard, particular mention must be made of the powerful political and cultural currents seeking to alter the legal definition of marriage (in the United States)," he added in a clear reference to gay marriage.

Last week Maryland legalized same-sex marriage. Massachusetts, Iowa, Vermont, New Hampshire, Connecticut, New York and the District of Columbia currently allow gay and lesbian weddings. Washington State will join the list in June unless opponents stop it ahead of a possible referendum, and Maryland will be added in January 2013 unless its law, too, is overturned by a threatened referendum in November....

Benedict called on American bishops to continue their "defense of marriage as a natural institution consisting of a specific communion of persons, essentially rooted in the complementarities of the sexes and oriented to procreation."

The Vatican and Catholic officials around the world have protested against moves to legalize gay marriage in Europe and other developed parts of the world.[21]

There are numerous prohibitions in God's Word against homosexuality, and they have been gone over many times in the articles on this website and in many other forums. I won't again go over those.

Always, the anger comes against us when we must denounce what God plainly calls an abomination and what He is against to the point that He has brought societies, cultures, and even empires that become immersed in such activity to their ends, according to my reading of the Scriptures and history.

"You hate those who are homosexual," is the hue and cry from those who want silenced the message that homosexuality is a sin. Nothing could be farther from the truth, of course.

We wish for those who engage in such sin to come out of that sin and into God's light. We want them to then walk in that light so their lives can be blessed by God, rather than condemned.

We are always asked when we address the homosexuality issue: "What about all of the other sins—those in which heterosexual individuals engaged? Why do you not condemn that activity—or other sinfulness?"

It isn't our place to condemn anyone or anything. And, we don't. But, God does have things to say about the issue of homosexuality, and He expects His children here on earth to carry His message. It is our duty to point to the Word of God as the only truth there is. God sees sin as contrary to His plan for human beings. He created us, thus has the exclusive right to write and hold the manual for living life properly, so that man is not destructive to himself or others.

To my fellow Christians, I say that if you "hate" homosexuals—or anyone else—you are as guilty of sin as the person practicing that vile activity. I say it not because I speak from my own authority, but because our Lord has said it many times and in many ways throughout His written Word.

Love is the opposite of hate. The word for "love" in the relevant sense here is *agape* in the Greek language. Jesus said the following, in answer to a question by a lawyer trying to trick Him:

> Jesus said unto him, Thou shalt love the Lord thy God with all thy heart, and with all thy soul, and with all thy mind.
>
> This is the first and great commandment.
>
> And the second is like unto it, Thou shalt love thy neighbour as thyself. In these two commandments hang all the law and the prophets.
>
> Matthew 22:37–40

Yet it is incumbent upon us who name the name of Christ to call those who practice homosexuality to repentance. So, to the extent that Pope Benedict XVI points out this grievous sin and exhorts corrective action, I say, "Kudos!"

APRIL 2012

April 2, 2012
Catalyst for End-Times Catastrophe

Mark Stein, substituting for radio talk show host Rush Limbaugh, was asked by a caller to the program on Friday, March 23, something like the following: "What do you think is China's reason for building their military at such a rapid rate? Is it because they think they need to prepare to defend their interests against an attack? Or is it because they intend to attack others in a first strike at some point in the future?"

The British-accented political pundit said he personally senses that China is trying to bankrupt the American economy in much the same way the U.S.—under Ronald Reagan's presidency—caused the Soviet economy to implode. The twist, Stein implied, is that China is accomplishing the bankrupting process through the debt owed China by this nation. Fully 80 percent of China's military buildup, he believes, has been funded to this point by the interest on the debt America owes the Chinese communist government.

I have pointed out in this column before that students of Bible prophecy have long wondered about the two-hundred-million-troop army described as the "kings of the east" in the Revelation 9: 5–16 and 16:12 prophecy. In context of the modern red Chinese army, it has been a long-standing question: How could such a force be outfitted, given China's weak economic position?

When Hong Kong again came under Chinese control, following a decades-long lease in which capitalists mostly from the West held sway over the city's tremendous economic influence, it was feared by some that the tyrannical Sino leadership of the time would clamp down and put all behind the communist Bamboo Curtain, thus ending that city's burgeoning economic growth.

To the surprise of all, a newer, younger Chinese leadership—far from imposing communism's draconian rule—joined China's economy to the methodologies and direction of that taken by Hong Kong's financial masters. The results are what we see now. China has been on a phenomenal economic growth track, and is—as Mark Stein pointed out—helping to bankrupt America and at the same time building its own gargantuan military with U.S. interest payments.

And now comes word of America's second-most-dangerous nemesis of the Cold War teaming up with our "friends" the Saudis, to feed the engines of their industrial expansion. The prospect adds one quite troubling element of confirmation to Stein's argument, in my view.

The new worry is that the petrodollar might go the way of the dodo bird, along with America's top position as the nation to which all others are linked in the global marketplace. This is because the largest oil producer in the Middle East and the second-largest petroleum consumer in the world are doing business in a way that troubles Western governments, especially some who worry about U.S. economic interests.

The following is how the deal was described in a recent *China Daily* article:

> In what Riyadh calls "the largest expansion by any oil company in the world," Sinopec's deal on Saturday with Saudi oil giant Aramco will allow a major oil refinery to become operational in the Red Sea port of Yanbu by 2014.
>
> The $8.5 billion joint venture, which covers an area of about 5.2 million square meters, is already under construction. It will process 400,000 barrels of heavy crude oil per day. Aramco will hold a 62.5 percent stake in the plant while Sinopec will own the remaining 37.5 percent.[22]

On top of this stunning development, which mysteriously has gone largely unreported by mainstream news media, China is making deals that indicate a grab for global economic power that will put it on track to replace America as the world's economic leader by 2014, or at the very latest, 2016, according to some economists.

Sino investment in petroleum refining capacity is unmatched by any other nation. It seems a master at implementing almost ingenious strategies for putting in place world-class refining facilities. Additionally, China is most successful as of late with developing relationships with new OPEC partners. Such relationships mean economic leverage that could soon subordinate U.S. relations with the same countries. The communist regime, with its newfound business development acumen, has partnered with Egypt by providing funding for a new refining project. Nigeria is another nation with which a partnership is being formed. Three new super-refineries are in the works there.

All of this is underway while America has to contend with regulations heaped upon other regulations. The current presidential administration fights every step of the way against constructing pipelines that would have oil flowing from near neighbor, Canada, and refuses to cooperate with U.S. oil interests in everything from drilling to gasoline production that would eventually be beneficial to the American consumer—thus to the creation of hundreds of thousands of jobs.

These developments, if carried to their ultimate extent, bring about some interesting prophetic possibilities. They also might answer, to some degree, the questions posed by Stein's caller the other day. Is China building its military at such a phenomenal pace in order to protect its interests from attack? Or, does China intend to initiate a first attack of some sort with its massive military forces?

Again, Revelation plainly foretells that there seems a barrier, the Euphrates River, that will separate the occidental from the oriental worlds until a specific time, as far as military conflict is concerned.

For most of the latter part of the twentieth century, the fear was that the Chinese communist leaders would one day use their overwhelming numbers to militarily invade all of the territory under their hegemony.

But then came the newfound economic-development brilliance within that leadership. And now, it is an invasion of another sort: replacing the petrodollar and the U.S. with another sort of power-wielding currency.

So, rather than sudden destructiveness through nuclear war exchanges, there is the growing economic bubble of trouble in the West and a growing threat of financial swamping by the Sino tsunami. It is a somewhat slower movement toward Armageddon. But, the same "slime" (petroleum material) that Nimrod employed to make the bricks with which he intended to build the tower to heaven (read Genesis 11) is at the center of—is the catalyst for—the building catastrophe Revelation foretells will bring all armies of the world to man's final war at the time of Christ's Second Advent.

April 9, 2012
Friends, Enemies, and Betrayal

Thinking on things pertaining to the death, burial, and resurrection of Jesus Christ—the remembrance of which Christians celebrated Sunday just past—set the story circulating about the Obama administration's apparent release of information involving Israel and Azerbaijan rumbling through my cogitations.

Betrayal of friends is the fodder of many a tragedy, both in fictional stories and in historical accounts. Judas Iscariot's treachery against the Lord Jesus is perhaps the most infamous of all such telling and retelling. Never was there a more wonderful and true friend than Jesus. He not only raised the dead, healed the blind, opened the ears of the deaf, healed the sick and lame, and fed multitudes with a miraculous breaking of the loaves and fish, but He gave God's Word to the people—God's love letter to all of mankind. He saved the souls of all the men who were His closest friends—His disciples. All but one, that is...

Judas Iscariot was of the devil, lost from the beginning (John 17:2). Judas had watched Jesus perform the miracles, had experienced Christ's love and comfort, and had sat in on the Master's breaking of God's Word on many occasions. But, the betrayal was accomplished without any thought of the friendship with which Judas had been blessed to enjoy on their travels together, leading to the night he sold Jesus out for thirty pieces of silver.

We who know Christ for salvation, which came about as a result of Christ's going to the cross, are nonetheless thankful for the betrayal. By that, I mean in the sense that God turned around the evil intended by Judas' father, the devil, and used it for absolute good, making reconciliation possible for all of lost humanity.

Betrayal is an ugly thing. It, when it is come to fruition, exposes the abscess in the core of character—lays bare the disease called sin that resides at the center of the soul. Sadly, there is an analogy to be made between Judas' betrayal of Jesus and the betrayals that have become increasingly manifest in recent months with regard to America's diplomatic interaction with our one-time best friend, in terms of international relations. I'm referring to Israel, the nation with which the United States has enjoyed what can only be described as a supernatural kinship, constructed by the God of heaven.

The prophetic portent presented by the betrayal, is, of course, less world-changing than was Judas' betrayal of the Lord. America's selling out Israel, in this and every instance it has happened as of late, is staggering in its implications.

The case can be made most effectively, I think, by exposing the current presidential administration's turning its diplomatic back on God's chosen people, while considering the dangerous drama building between Israel and Iran. The following news excerpt helps portray the subterfuge perceived by a well-known former diplomat.

> Former U.S. diplomat John Bolton alleged Thursday that the Obama administration leaked a story about covert Israeli activity in order to foil potential plans by the country to attack Iran's nuclear program.
>
> Bolton, who served as U.S. ambassador to the United Nations in the George W. Bush administration, was responding to an article in Foreign Policy magazine that quoted government sources

claiming Israel had been granted access to airfields in Azerbaijan—along Iran's northern border.

The article did not state exactly what the Israelis' intentions were, but it suggested it could point to a possible strike on Iran.

"I think this leak today is part of the administration's campaign against an Israeli attack," Bolton claimed on Fox News.[23]

Azerbaijan is a small country strategically located along Iran's northern border. Israel has had an ongoing relationship of relative goodwill with that country's leadership. Observers of the diplomatic world report that the friendship goes much, much deeper than simply diplomatic courtesies. The relationship between Azerbaijan and the Jewish state has been compared to an iceberg, meaning that things of great diplomatic weight going on beneath the surface belie the almost insignificant-appearing niceties for public consumption.

Reports are that those within the Obama administration fear that the Azerbaijan-Israeli friendship has resulted in the selling of an air base to Israel for the purpose of providing a place to land, once a strike takes place on the Iranian nuclear development facilities. Thus, the planes would not have to risk refueling in air, necessarily, or risk returning to home base in Israel proper without taking on more fuel.

According to an interview with Lt. Col. Oliver North, the biggest concern within the administration is for the dangers posed to the re-election of President Barack Obama. North said those within the Obama campaign will do anything and everything it takes to keep the president out of trouble as the 2012 effort at re-election runs its course. The Israelis must be prevented from attacking Iran's nuclear facilities at all costs is the re-election imperative.

North spoke to Fox News host Sean Hannity on Monday, April 2:

"Sean, what is happening here is a full-court press that is political and ideological because there is this naive utopian hope within the Obama administration that if they can simply bring about some kind of Palestinian-Israeli peace accord, all the problems of the Jihad being waged against us will go away—it won't work...."

"All of it is being done to prevent Israel from launching an attack on Iran's nuclear sites," North said. "If the only goal is to have Barack Obama survive this presidential election, it makes political sense and the ideology of this blissful hope that some kind of Palestinian-Israeli peace accord is going to solve all of our problems—again, extraordinarily naive and utopian."[24]

Colonel North went on to say that no Israeli prime minister, whether Benjamin Netanyahu or some other, less hawkish, leader can ever fail to remember Israel's uncompromising principle for survival: "Never again!"

American leaders should never forget a principle that is much more important. Friendship with Israel—even if it means conflict with Israel's enemies that might lead to war—must never be betrayed. That principle is issued by the very Creator of all things:

> And I will bless them that bless thee, and curse him that curseth thee: and in thee shall all families of the earth be blessed.
>
> Genesis 12:3

April 16, 2012
Waging Race War

America is at the forefront of a significant end-times prophetic signal while the 2012 presidential battle enters the stage of all-out fury. It is not only warfare of a political race we are witnessing, but also what just might be something that will grow to be all-out racial warfare.

Trayvon Martin's death at the hands of George Zimmerman in Sanford, Florida, might be the spark that ignites the U.S. theater of the racial war that has for decades been raging around the world, spawning genocide and dictatorships of every description. It is beyond any doubt warfare strategically planned by the father of all hatred, the old serpent.

Mainstream media and leftist ideologues—in my view—are at the heart of stirring the cauldron of racial strife. These consistently incite, and constantly hold up before the American public the inciters' own bigotry—that of bias against white citizenry. They incessantly imply and outright declare that the present generation of the Caucasian community of this nation is responsible for the slavery that stained America's early history.

Their "reporting" and "declaration," however, are disingenuous. The "journalist" race-baiters—and that's what they are—do their inciting in order to make exciting news, not simply report it. The ideologues do their race-baiting for political gain. Their thinly veiled purpose is to, in effect, hold their voters on the politico-economic plantation. They promise to redistribute wealth and make the haves forfeit their wealth to the have-nots.

The truth is that both factions within the race-baiting industry mentioned here do so to accumulate to themselves the filthy lucre—the money—to be made by keeping the racial strife on the front burners of culture and society. They want power that such wealth buys them. They thus embrace the very love of mammon they claim to so disdain. Mainstream media has to go through all sorts of verbal gymnastics to make their point. But, they will work as hard as necessary to accomplish their destructive mission.

The prime example I offer is, again, found in the case of Trayvon Martin's death at the hands of George Zimmerman. Mainstream news organizations such as Reuters displayed a photograph of a young, preteen boy, and describe Trayvon Martin as a black teenager who was carrying only some candy and other nonthreatening articles with him when he was found. George Zimmerman was described by the same news sources as a "white" Hispanic who was a self-appointed security cop vigilante, and who followed the seventeen-year-old and shot him, despite having been told by a 911 operator to stop following Martin. The reporting of the event was in both cases, if not totally inaccurate, certainly incomplete.

There were no awaiting details of police investigative reports. No waiting for eyewitness accounts to be gathered and told. The template was set. That template mandated that the story unfold as a hate crime, perpetrated against an innocent black child by a white person. And, that's the way it was presented—and is still presented, with the obvious intent to generate a national, political mood that will ultimately benefit a political party that is the choice preferred by the elite media and the liberal left.

The Florida state prosecutor appointed to look into the shooting seems to have, for several weeks after the case finally reached headline status, not found enough evidence to pursue an arrest in the case. And, remember, the case was a month old before the recent publicity brought it to the forefront of national news. Then tremendous pressure revved up by the likes of Jesse Jackson and Al Sharpton, fanned by media propaganda designed to whip up social and cultural unrest, apparently helped her decide to formulate charges against Zimmerman.

The president of the United States could have—like presidents have done before in powder-keg situations—calmed the building racial firestorm. Instead, he threw fuel on the fire by stating from his high office that if he had a son, he would look like Trayvon. His Department of Justice has weighed in. U.S. Attorney General Eric Holder sent several from the Justice Department to meet with the family of Trayvon Martin. The attorney general has given his verbal approval in a speaking forum to Al Sharpton for Sharpton's leading rallies that stirred up residents in the black community to which Trayvon Martin belonged, as well as elsewhere in Florida.

Holder called those doing the revving up, as well as his Department of Justice representatives, "peacemakers"—despite the fact that Sharpton's call was for justice against George Zimmerman and was invective against the state attorney general before any of the evidence was presented. It was community activist pressure, pure and simple, and something to which the obviously prejudiced U.S. attorney general should never have lent his national public office.

Holder didn't reach out to the "white" Hispanic Zimmerman family in order to "make peace." Neither did he come down against the New Black Panther Party, which has put a large bounty on Mr. Zimmerman—a thing illegal in every sense in both Florida and the United States of America. Am I saying that I think Trayvon Martin should have been killed? Of course not. It is a tragedy in every sense. Any racial bigotry—and it remains to be seen if bigotry was at the heart of this tragedy—is absolutely against God's love for all humanity, and He will deal with it in great judgment.

What I am saying is that racial strife is being stirred by the mainstream media and by some elements within the U.S. government. Regardless of the degree of Mr. Zimmerman's innocence or guilt, the bigotry—the race-baiting—is being contrived and carried out by our nation's government, which is supposed to be there to promote the general welfare and ensure domestic tranquility.

The true peacemaker, the Lord Jesus Christ, prophesied that there would be ever-increasing racial strife at the time His Second Coming nears. We are seeing that prophecy in the process of fulfillment in these final hours of the Church Age. Jesus foretold the following:

> For nation shall rise against nation, and kingdom against kingdom:
> and there shall be famines, and pestilences,
> and earthquakes, in diverse places.
>
> Matthew 24:7

We have written before in these commentaries that the word "nation" is *ethnos* in the Greek language. We get the English word "ethnic" from this term. "Nation will rise against nation," then, means that Jesus was saying that there will be great "ethnic" upheaval. The definition of "ethnic" is "racial" or "race." Jesus prophesied tremendous racial strife in the days immediately leading up to His next catastrophic intervention into human history.

We are talking here about one more signal that forewarns that we will soon hear the shout from heaven: "Come up here!" (Revelation 4:1).

April 23, 2012
Mid-East War This Summer?

It's like the proverbial broken record—or, I guess that would be "broken CD" in today's jargon. This summer will be the time of that explosion in the Middle East that will set the world aflame, with petroleum the accelerant that ignites the conflict. We have heard the same dire predictions for at least the past five years. Still, the explosion hasn't come.

I've received numerous copies of Joel Rosenberg's blog article with the title, "War This Summer?" and I've heard him talking about all-out war in the Middle East since before he spoke to the Pre-Trib Research Center group in Dallas a number of years ago. Rosenberg is not the only one who has declared early in every year recently past that war will erupt during the summer. Many have predicted that something would happen to spark war so violent that that prophetic region will not be able to contain the devastation. The likely results, it has been said by some, will be the "presumed" Psalms 83 war, or even the Gog-Magog war of Ezekiel 38–39.

Iran's incessant movement toward developing a nuclear capability continues to raise the fear level of the international diplomatic actors. This is not without good reason. Iran's chief political leader, Mahmoud Ahmadinejad, has, as we have pointed out many times, spewed hatred that includes the threat to wipe Israel off the map. But the same diplomat elitists seem to fear even more what Israeli Prime Minister Benjamin Netanyahu might do as a preemptive action against Iran's nuclear weapon ambitions.

The worried diplomats talked with Iran about their nuclear program on Friday, April 13. Rosenberg relayed the gist of the talks by writing: "International negotiations with Iran went nowhere on Friday. More discussions are schedule for May, though Israeli Prime Minister Netanyahu said this was a gift to the Iranians who will have more time to enrich uranium and accelerate their weapons development program."[25]

The displeased Israeli prime minister said in a meeting with U.S. Senator Joe Lieberman: "My initial impression is that Iran has been given a freebie…[Iran] got five weeks to continue enrichment without any limitation, any inhibition."[26]

Rosenberg wrote that the "fruitless" talks had no sooner ended than speculation of imminent war began revving up in Israel. The Times of Israel website reported:

> A major Israel TV station on Sunday night broadcast a detailed report on how Israel will go about attacking Iran's nuclear facilities in the event that diplomacy and sanctions fail and Israel decides to carry out a military strike.[27]

The newspaper's reporter was apparently given unusual access to Israeli military inside planning, according to Rosenberg's blog:

> The report, screened on the main evening news of Channel 10, was remarkable both in terms of the access granted to the reporter, who said he had spent weeks with the pilots and other personnel he interviewed, and in the fact that his assessments on a strike were cleared by the military censor. No order to strike is likely to be given before the P5+1 talk with Iran resume in May, the reporter, Alon Ben-David, said. "But the coming summer will not only be hot but tense."[28]

Avi Lipkin, a well-known Jewish author and speaker on the Middle East war tensions and Islam's likely part in Bible prophecy, drew my attention the morning of Tuesday, April 17. He was being interviewed by Dr. Larry Spargimino of Southwest Radio Ministries. His observations presented some rather unorthodox, but fascinating, food for prophetic thought. I want to share some of it with you.

The host asked his guest about the "horrific situation" that seems to be getting worse every day—referring to the building threat of war with regard to Iran and Israel. Lipkin launched into reasons to be considered and speculated upon what might happen in the region. He said that the Iranian people are "good people," and there is a need for a regime change to make life better for them.

Then he made some rather startling statements.

Lipkin says he believes that President Obama, "the international conductor of the orchestra," is going to lead a war against Iran, probably a month or two before his re-election. He then brings up the nuclear threat. But, this is not a major reason, he says, because the international community really doesn't care if Israel is nuked out of existence.

Lipkin said the more important reason, in the eyes of the international diplomatic community, is the following:

> The Saudis are more threatened than the Jews are. The Saudis are Sunnis. The Saudis will have their heads chopped off by the Iranians, because the Iranians see the Saudis as heretics, infidels and traitors.... The Saudis are commanding Obama, and they say that your job is to destroy the Shiite threat—meaning the ayatollah regime. Replace it with another regime. And, secondly, your job after you get reelected is to destroy Israel.

Lipkin said:

> [Another] reason for the war [that is coming] is that President Obama needs this war to get re-elected. But, the war should not be now, according to Obama. The war should [take place] into the summer, or late summer, so that he can ride on this crest of new popularity. That the Jews and Christians will vote for him, because he saved Israel.

Further, Lipkin stated that the real reason for the war is oil.

> The world is thirsty for oil. And, the one world order, which is in bed with the Moslems, is the harlot riding the dragon, in my opinion. The one-world government wants the oil. You cannot get to that oil until you destroy the Iranian regime and bring in an international regime that will be subservient to the oil companies.

Avi Lipkin concluded by saying:

> So, I think that these are the [reasons] for the war with Iran. I think it will happen sometime this year, probably much closer to the election than now.

But, I think that the Iranian regime will be removed, and then what we will see is that the Shiites in Syria, the Shiites in Lebanon will be terminated.

Then we are going to see a monolithic Sunni Armageddon army marching on Israel—which will probably be four or five years from now.

I've noticed that Lipkin's outlook on these matters—much of which doesn't fit my own perspective—is in agreement with a growing number of opinions I come across on a daily basis these days. The cynicism is rampant. Many believe there will be a war this summer or in the early fall, and, like Avi Lipkin, believe it will be a war contrived in large part for political reasons in this presidential election year.

One thing certain is that the prophetic players are almost in alignment for the wind-up of the age. The shout from Christ to His church, therefore, can't be far distant!

> After this I looked, and, behold, a door was opened in heaven:
> and the first voice which I heard was as it were of a trumpet
> talking with me; which said, Come up hither,
> and I will shew thee things which must be hereafter.
>
> Revelation 4:1

April 30, 2012
China's Patience

One of the literary descriptions of the Chinese people is often wrapped in one word–inscrutable. Among that word's synonyms are the following: incomprehensible, unexplainable, unfathomable, impenetrable, inexplicable, ambiguous, and difficult. I think of the nation of China, in general terms, as one thing more–extremely patient.

One of the most validating proofs of the patience of the Chinese is found in, I think, the matter of the debt it has purchased and maintained on its financial books—especially the debt of the United States of America. It is estimated that China holds U.S. Treasury bonds and other debts totaling approximately $1 trillion. The Chinese nation holds indebtedness of other nations, also, to the approximate tune of $2 trillion. It is a troubling matter that this is the case, when one considers that China has been, since the revolution that brought communism to power, America and the world's most dangerous adversary. It is the most dangerous because of the synonyms above that define the Chinese communist leadership since, particularly, the time of Mao Zedong. They have been all of those things: incomprehensible, unexplainable, unfathomable, impenetrable, inexplicable, ambiguous, and difficult.

And now they hold the wealth of America and the world in the palms of their inscrutable hands. The question arises: Why do they keep purchasing debt, when they might never collect, seeing as how all nations are headed, obviously, toward the fiscal abyss?

Is it just that they, like most of the world's economic gurus seem to think, believe that no matter how bad it gets, a solution will magically be found, and the indebted nations will make good on their restoration to financial health? They have been, since that communist revolution, the most bellicose of enemies in terms of threatening anyone who crosses them. Why the patience now, gladly holding the debt of their enemies, who by any stretch of the imagination have no hope of repaying the debt that is growing exponentially?

Now, I know the Chinese have made protests and even threats of fiscal action if their debtors don't straighten up their economic acts. But, for the most part, the Chinese leadership's patience is...well...inscrutable. Add to all of this perplexity another piece of the Chinese puzzle. The following brief excerpt from a recent news story is interesting to consider:

> North Korea has almost completed preparations for a third nuclear test, a senior source with close ties to Pyongyang and Beijing told Reuters, an act that would draw further international condemnation following this month's failed rocket launch which the United States and others said was a disguised missile test.

> "Peace and stability on the Korean peninsula and in Northeast Asia bears on China's national interest and also bears on the interests of all relevant parties," Chinese Vice Foreign Minister Cui Tiankai told a news briefing.
>
> "China will oppose anything which might jeopardize peace and stability on the Korean peninsula and in Northeast Asia, as this would damage China's national security interests and the interests of the relevant parties as well," he said, when asked about the possibility of a new nuclear test by North Korea.[29]

This is the same China that threatened to bring its hordes into the Korean peninsula in support of the North Koreans during the Korean conflict. It was even willing to go to nuclear war with the West if the North Korean regime looked to be losing, according to reports back then. Now China is acting like the peacemaker, even set to discipline its rabid North Korean pet, if necessary to preserve world stability.

Why the present level of civil comportment?

To my way of thinking, the answer is China is exerting extraordinary patience for very special reasons. We are paying to outfit the army of two hundred million we read about in Bible prophecy and in accounts from news sources that tell us China and its Asian allies could easily outfit such a military juggernaut today.

They are confident—I believe their patience shows—that they will recoup their losses when they one day have enough, in terms of superior military assets, to become bill collectors on an unprecedented scale. We begin to see how even the kings of the East—as inscrutable as that part of the world is—fit into the end-times prophetic puzzle.

MAY 2012

May 7, 2012
Evil Seducers in the Limelight

It seems the prophetic moment has arrived that the apostle Paul warned about in more than one epistle:

> But evil men and seducers shall wax worse and worse, deceiving, and being deceived.
>
> 2 Timothy 3:13

> Wherefore take unto you the whole armour of God that ye may be able to withstand in the evil day, and having done all, stand.
>
> Ephesians 6:13

Unfolding events of recent days make clear the accuracy of God's Word in foretelling things to come. Paul, in his perilous-times prophecy of 2 Timothy, speaks to some very specific characteristics of end-times mankind that will mark the very end of the Age of Grace—the time just before Christ calls His church into heaven (John 14:6; Revelation 4:1).

He writes in that 2 Timothy, chapter 3, forewarning, as I've picked and chosen, the following:

> This know also, that in the last days perilous times shall come. For men shall be lovers of their own selves...proud, blasphemers... unholy, without natural affection...false accusers, incontinent, fierce, despisers of those that are good.
>
> 2 Timothy 3:1–3

Issues and events, as they have developed in very recent days, are accurately described and defined by words I've chosen from Paul's "perilous-times" prophecy. It's almost as if the public carrying on of one individual in particular epitomizes all of the characteristics that Paul prophesies for the very days in which we find ourselves. It's as if we see personified the end-times characteristics of Paul's prophecy manifested before our very eyes and ears in the news reports. Specifically, I see these characteristics displayed: unholy, blasphemers, false accusers, fierce, and despisers of those that are good.

The individual—the human subject of all the recent attention—displays the last-days evil that has become a visceral part of American culture. Media—both news and entertainment—seem to proudly put it all in the limelight for the eager eyes and ears of the American public. The nation's youth seem to me to be the particular recipients of the evil's focus.

The Obama administration has stated it has made it a priority to attack bullying whenever and wherever it raises its ugly head. But, like so much of the surface promises of transparency and action on behalf of the American public, its true intentions and nature have been exposed by the light of truth. Administration propagandists have at their disposal mainstream media sycophants—both entertainment and news—that have done all they can to cover the recent hubbub created by one of its chosen in the ongoing war against Judeo-Christian-value-based morality in this nation.

Dan Savage, spokesman for the so-called anti-bullying organization, "It Gets Better Project," behind which the Obama administration has thrown its presidential weight, viciously attacked, verbally, a group of Christian high school students who walked out on one of his what has been described as "vulgar and vitriolic" presentations. This excerpt of a blog-report on the matters involved explains further:

> This is the same Dan Savage who spoke at the National High School Journalism Conference last week, where he ripped into the Bible and called religious students "pansy-assed" for walking out on him. But, there's much more to Dan Savage than just anti-

> religious bullying. He's one of the biggest bullies on the planet. And he's the point person the White House specifically chose—and fundraised for—in order to push their anti-bullying agenda. Now, it's not as though the White House was ignorant of the fact that the "It Gets Better Project" is run by Savage. On the contrary—search the White House website for Savage's name, and two "It Gets Better" links come up.... The Obama Administration has placed significant support behind the so-called "It Gets Better Project." The White House has devoted a specific section of the White House.gov website to the project. President Obama, Vice President Biden, Secretary of State Hillary Clinton, House Minority Leader Nancy Pelosi, Secretary of Labor Hilda Solis, Secretary of Agriculture Tom Vilsack, and many other administration officials have cut videos on behalf of the Project.[30]

The organization's goal, at first glance, seems honorable. Its stated purpose is designed to protect children from bullying:

> Everyone deserves to be respected for who they are. I pledge to spread this message to my friends, family and neighbors. I'll speak up against hate and intolerance whenever I see it, at school and at work. I'll provide hope for lesbian, gay, bi, trans and other bullied teens by letting them know that "It Gets Better."

However, it is the latter part of the pledge to which Savage—and a vast number within the administration—are truly devoted. The homosexual agenda is all important in their scheme to affect and infect the morality of America's youth.

The kinds of "bullying" verbiage from the "lectures" Mr. Savage presents—as he did the day the high school students walked out, thus igniting his wrath—are actually more salacious than I'm willing to post here. But, suffice it to say that he has made the following statement that he wishes "all ****ing Republicans were dead." He has used the same kind of language in wishing Christians were in the same condition.

We are indeed in Paul's perilous times. This generation is facing a most evil day. We had better gird for the evil men and seducers—which includes the mainstream media—who are out to remove every trace of morality from the face of America and the world. But, the same apostle who forewarned of this very hour was given the following from the Holy Spirit to comfort and reassure Christians alive in these troubling but exciting days:

> For God hath not given us the spirit of fear;
> but of power, and of love, and of a sound mind.
>
> 2 Timothy 1:7

May 14, 2012
At Sodom's Gate

My mind is impressed, as Israel's sixty-fourth year into the modern era arrives on May 14, that God's dealing with man seems about to make full circle. By that, I mean that the Book given to humanity that is His love letter and His manual for living life on this planet, given through His chosen nation, opens, in my spiritual mind, to the pages of the time of Lot and his life in Sodom.

It seems to me that we can sense, if we consider the headlines today, the angels of judgment at the gates of our own nation. Are they there, sent by the Lord of heaven, after having entertained the efforts of God's servants—like Abraham those thousands of years ago—to find, percentage-wise, ten righteous people who have a heart for the things of the Lord?

Israel is the prototype nation—i.e., all successive nations have had Israel to use as a template of how to act, not act, react, and conduct the affairs within the human conditions of their time in the spotlight of history. We are at just such a time of examination, in my estimation, of our own much blessed country.

It is striking to me that a first-time author has hit it big with a book that deals almost precisely with the premise of this commentary. *The*

Harbinger by Jonathan Cahn uses just such a template to dissect the Almighty's dealings with Israel as juxtaposed against the recent history of America.

This isn't a review of that book, so I won't say a great deal about it. Suffice it to say that I find the relevant points of similarities between the two nations quite remarkable, as presented by the author. I recall my own opening remarks in a book written not long after the attacks on the U.S. of September 11, 2001, as I reflect on what Mr. Cahn has written.

> Television screens across America and the world repeatedly flashed videotape of the huge passenger jet crashing full-throttle into the enormous building. Dazed people watched in awestruck disbelief while trapped victims leaped from the building's top floors, some holding hands with others when they jumped. The massive twin towers disintegrated and crumbled to flaming rubble. It was the most heinous terrorist attack ever recorded. Almost immediately, angry, frightened people began demanding answers to the insanity now forever etched in their memories. Many churches were filled the Sunday following the attacks in New York and Washington, D.C. There was an instinctive sense that those murderous acts of terrorism were somehow foreordained. That the carnage now known as "Ground Zero" and the uncertain future is, in some troubling way, linked by prophetic destiny. *(Prophecy at Ground Zero: From Today's Middle East Madness to the Second Coming of Christ.)*[31]

The author of *The Harbinger* reaches much of the same sorts of conclusions as did the authors who collaborated with me in our book, released in 2002. He gets much more specific about Ground Zero in Lower East Manhattan than did we, providing some really chilling similarities between things written in prophecy about Israel and their fulfillment, and what has happened in America since that fateful 9/11 date. He does a credible job of postulating—with strong scriptural backing—on how the

U.S. judgment looks to have begun taking place in earnest at the time the towers fell on September 11, 2001.

The bottom line is that events just this past week bring home in an almost eerie way that the angels of judgment must be at the very gates of our own nation. We have long recounted the many signals of impending prophetic fulfillment. The nation Israel is at the center of hatred in the U.N.; the reviving Roman Empire is rearranging daily into prophetic configuration; the Roadmap to Peace plan is being pushed to make Israel conform to the wishes of the international community; the world is moving swiftly toward one world—especially toward global economy that threatens to bring the dollar down and install some sort of electronic funds transfer system.

As if that weren't enough evidence of where we stand on God's prophetic timeline, there is Russia, Iran, Turkey, and the whole Islamic world coming together in a way that indicates the Gog-Magog prophecy of Ezekiel 38–39 is shaping for soon fulfillment. China represents a growing hegemonic threat not only in all of Asia, but in the whole world, economically speaking.

And now, astonishingly, the first sitting president of the United States in history, on the heels of his vice president first doing so, puts America directly at the gates of Sodom with his declaration that marriage should be made legal as between a man and a man and a woman and a woman. That is, it would indeed be astonishing—except that the U.S. citizenry has been desensitized by years of news and entertainment media inculcation, putting forward the idea that there is no difference between heterosexual and homosexual relationships. So, where at one time—no more than a decade ago—an incumbent president proposing such a thing would have sealed his own defeat, we now have no way of knowing if it will adversely affect his election chances.

Again, we hear the words of Jesus echo in forewarning of when He will next catastrophically intervene into earth's history:

> Likewise also as it was in the days of Lot; they did eat, they drank,
> they bought, they sold, they planted, they builded;

But the same day that Lot went out of Sodom it rained fire and brimstone from heaven, and destroyed them all.

Even thus shall it be in the day when the Son of man is revealed.
Luke 17:28–30

May 21, 2012
Welfare World Order

Watchmen on the wall should be alert as never before. It is becoming clearer by the day. The self-appointed governing elitists of planet earth are using the slothful inclination of fallen mankind as fuel for the engine of their drive toward a New World Order.

We witness time after time the bringing down by angry voters European leaders who aren't totally sold out to the socialistic promises of something for nothing—or at least many handouts for very little work in return by the citizenry of the nations they serve. We thereby begin to understand the means by which the Antichrist regime will eventuate. Chaos in the streets translates to first untenable, unsustainable promises by elected politicians to quell the unrest. Then, eventually, an absolute iron fist of control as forecast in Revelation 13:16–18 will be used to bludgeon resisters into submission to the beast-state.

One blog pundit recently interviewed an insider to the world economic elite. I'm not certain about the multi-billionaire interviewee's position within the global economic order of things, but his commentary in answering seems to indicate he sees great danger in the machinations of his peers who are part of the new tower of Babel builders.

Multi-billionaire Hugo Salinas Price told the blogger news service interviewer that the globalists elite plan to control the world. Now, that's not a surprise to biblical prophecy watchmen. We here at Rapture Ready have written countless times about this plan. We have done so, resisting the conspiracy-theorist mentality that tends to set dates and name names as if we were Old Testament prophets. The observations from a globalist insider, on the other hand, present possibilities too fascinating to resist reporting. Salinas Price told his interviewer that the globalists' plan to completely rebuild the world order into a new one is a disturbing fact as time moves forward. He said:

> The problems we are seeing in the West are not going to be resolved in any positive way. What we have had in the West, in recent decades, has been the welfare state. The welfare state is, in my view, what I would call, "socialism light." We've had "socialism light" and now we're going to transition to full-blown socialism.... [It is these] elite, who do not want to give up their control. The furtherance of their control lies in socialism.
>
> I think this comes from a central idea that has possessed the imagination of the world. It's the idea that authority comes from below. In other words, that authority comes from the people. This idea of authority from the will of the people is a myth of our civilization....
>
> I'm just saying that those who control the world know they have to curry the favor of the people. To do this they went the way of the welfare state, and democracy to give people the fiction they (the people) are in control. Well, they are not and never have been.[32]

To watchmen on the wall, it is increasingly clear that what Mr. Salinas Price reports is based in truth. And it is easy to observe that America is in the crosshairs of those who are targeting the United States for the New World Order methodologies with regard to bringing about the ever-increasing welfare state. This nation is on the fast track to becoming the completely changed nation Barack Obama promised during the last presidential campaign.

May 28, 2012
Jerusalem's Burdensome Stone

Israeli Prime Minister Benjamin Netanyahu has once again thrown down the proverbial gauntlet. Despite his playing to the news cameras and to the international community diplomatic forces trying to force the Jewish state to divide the city where Jesus was crucified, when push comes to shove, Netanyahu says a resounding "NO" to Jerusalem being divided.

The prime minister has, as pointed out before, learned to talk the talk in playing the game to agree on matters of forging some sort of a peace. This is a trick long utilized by PLO head Yasser Arafat and most other Islamists when it comes to seeming to agree to move ahead with peace, but always changing some things at just the right time in the process to prevent negotiations from ever actually coming to fruition. Netanyahu, however, makes no bones about the status of Jerusalem in his thinking.

He said, upon becoming prime minister the first time around:

> I will never allow Jerusalem to be divided again. Never! Never! We will keep Jerusalem united and...we will never resurrender those ramparts....
>
> Jerusalem has been the capital of Israel for 3,000 years since the time of King David and we don't expect to change that for the next 3,000 years!

His present position, despite all of his jockeying to produce sound bites that make it seem he's for doing most anything to bring about the Roadmap to Peace, is as firm as ever. Netanyahu's position with regard to Jerusalem is unchanged. He recently made his thoughts even more adamant about Jerusalem and what he considers the most vital matter involved in keeping the city undivided, according to the following news excerpt:

> Whoever proposes that giving up the heart of Jerusalem—the Temple Mount—will bring peace, is fatally mistaken, Prime Minister Binyamin Netanyahu declared on Monday evening. Addressing the Knesset plenum at a special session held to honor Jerusalem Day, Netanyahu said that taking the Temple Mount out of Israeli hands, would bring decline, and the rise of radical Islam in the region and in the world...

> "Only under Israeli control, will this accessibility...and freedom of religion continue," he said. "The Temple Mount is in our hands and...it shall remain in our hands."[33]

Netanyahu's assessment of the vital importance of the Temple Mount is far more profound than even he realizes, I suspect. If I might be so bold, I refer to my own writing on the matter, written some years ago.

> Mt. Moriah sits at the southern end of the ancient city, crested by a golden dome that represents hundreds of millions whose religion demands of its adherents' blood-vowed opposition to God's chosen nation, Israel. This is the place God picked to have His temple on earth constructed. It is the precise location where the third temple will sit, the temple that will be desecrated by Antichrist, earth's last and most beastly tyrant. Even more importantly, the Temple Mount will be the home of Christ's Millennial Temple. Moriah, then to be known as Zion, will be supernaturally elevated by the tremendous topographical changes caused when the Lord's foot touches the Mount of Olives at His return.
>
> Diplomats of the world have, for the past four decades, engaged in effort after effort to bring stability to the region, at whose heart the city of Jerusalem sits. We remember the many jettings to and from Washington, D.C., Jerusalem, and other capitals of the Mideast. From Henry Kissinger, James Baker, Madeleine Albright, and Colin Powell to Condoleezza Rice. America's secretaries of state have burned mega-gallons of jet fuel in trying to find the formula for peace that would defuse the Armageddon bomb. And, the former British Prime Minister, Tony Blair, immediately upon resigning, was named by the so-called "Quartet" (U.S., E.U., U.N., and Russia) as the overseer of continuing efforts toward constructing Mideast peace, which has eluded mankind for thousand of years....

To be even more specific about the importance of the temple mount, here is what one of the foremost Christian Hebrew scholars, Arnold Fruchtenbaum, tells us.

> The significance of Israel' s reinstituting the Sanhedrin may be another event that leaves in place the possibility of how the Lord will work out His will with His people. Almost sixty years after a 1,900-year absence, the nation of Israel came into existence. Jewish people from the four corners of the world have made aliyah to live in the Land. The Temple Institute in Jerusalem has reconstructed the instruments for Jewish Temple worship; Jewish men determined to be descendants of Aaron, known as the Kohanim, are being trained in ritual practices to serve as Temple priests; and now we have the establishment of an authoritative body to speak to the nation of Israel on matters of Jewish religion. This is significant in light of such passages as Zechariah 12:10 and Hosea 5:15, which speak of a time when the people of Israel will be led into the acceptance of Jesus as their Messiah. The existence of a religious authority for the entire nation will facilitate the multitudes coming to faith. (Arnold Fruchtenbaum, *Ariel Ministries Newsletter,* Fall/Winter, 2004)

Make no mistake, the Temple Mount—Mount Moriah—is the burdensome stone that Zechariah the prophet foretold:

> And in that day will I make Jerusalem a
> burdensome stone for all people:
> all that burden themselves with it shall be
> cut in pieces, though all the people of the earth
> be gathered together against it.
>
> Zechariah 12:3

JUNE 2012

June 4, 2012
Damascus' Cup of Wrath

Reports of atrocities coming out of Syria are reminders of the ongoing rage of man against man. We live in a world headed for a time in which God must deal in judgment with planet earth. We get an inkling of what faces the cities of this world with the declaration found in the book of God's most terrible judgment.

> And the great city was divided into three parts, and the cities of the nations fell: and great Babylon came in remembrance before God, to give unto her the cup of the wine of the fierceness of his wrath.
>
> Revelation 16:19

The great commercial center at the time of that judgment will suffer as perhaps no city or people have ever suffered, when God's cup of wrath is full, and He gives it to Babylon to drink. Jesus Himself said it would be the most terrible time in human history—and that's saying something! This earth has been witness to regimes that have dealt so fiercely with their peoples that we sometimes wonder how the Creator of all things could have allowed such treatment.

The Lord has acted at times to judge the murderous governments throughout history, of course. The Third Reich is an example. Hitler's Reich was to last a thousand years, but lasted barely twelve, and is today looked upon as among the most heinous—certainly considered the most horrendous of the modern era. Yet there are elements among us that view the Nazi regime as a good idea, particularly because of the way that government treated the Jews.

Syria's present tyrant-ruler is one such admirer of the Nazi attitude toward God's chosen people. Like all Muslim states of the radical sort—and it's difficult to find one that isn't radical—the brutal Syrian dictatorship of Bashar al-Assad, successor to his father, Hafez al-Assad, hates Jews with satanic passion and has Israel in its crosshairs for annihilation. For this reason it can be said with certainty that, barring repentance, the Syrian leader and his ilk are in for some very rough times indeed. God's Word says about the people of earth and their treatment of Abraham's progeny:

> And I will bless them that bless thee,
> and curse him that curseth thee:
> and in thee shall all families of the earth be blessed.
>
> Genesis 12:3

But, it is not the Jews alone the Syrian dictator comes against with luciferian anger. He slaughters anyone who would defy his self-anointed right to rule with an iron fist of oppression. He is doing so with abandon these days, even in the face of pressure—although milquetoast pressure—by the international community.

The world of opposition to what's going on in Damascus and the surrounding area is of the spineless sort because of threats from Russia and China. Putin and the Chinese leadership have made it clear that any military action to put Assad out of power will be met with Russian and Chinese force. It is much like in the cold-war days when the Soviets and the Maoists held the nuclear threat over the heads of the world's diplomatic community.

As the death tolls rise with Assad's military murdering people in plain view, yet blaming the opposition rebel forces of perpetrating the killings, the international community sends the likes of former U.N. head, Kofi Annan, to plead with the Syrian dictator to stop the genocide.

During his meetings, Annan renewed an appeal to the Assad regime to end the violence against its people. Annan said he expressed the international community's concerns about the government attacks, including last week's slaughter in Houla.

"We are at a tipping point," Annan said. "The Syrian people do not want the future to be one of bloodshed and division. Yet the killings continue and the abuses are still with us today."[34]

Eleven nations, including the United States, said they are expelling Syrian envoys in a coordinated action over the killings. Besides the United States, Japan, the Netherlands, Australia, Britain, France, Germany, Italy, Spain, Bulgaria and Canada announced that they are expelling some Syrian diplomats.[35]

There seems no chance of a Jonah-Nineveh sort of repentance by Assad and his ruling henchmen. We can say with certainty, then, that God's judgment is on its way to Syria. But, it's not just the fact that God will judge anyone who hates Abraham's seed, or that judgment will come because of the obvious sins of the regime in murdering the Syrian people. We can know with certainty God's judgment is coming because of the prophecy, with which most Bible prophecy students are familiar.

> Behold, Damascus is taken away from being a city,
> and it shall be a ruinous heap.
>
> Isaiah 17:1

Damascus' cup of wrath is about to be poured by the mighty hand of God. But, lest the rest of the world thinks this city that harbors most every Islamist terrorist organization that is blood-vowed to destroy Israel is alone in the prophetic promise to drink of that cup of wrath, consider again the following forewarning to all cities of earth:

> And the great city was divided into three parts, and the cities of the nations fell: and great Babylon came in remembrance before God, to give unto her the cup of the wine of the fierceness of his wrath.
>
> Revelation 16:19

June 11, 2012
The Harbinger's Bottom Line

The Harbinger, a novel, meaning that it is a work of fiction, has fallen under a furor of opposition to the book, which is high on the *New York Times* Best-Seller list. Its author, Jonathan Cahn, a first-time author, astonishingly has been cast by some critics into the "brute beast" heap reserved for Jude's anti-God crowd (Jude 1:10–13).

I am astonished—not because Mr. Cahn is so castigated, but because he is categorized in such a way by a few of those I respect putting forth the particular critiques in question. I mentioned in my recent review of *The Harbinger* that the book is a phenomenon because it defied all odds to become a New York Times Best Seller. Those who govern such things usually have a bias against anything to do with Jesus Christ or His Name, except in cases in which He is slandered or His Name is used as profanity. Yet, these have accepted the novel and even made it one of their top-rated books. Some of the critics of whom I write—the ones attempting to cast Cahn and *The Harbinger* in the brute-beast mold described by Jude, comparing it to the likes of *The Shack*—are from the group well known as purveyors of Bible truth.

This is puzzling and quite disturbing to me, especially when Mr. Cahn is implied by some (not all) of his critics of the condemning sort to not have Jesus Christ or the gospel message of salvation anywhere in the book. Chapter 21 of *The Harbinger* has one of the strongest, Christ-centered salvation messages to be found in fiction or in nonfiction, if anyone cares to check the facts. What is most distressing is that those critics—again, among the most respected Christian apologists—would write such things, knowing they aren't telling the truth.

They wouldn't do this, I'm convinced. This leaves only one conclusion, in my estimation. They didn't read the whole novel—rather, skimmed it, missing this most important part. This is, in my opinion, an egregious act of slothfulness, which calls for an apology, not an unsubstantiated-by-the-facts apologetic. It might be said—and most likely was said—that the very fact that *The Harbinger* is accepted by the likes of the New York Times Best-Seller list is proof that Cahn's book is in the camp of Jude's brute-beast sort. Oh, really? I saw no such criticism of the Tim LaHaye-Jerry Jenkins Left Behind series coming from these same critics. Tim and Jerry used literary device—some that certainly could have been questioned—much in the same way Jonathan Cahn uses such device in his novel.

And, the fact that it is a novel, and stated as being a novel by Cahn—even is listed as fiction in the New York Times list—gives license to use such literary device. Yet, the critics in question treat *The Harbinger* differently than the LaHaye-Jenkins fiction series, choosing to almost seem to serve as a seminary board dissecting a doctoral dissertation on Bible exegesis.

It is NOT a doctoral dissertation. It is not a nonfiction book. It is a novel. It is a fictional account of a biblically prophetic truth, in the same way as was the Left Behind series.

Some among the critics in question use the words "fiction" and "novel" together. This shows a lack of understanding of the process of using fictional literary device. It is a redundancy of terms that anyone using such reference should make the effort to comprehend, or else just not pontificate upon the matters involved. These critics have overanalyzed, to an unwarranted degree, this work that God is using to forewarn our nation.

What has the author written that in any way detracts from God's great purpose—to draw men, women, and children to repentance? Why won't those who consider themselves the end-all purists recognize the nuances the Lord uses to accomplish that purpose? As mentioned, the LaHaye-Jenkins series is one such device the God of heaven used to draw people to repentance. That series was picked apart, too, but not to the degree *The Harbinger* has been dissected—and, certainly not by Bible students steeped in prophecy from the Scripture who should know better.

So far, I have attempted to give a broad overview of what I believe is an injustice done to a Christian author whose book our Lord is using to accomplish things some of us—including yours truly—have not been able to accomplish with our many nonfiction volumes on eschatology. It is obvious to me that *The Harbinger* is reaching millions in a short time, while our multitude of books has reached millions, collectively—but over decades. I see great importance in that fact, regarding the nearness of Christ's return. We should be cheering God's using this work in this way; but instead, there is division—division that is counter to God's purpose.

I will now point to some specifics as to why the criticisms against Jonathan Cahn and *The Harbinger* are unjust and unwarranted. Some of the following is a mixture of my own thoughts and the words of others who agree that the assault on this novel should not stand. I won't give attribution because I don't feel it is necessary. Those who have weighed in want only to see that this book is allowed to accomplish what the Lord has for it to accomplish in this time so near to Christ's calling the church into His presence.

Neither will I name names of those who have, in my opinion, been unfair and inaccurate in their condemnation. Again, I don't think that is necessary. I apologize if the following seems disjointed in some ways, as I have tried to meld and synthesize some of the conversations and emails in which I've been engaged involving these matters.

Some of the critics of *The Harbinger* who are in question begin with an erroneous assumption about eschatology, claiming that Cahn and we can only depend on the writings of Jesus and the apostles for an accurate eschatology. This smacks of hyper-dispensationalism. The entire Bible is eschatological, from Genesis through Revelation. In fact, it is very hard to get a complete, accurate picture of what Jesus and the apostles were referring to without studying the Tanach, especially the Prophets, since they are pregnant with end-times passages. If it were true, as the critics in question believe, that Isaiah 9 cannot in any way be applied to us, then we would indeed, perhaps, be luciferian, as one of the critics claims regarding the tenets of this novel.

However, when the apostle Paul said, "all Scripture is profitable," he meant ALL Scripture. Consider, for example:

> For whatsoever things were written aforetime
> were written for our learning.
> Romans 15:4

Consider also that 2 Timothy 3:16 tells us that the Scripture is inspired and "profitable." Jonathan Cahn, in *The Harbinger*, takes some general biblical principles and makes application of them much in the same way that some pastors have used the Song of Solomon to speak of the love relationship between Christ and the church. We all believe that God is the One who saves people, yet Paul wrote:

> I am made all things to all men,
> that I might by all means SAVE some.
> 1 Corinthians 9:22 (emphasis added)

Are we to attribute heresy to the apostle because of this statement?

Further, a chief element of the criticism I've read is that Cahn equates America to Israel in the matter of covenants made with and promises given the Jewish people.

The author brings out points of connection between the U.S. and Israel of old that simply are unmistakable linkages—not to God's covenant promises, but to the nation Israel as a prototype of how He must deal with sin in a corporate way.

Wasn't Nineveh given a chance to repent—and did so, thus sparing that corporate city-state? Why should America be immune from such restoration, if it is offered? And surely, it is offered. Isn't God (Jesus who is God) the same yesterday, today, and forever? Isn't He unchanging, with no shadow of turning?

One critic assumes that Cahn totally disregards the book of Revelation or does not believe in it because he never quoted it. That is ridiculous, since the subject was not the entire tome of eschatology, but a specific event, 9/11, and the aftermath of it. Cahn would have had to write an encyclopedia to meet this critic's standard (something that even these critics have not done). Our salvation is not based on pre-trib, mid-trib, or post-trib eschatology, but on Jesus' finished work on the cross and our belief in His literal return to establish His kingdom.

The critic in question accused Cahn of being an occultist, and then assumes the author is saying that a real prophet actually visited Cahn, and then tries to prove that the visitor could not have been a prophet because he seems to always be in the right places or appear mysteriously. Jonathan made it very clear that he was taking literary license to create the story. There was no prophet who in actuality visited him and gave him seals. The characters were fictional. The events and the Scripture were factual. He made that clear in interviews. That is part of why it can be said with a high degree of assurance that the critic in this case did not read the book objectively or do much other research.

And then there is biblical evidence for people showing up suddenly, seemingly out of nowhere, to give a prophetic word, then disappear like described in 8:38–39 when the Holy Spirit snatched Philip from the Ethiopian eunuch. Was Philip an occultist practicing astral projection? Of course not. Did not the Lord tell Ananias to go to Paul and give him specific directions as to where to find him? Do you not think Paul was a little freaked by having a stranger suddenly appear at his dwelling, lay hands on him, give him a message, and then restore his sight?

The critic in this case then accuses Cahn of subscribing to replacement theology, but again shows no evidence. One brother in Christ who wrote me said:

> I have known, studied with, and read the works of many Messianic Rabbis from Michael Brown to Arnold Fruchtenbaum to Kurt Schneider to many others. I have never found one yet that teaches "Replacement Theology." Though I could be wrong, they would be rarer than hen's teeth. Messianics despise "Replacement Theology" more than we do. Not only is it unbiblical, it is repugnant to them since it was the primary motivation that justified almost two millennia of inquisitions, torture, pogroms, and genocide of their people. Jonathan and I discussed this during a long phone call. He rejects replacement theology. First [this critic]

makes the statement that he can prove this, then backtracks and says he cannot.

The writer of the email then says the following:

> [The critic,] in [a] radio broadcast, suggests that Cahn is a Kabbalist. Again no evidence—and ridiculous. Messianics reject the Kabbala[h] as occultist. Only the most radical Orthodox, like the Hassidim or Haredim, practices Kab[b]ala[h]. Neither do they believe in the authority of the Talmud, only Biblical Judaism. This shows [the critic's] total ignorance of what Messianics believe.
>
> [The critic] then alludes to the idea that Cahn may be a Preterist or Dominionist, but again admits that he has no evidence to back it up. I have never met a Messianic that holds to Preterism or Dominionism. Those beliefs are Gentile in origin. All of them that I have read, and I have studied many, were all Pre-Millennial and Pre-Trib, Like Prasch and Fruchtenbaum. Even Sid Roth, who I do not advocate, prefers the Pre-Trib view but admits he is not dogmatic about it.

Examining the bottom-line results of any endeavor intended to produce something worthwhile is the way to gauge success. *The Harbinger* is a work, I'm convinced, thoroughly meant by its author to produce repentance. This is in alignment with God's grand purpose throughout His Holy Word, the Bible. So, let's look at *The Harbinger's* bottom line.

It has attained best-seller status on the most exclusive list of the book marketing industry. It is there against all odds—despite the world's hatred for Jesus Christ and His one-way only exclusivity in the matter of salvation and eternal life. The gospel (as given in chapter 21 of the book) is now in the hands of literally millions of people who likely would not get the message through books such as mine and those of the critics who have come down so hard on this novel. So many will read novels who would never pick up a book of nonfiction in the Bible prophecy genre.

The Harbinger uses Scripture—even if through literary license—to call people to salvation and America to repentance. Again, it makes linkage to Israel and the U.S. in ways that cannot be denied by anyone with half a brain to see things from the recent historical perspective. America has been so intricately linked to the Jewish state in its modern incarnation that the supernatural elements of the relationship can be denied only by those who deliberately wish to rewrite history. The prophetic import of the 9/11 event, with Cahn's putting facts together—again, using novelistic, scripturally suggested ties in the matter of calling those who will listen to repentance—is something that anyone who truly reads this book can't help but see clearly. The key is that you must actually read it to understand what the Lord is saying through this story.

Being on guard against deception and false prophecy is a God-ordained directive—especially for these troubling days in which we find ourselves. We are all called to be watchmen and Bereans. However, the bottom line—the question, "What is a work doing for the great cause of Christ?"—must be at the heart of that watchfulness. I implore my fellow watchmen on the wall: Save the blowing of the sirens of forewarning for activities that are truly against God's program for His human creation. Please do not render ill-thought-out criticism that is counter to our Lord's purposes.

To do otherwise than remain faithful to accurate, just, and fair examination of such works as *The Harbinger* is to engage in ministry that is putting out a noneffectual, little-boy-who-cried-wolf message to a world already headed for destruction because of unbelief.

June 18, 2012
Surveillance Society Surging

America is about to experience what citizenry in Britain has been going through for some time. The assault on U.S. privacy has been undergoing a metamorphosis for decades, but until very recently, the barriers have seemed to at least hold back unbridled Big Brotherism in this nation.

One journalist reported from England in a chapter for one of my books:

> If you want to be a film star, come to Britain. We're all on camera. All you have to do is walk through any town or drive down any road and you are watched, filmed, and monitored. When my wife, Pat, and I tour America, we feel neglected because the roadside cameras are no longer ever-present—not yet. As the world moves towards a "Big Brother" society beyond the nightmares of author George Orwell, who predicted a world in which the state watched everyone in his 1948 classic novel, *1984,* it is like we are inmates of a high-tech prison. Big Brother really is watching us in Europe. The rest of the world is not far behind.[36]

It seems that now Alan and Pat won't be sensing that they are neglected when they come to America. Strides are being made—in the name of commerce—to make sure that we are all on *Candid Camera.*

We have been listening to the debate for some time now about the drones that have spied on, then, in some cases, hunted down and taken out high-priority terrorist targets in some places in the Middle East. Now, the drones are being seen and reported more and more in the homeland. The most recent flap has been brought to our attention by U.S. Senator Rand Paul, who says such surveillance is becoming akin to violating the Fourth Amendment of the U.S. Constitution. That's the one that, in part, prohibits illegal searches and seizures of private citizens and their properties.

This past week, a story surfaced outlining the technology's invasive nature.

> Planes able to photograph sunbathers in their back gardens are being deployed by Google and Apple. The U.S. technology giants are racing to produce aerial maps so detailed they can show up objects just four inches wide. But campaigners say the technology is a sinister development that brings the surveillance society a step closer. Hyper-real: 3D mapping services used by C3 Technologies (as purchased by Apple) will form the main part of the software giant's new mapping service. Google admits it has already

> sent planes over cities while Apple has acquired a firm using spy-in-the-sky technology that has been tested on at least 20 locations, including London. Apple's military-grade cameras are understood to be so powerful they could potentially see into homes through skylights and windows. The technology is similar to that used by intelligence agencies in identifying terrorist targets in Afghanistan.[37]

People have embraced their satellite-to-vehicle capabilities in searching out locations while traveling. Browsers on the Internet love sometimes taking the virtual tours down the streets of cities throughout the nation. The convenience and entertainment presented by technology continues their desensitizing effects on the American public to the dangers inherent in such surveillance advances.

Homeland security agencies—which have proliferated since 9/11 and the radical Islamist attacks—seem oblivious to complaints that they are becoming increasingly invasive. It is troubling, although thoroughly fascinating, to witness how global control, long ago prophesied by the only source who knows the end from the beginning, is coming to fulfillment in our time.

It is no longer difficult to imagine how Antichrist and his regime of absolute control will have the technological facilities to keep tabs on every victim during the Tribulation. Developments in the global monetary world are moving along the necessity of bringing about that end-times system of control. The powers that be must find a way to make all conform to a singular methodology in transacting business. There must be a completely changed economic order in order to establish even a modicum of stability to a world gone mad in terms of economic insanity.

Satan moves malevolently on the minds of mankind, as the apostle Paul told us:

> For we wrestle not against flesh and blood, but against principalities, against powers, against the rulers of the darkness of this world, against spiritual wickedness in high places.
>
> Ephesians 6:12

All people of planet earth must be made to cooperate with the regulations the powers dictate. This means everyone must be observed at all times, which is where this is all leading. In my view, this is the major reason for the surging surveillance society we are considering here.

June 25, 2012
Principalities and Globalism

The G-20 met this last week in Mexico to try to reach some degree of consensus on how to globally govern the rest of us. The phrase "some degree," in combination with the word "consensus," constitutes what is known as a non sequitur, or nonstarter. The sentiment, thus expressed, does not follow. Consensus is just that—consensus; i.e., it strongly implies harmony without substantial opinion to the contrary.

In international community diplomatic parlance, however, "some degree" is as close to consensus as it gets. And, this quandary is at the heart of the distress and perplexity world leaders face in trying to govern the rest of us in a global way. Globalism—as it has always been attempted—has been an abject failure. The contentiousness is just too great when efforts are made to get the nations of the world to agree on anything, much less on things as monumental as creating a one-world order. All such monolithic projects have failed miserably since the Babel builders saw their attempt at world order under one man, more or less, come crashing down when God destroyed the tower under construction and scattered the would-be, new-world-order masters and their subjects to different locations around the world (Genesis 11). There simply is not consensus in the matter of globalism.

The individual egos among world leaders are themselves monumental—as titanic as the tower of that Genesis 11 account. The lyrics in a country song sum up the gargantuan egos of today's national leaderships: They are "legends in their own minds."

Because of the pride and arrogance—not to mention the greed and lust—rampant within so many countries, neither consensus nor anything close to it can ever be reached to produce a single, governing global entity. Yet those of us who study God's prophetic Word believe there is ultimately to be a global order under one dictator, the man of sin, the Antichrist.

Since there can never be harmony on a worldwide scale that will bring order like that indicated in Revelation 13:16–18, how will the beast's regime come to fulfillment? While thinking on such things, I was struck with the realization—upon reading an article by my friend Wilfred Hahn—that globalism is, itself, a non sequitur, a nonstarter.

Hahn, an expert on global economic matters whose articles appear on Rapture Ready, wrote the following, quoting Moisés Naím, the well-known former editor-in-chief of *Foreign Policy* magazine and former executive director of the World Bank:

> When was the last time you heard that a large number of countries agreed to a major international accord on a pressing issue? Not in more than a decade....
>
> These failures represent not only the perpetual lack of international consensus, but also a flawed obsession with multilateralism as the panacea for all the world's ills. It has become far too dangerous to continue to rely on large-scale multilateral negotiations that stopped yielding results almost two decades ago. So what is to be done? To start, let's forget about trying to get the planet's nearly two hundred countries to agree. We need to abandon that fool's errand in favor of a new idea: minilateralism. By minilateralism, I mean a smarter, more targeted approach: We should bring to the table the smallest possible number of countries needed to have the largest possible impact on solving a particular problem.[38]

This recommended minilateralist approach seems to precisely foreshadow the global configuration that will vault Antichrist to his dictatorship and sustain his power. It will be constructed by the principalities the apostle Paul exposes as recorded in Ephesians 6:12. We see this global arrangement for the climax of history just prior to Christ's return in the following scriptural passage:

And the ten horns which thou sawest are ten kings,
which have received no kingdom as yet; but receive power as kings
one hour with the beast. These have one mind,
and shall give their power and strength unto the beast.
Revelation 17:12-13

Since the prideful human power wielders will never easily come to consensus on governing on a worldwide basis, the most powerful dictator ever to be upon planet earth will use his demonic force of will to wrest control from the holdouts.

After this I saw in the night visions, and behold a fourth beast,
dreadful and terrible, and strong exceedingly; and it had great
iron teeth: it devoured and brake in pieces, and stamped
the residue with the feet of it: and it was diverse from
all the beasts that were before it; and it had ten horns.

I considered the horns, and, behold, there came up among them
another little horn, before whom there were three of the first horns
plucked up by the roots: and, behold, in this horn were eyes like
the eyes of man, and a mouth speaking great things.
Daniel 7:7-8

Watching the G-20 in action last week—or perhaps watching the inaction of the G-20 would be more appropriate terminology—makes ever more obvious that the minilateral approach is likely the methodology that will be used by the powers and principalities of Ephesians 6:12 to bring about Satan's final form of globalism.

JULY 2012

July 2, 2012
End of Days on Track

Much of the email traffic and conversation in which I've been involved of late has dealt with the concerns about the Isaiah 17:1 prophecy, because of some reports that Damascus, Syria, might be targeted for attack by Israel, or even by the United States. There are fears that some of Syrian dictator, Bashar al-Assad's regime has chemical and even, possibly, biological weapons of war. These, it is thought, might fall into the hands of terrorist types even more diabolical than Assad's, should he—as it looks at present—have to give up his ruler ship over Syria.

Before Israel would let that happen, it is conjectured, the Israeli Defense Force (IDF) would wipe out the entire city—or whatsoever territory it takes—in order to eliminate the threat from such weapons of mass destruction. The present set-up, it is put forth, fits perfectly the Isaiah prophecy:

> The burden of Damascus.
> Behold, Damascus is taken away from being a city,
> and it shall be a ruinous heap.
> Isaiah 17:1

The fears that this prophecy is nearing fulfillment comes from reports such as the excerpted portion of the article that follows.

> U.S. intelligence agencies are closely watching Israel's military for signs it will conduct strikes on Syria's stockpiles of chemical

weapons, amid concerns the deadly nerve agents could fall under the control of Hezbollah or al Qaeda terrorists, U.S. officials said.

Syria's arsenal remains vulnerable as the result of the internal conflict currently underway in Syria between government forces and opposition rebels, one official said.

"Everyone suspects Syria maintains an active chemical weapons program; and it would be dangerous not to plan accordingly," the official said.[39]

I wrote an article several years ago with the title "End of Days." I used the title as indicative of mainstream journalists' favorite term for matters of end-times prophecy.

The commentary was about my view of how biblically prophesied things would possibly play out from that point in time forward. The piece was written in scenario fashion, dealing, in particular, with issues and events involving America, Europe, and the Middle East. I have seen no reason to change the scenarios presented within that article to any great extent, with one caveat. I would have made some mention of the tremendous economic upheavals, if writing it today.

The following represents a small excerpt of that article. It continues to be my perspective on how things are shaping up, especially in light of our current news headlines.

> Following the rapture of all born-again believers, the leadership of Israel will look around to find its world support gone with the disappearance of millions of people. All who truly believe Israel has a God-given right to the land, based upon Scriptures in Genesis, will be missing. America will be in total turmoil, and desperately searching for ways to regain its national equilibrium.
>
> This can only be accomplished by reestablishing government that will provide structure for restoring order. The European Union, somewhat shaken, nonetheless will remain solid. All civilized parts of the western world will rush to the EU for help in

trying to regain and/or preserve things lost in the greatest catastrophe in recorded human history.

The Islamists of the Middle East, who have for centuries held the people under their despotic thumbs, will not be cowered by the disappearances—even of all of their young children. Rather, they will be emboldened to look toward Israel and see an Allah-sent opportunity to once-and-for-all scour the Jew from the face of what they consider to be their land. This rumor of war will not escape Israel's leadership.

While the Arab-Islamic forces gather in council of war, the military leadership of Israel will be given the top spot in doing whatever is necessary to insure the nation's continued existence. The liberals and woolly-minded who harbor delusional thoughts that peace is primary will be pushed to the margins. Israel must survive.

Gamal Abdel Nasser will be remembered in the councils of both Israel and her enemies who spawned that Egyptian warlord. Nasser gathered the combined forces of Arab nations and attacked Israel in 1956. He was in the process of again doing so in 1967, when the Israeli Defense Force pre-empted the Egyptian dictator's plans, and thoroughly defeated that collective foe. The people who declare they will never again sit still while forces gather to destroy the nation will now be in charge in Israel. Dramatic action is called for; it will be taken.

Leadership of the major Mid-East terrorist organizations will gather at the one place they are all headquartered—the oldest inhabited city on earth, Damascus, Syria. Their drum beat of blood-vowed hatred will make the inevitable obvious to the Israeli hawks—most all within Israeli leadership. They will decide to cut off the heads of the hydra-headed serpent in one mighty blow. That blow will be delivered by the nuclear sword: "The burden of Damascus. Behold, Damascus is taken away from being a city, and it shall be a ruinous heap" (Isaiah 17:1).

One Israeli jet with a 15-kiloton bomb will cut off the heads, bringing much of Islam into confusion and immense rage. Then, there will be jihad of the most nightmarish sort. But, preparation for such jihad will take time. Much of the diabolical terrorists most proficient at planning such a holy war will have gone to their seventy-two virgins.

Now, America will agree to agree with EU brainstorming. Something, all agree in the western power sphere, must be done—immediately. World War III—that some have said has already begun with the War on Terrorism—will be about to get underway in full-blown fury. Israel will then sense the collective wrath not just of its Islamic neighbors, but of the entire world, including its former staunchest ally—the United States of America.

Israel, through its preemptive destruction of Damascus with a nuclear weapon, will have enraged everyone, who now looks at the tiny Jewish state as the number-one trouble maker on the planet:

> The burden of the word of the Lord for Israel, saith the Lord, which stretcheth forth the heavens, and layeth the foundation of the earth, and formeth the spirit of man within him. Behold, I will make Jerusalem a cup of trembling unto all the people round about,when they shall be in the siege both against Judah and against Jerusalem. And in that day will I make Jerusalem a burdensome stone for all people: all that burden themselves with it shall be cut in pieces, though all the people of the earth be gathered together against it. (Zechariah 12:1–3)

Israel will be friendless. Most all Jews will know they are doomed. There will be no choice but to invoke the Samson Option. They will bring all who come against them down with their own deadly fall. But there will be one man within the hier-

> archy of the EU who wants to try a diplomatic tact others haven't considered.[40]

I'll stop there and let you read the balance of the article for yourself, if you so choose. Certainly, we are seeing things shaping in geopolitical areas specific to things prophesied for the very end of the age. Again, Luke 21:28 is a most apropos Scripture for our day.

July 9, 2012
Denying the Power...

The year 2012 has brought with it strange geophysical manifestations. The heat and storms of recent days are unprecedented in many cases, in terms of records falling. Power outages in parts of the nation are particularly thought provoking. The following excerpt encapsulates the plight of many Americans as I write this commentary.

> WASHINGTON—Millions of people in a swath of states along the East Coast and farther west went into a third sweltering day without power Monday after a round of summer storms that killed more than a dozen people.
>
> The outages left many to contend with stifling homes and spoiled food over the weekend as temperatures approached or exceeded 100 degrees.
>
> Around 2 million customers from North Carolina to New Jersey and as far west as Illinois were without power Monday morning. And utility officials said the power would likely be out for several more days. Since Friday, severe weather has been blamed for at least 22 deaths, most from trees falling on homes and cars.[41]

This outbreak of devastation is joined by myriad earthquakes, volcanic eruptions, and other geophysical phenomena that seem to be ratcheting up by the hour around the world.

Paul the apostle's words provide the thought-provoking impetus for this commentary:

> This also know, that in the last days perilous times shall come, for men shall...have a form of godliness, but deny the power thereof.
>
> 2 Timothy 3:1, 2, 5

My own cerebral meanderings on what's going on conjured the thought. This generation, through denying even the mention of the power of God's dealing with mankind, might be resulting in an increasing lack of power of the electrical sort to energize the households and businesses of large parts of America.

A stretch, you say?

The supposition/postulation isn't as far-fetched as might be thought at first assessment. To begin, we must ask: Using Paul's perilous-times indicator, what is the "power"—albeit of spiritual nature—within the "form of godliness" that this generation is denying? The answer is found in the following Scripture. That power is the One described as follows:

> Who is the image of the invisible God, the firstborn of all creation;
>
> For by him were all things created, that are in heaven,
> and that are in earth, visible and invisible, whether they be
> thrones, or dominions, or principalities,
> or powers: all things were created by him, and for him;
>
> And he is before all things, and by him all things consist.
>
> And he is the head of the body, the church:
> who is the beginning, the firstborn from the dead;
> that in all things he might have the preeminence.
>
> Colossians 1:15–18

The name is Jesus. It is the name above every other name—now, and in the ages to come (see Ephesians 1:21; Philippians 2:9). Come to think of it, it is totally relevant to analyze these matters in this way. The One who owns that holy name holds in His mighty hand all power, whether of the natural or supernatural variety, according to God's Word as given above. Without the Lord Jesus Christ, there would be nothing whatsoever upon which to cogitate—nor would you and I be here to think upon anything.

But, this is not the way many people in America now view the God of all creation. Jesus, in this country whose founders and other leaders invoked that holy name in many of their writings, is now considered persona non grata. His name can be used as a curse word in film and other public entertainment venues, and in private conversations. But, He isn't to be mentioned in the public school systems, nor can public prayers be ended with His name for fear of offending those of other religious belief systems.

As a matter of fact, the Supreme Court ruled in 1963 that God will no longer be allowed in public classrooms. Our leaders have turned their backs on God, and, sadly, many of America's citizenry prove by their daily way of life that they indeed follow the leaders. Jesus, as we've written before in these commentaries, spoke to the very conditions we see developing with regard to geophysical upheaval. While the Lord rode the little donkey toward Jerusalem to offer Himself as Israel's Messiah, the people laid palm fronds before the animal's path. They praised Jesus, shouting, "Hosanna!" They were shouting, "Blessed is the king who comes in the name of the Lord!"

The pharisaical religionists told Jesus to make the people stop their praise of Him. These considered it blasphemous for the people to attribute the title of Messiah to this carpenter from Nazareth. The Judaizers hated Him and wanted Him dead. They would shortly get their wish, because Jesus would soon be crucified upon Golgotha.

The modern-day religionists and those who hate the name of Jesus Christ, because He represents to them a narrow-minded way of righteous living to which they will not conform, are doing all within their power to keep the people of the nation from seeing Jesus as the Savior of the world. The name of Jesus is suppressed at every level they can manage to influence.

Luke recorded Jesus' words to the God-despisers of those times—those who had a form of godliness but denied the power thereof:

> And he answered and said unto them, I tell you that, if these should hold their peace, the stones would immediately cry out.
>
> Luke 19:40

Jesus is again about to interject His majestic presence into this Christ-rejecting world. It seems to me that nature is shouting, "Hosanna!"

July 16, 2012
Liberty's Last Gleaming

My laptop is new, just out of the box. There wasn't time enough to program it with the things I need in order to use it before leaving on a trip last weekend to San Antonio, Texas. I am, as Dr. J. Vernon McGee used to say, "a back number" when it comes to acumen and literacy. I need all of the assistance I can get in navigating the Internet. On top of that, I need JAWS (Jobs Accessible Word System)—a voice synthesis computer program—to tell me what I'm doing on my computer, because I've been blind since 1993.

So it was that I didn't have my anytime-I-want-it Internet access and email available to me while on the trip. This was quite disconcerting, as I am constantly online and using email during the course of any given day. I felt at times imprisoned at the loss of liberty to get into cyberspace any time I wished.

I reflected during those hours without my computer much like we old-timers sometimes get hung up on nostalgia about our days of yesteryear when we didn't have air conditioning in the hot summers. How in the world did we ever do without those environment-controlling technical wonders? I wouldn't have to worry about returning to those humidity-filled, sweat-inducing days of yore, I was pretty sure. And, at least I knew I could hang on until I returned to the computer, Internet, email, and the like. My time in lock-up, away from Internet access, was not permanent.

However, a just-issued executive order by the president of the United States could, at any moment in the future, end freedom from worry about loss of ability to conduct business through such electronic communications. According to some experts, liberty's last gleaming, so far as cyberspace is concerned, is as near as the next crisis deemed severe enough to invoke pulling the plug on our Internet availability.

The presidential dictate of Friday, July 6, gives government unprecedented new authority to take over wired and wireless private communication networks under pretext of national security. The White House edict will permit such national security entities as the Department of Homeland Security (DHS), Department of Defense, Department of State, and the Office of the Director of National Intelligence to formulate, implement, and direct policy recommendations and plans for ensuring continuity of government communications capabilities in time of crisis.

The Obama directive authorizes the establishment of a new National Security and Emergency Preparedness Communications Committee (NS/EP). Representatives from each of the agencies will constitute the crisis-management system for controlling all communications within the nation.

According to the executive order, "The Federal Government must have the ability to communicate at all times and under all circumstances to carry out its most critical and time sensitive missions."[42]

A watchdog group, the Electronic Privacy Information Center (EPIC) issued a statement that said, "The problem with the executive order is that it also grants the DHS new authority to seize private communication facilities when necessary and to effectively shut down or limit civilian communications in a national crisis."[43]

Amie Stepanovich, associate litigation council at EPIC, said the provision that grants the government such encompassing control over private communications is troubling. She maintains that the complete takeover of private networks for government communications purposes during a crisis could degrade or severely compromise the civilian population's ability to communicate in an emergency.

Stepanovich said, "This specific authority is something that should have been granted through Congress," rather than through executive order.[44]

And therein resides the reason for the phrase liberty's last gleaming for the title of this commentary. This president has taken every opportunity, it seems to me, to dilute American liberty through presidential edict, as opposed to seeking approval through constitutional means. We have watched this process take place time after time, even to the point of foisting Obamacare upon a population that overwhelmingly disapproves of the enslaving legislation—legislation that was found unconstitutional under the guise of which it was congressionally proposed and approved—as a mandate to require the purchase of health insurance.

It took a Supreme Court chief justice to find a surreptitious way to make it constitutional by calling the legislation not a mandate, but a tax, in order to get the forced payment strapped upon the backs of the already national-debt-laden American people.

Another deep gully just materialized in America's landscape of liberty, caused by the flood of executive orders that are eroding our freedoms. No doubt, the biblically prophesied great world leader that is soon to appear will completely control all communications, ostensibly for purposes of instituting measures that the people of planet earth will believe are the answer to the great crisis of the time.

I'm convinced that the crisis that will be too good for Antichrist to waste will be the crisis created in the wake of the Rapture of the church. But, for believers who go to be with Christ, it will mean true liberty forever.

July 23, 2012
The Damascus/Psalms 83 Question

Most of the following worries in the Middle East center around a number of factors: 1) Israel's impatience with threats from its enemies; 2) Iran's bellicose posturing in threatening to use its missiles; 3) the Syrian regime's feared ability to wage biological and chemical warfare; and 4) (of particular concern for many Bible prophecy students) the so-called Psalms 83 war.

I term it "so-called" because I remain unconvinced that the Scriptures involved indicate a prophesied war—for reasons I will address in due course. Other factors just mentioned dominate news coming out of the region where Armageddon is foretold to bring the world together for the final and most horrific war of the age.

Israel has good reasons to be short of temper and of patience, although the leadership has shown remarkable restraint to this point. The Jewish state has been threatened with annihilation by all leaders of the Arab League at one point or the other. With the record of that leadership's predecessors attacking viciously in the relatively recent past, Israeli President Benjamin Netanyahu can hardly disregard current Arab League semi-encirclement, the ring of hatred having tightened rapidly with the Muslim Brotherhood-spawned Arab Spring uprisings of the past couple of years.

The Persian branch of Islamist rage has superseded the Arab rage to the point that Iran now threatens to produce weapons that can indeed do what Arabs from Gamal Abdel Nasser to Anwar Sadat and beyond could not. And now, the concern is that Bashar al-Assad has weapons of mass destruction in the form of biological and chemical agents that his Syrian regime might rain down on Israel's citizenry, should the dictator begin to lose in his effort to stay in power.

The Iranian leadership, as well as Russia, and to some extent, China, continues to back al-Assad. The Russians and China do so for the most part by refusing to allow U.N. action against the al-Assad regime in the Security Council, where each holds veto power. This veto power was exercised most recently July 19, in refusing to go along with U.N. sanctions against the Syrian regime. Russia has given somewhat stronger backing by moving some naval military assets into the waters nearby.

Iran, on the other hand, backs Assad with threats of military action, all the while displaying a growing missile arsenal—even demonstrably proving it can have an intercontinental ballistic missile by 2014 that is capable of reaching the U.S. homeland. Iran's apparent determination to stand by the al-Assad regime's refusal to give up power is doubly troubling. Reports of weapons of mass destruction hidden away in Syria's military arsenal, if more than rumors, make the threat of a Middle East conflict of major magnitude a real possibility. Iran apparently possesses the technological knowledge and hardware to assist Assad in raining terror upon Israel in order to divert attention from his own possible overthrow. He might choose all-out war if he is about to go the way of Saddam Hussein, Hosni Mubarak, and Moammar Gadhafi.

My respect for DEBKA file information, as some might be aware, has greatly eroded over the years. The reports, though very professional sounding and steeped in jargon akin to that disseminated by some of the more credible such reporting services, have proven time after time to be filled with too much hyperbole and unacceptably inaccurate. Nonetheless, the following offering, under the DEBKA banner, rings true, so I'll go out on a limb and embrace the assessment.

> As the already unthinkable pace of slaughter in Syria accelerates further, Western military sources warned Saturday, July 14, that not only Israel, but additional strategic targets in Middle East lands deemed enemies by Bashar al-Assad should prepare for him to launch surface-to-surface missile attacks. The assaults would start out with conventional warheads, but as the regime continued to be hammered, the beleaguered ruler might well arm the next round of missiles from his huge stockpile of mustard gas—not to mention sarin nerve poison and cyanide. Western intelligence sources say al-Assad has a list of targets ready to go. Analyzing the Syrian war game taking place last week, they calculated that Wednesday and Thursday, July 11 and 12, the Syrian army practiced shooting missiles at strategic centers in Israel, Turkey and Jordan.

All of this is going on among confusing rumors that Bashar al-Assad has left the country, or is in hiding, while violence increases by the hour with fierce fighting in Damascus. Whether Assad stays or goes, Bible prophecy marches on and events are shaping most interestingly.

Enter one more worry voiced by many emailers of late: the Isaiah 17:1 prophecy, which follows:

> The burden of Damascus. Behold, Damascus is taken away from being a city, and it shall be a ruinous heap.
>
> Isaiah 17:1

The Syrian capital city is, like so many other prophetic indicators today, front and center in the news headlines. The question is: Will we soon witness the complete destruction of Damascus as given in the Isaiah 17 prophecy?

Further: Might an attack on Israel on that city bring about the Psalms 83 war, bringing all of Israel's enemies into coalition that will declare that war on the Jewish state? As stated many times in this column, most every major Islamist terrorist organization is headquartered in this, the longest continuously inhabited city in world history. A single strike of a relatively low yield nuclear weapon could do the job in a single flight of an Israeli fighter-bomber. The heads of the terrorists' hydra-headed serpent could be lopped off in that single blow.

My belief is that the Psalms 83 matter is a prayer for God's protection, and that it will be answered when the "many people with thee" of the Ezekiel 38–39 Gog-Magog war will be destroyed, except for one-sixth of those forces. My assessment is that whether the Psalms 83 Scripture indicates an actual war or is an imprecatory prayer for God to vanquish Israel's surrounding enemies, the attack on Damascus—if the destruction does come from an Israeli attack—and such a war won't happen until after the Rapture of the church.

Such an event would take the world out of the time of "business as usual," as Jesus prophesied in Luke 17:26–30 and Matthew 24:36–42, 44, in my opinion.

Such an attack and a war would be catastrophic to the world's economy, and in other ways that are almost incalculable. Sudden destruction comes, according to Jesus' words in those passages, similarly to the situation in the cases of the Flood and the destruction of Sodom and Gomorrah—that is, after Noah and Lot were safely out of range of harm at the time judgment fell. It fell immediately after they were safely in the ark and in the city of Zoar.

He said that as it was at that time, so will it be at the time He intervenes again into the affairs of men in a catastrophic way. Again, Luke 21: 28 is applicable:

> And when these things begin to come to pass, then look up, and lift up your heads; for your redemption draweth nigh.

July 30, 2012
End-of-Days Violence—Part 1

The most profound foretelling in Bible prophecy is done by the Lord Jesus Christ. He is the Great I Am, and no prophet of the Old or New testaments speaks with greater authority. Other prophets speak with authority equal to His, the argument can be made, but only because Jesus gave them the prophetic truth to pass along to the rest of us. It is His prophecy in the first place.

Despite the tremendous importance of and power manifested in Jesus' Olivet Discourse, the earliest part of that reporting of end-times matters takes second place to another area of prophecy, as far as we are concerned today, in my view. I find Christ's words in the following passages to be the most relevant to this very hour in which this generation finds itself:

> And as it was in the days of Noe, so shall it be also in the days of the Son of man.
>
> They did eat, they drank, they married wives, they were given in marriage, until the day that Noe entered into the ark, and the flood came, and destroyed them all.

Likewise also as it was in the days of Lot; they did eat, they drank, they bought, they sold, they planted, they builded;

But the same day that Lot went out of Sodom it rained fire and brimstone from heaven, and destroyed them all.

Even thus shall it be in the day when the Son of man is revealed.
Luke 17:26-30

As many who read these commentaries are aware, I consider this to be the most relevant prophecy to our time because of specific factors. Jesus was prophesying here about exactly how things will be in culture and society upon the earth at the time He intervenes catastrophically into the affairs of mankind. He said in these and other similar passages that things would be pretty much normal for the times, so far as human activity is concerned, at the time of His thief-in-the-night interjection into earth's history. People will be eating, drinking, buying, selling, building, marrying, planting, and doing other things that seem to be normal activities at the time He breaks in and reveals Himself.

As I've written numerous times, this cannot be referring to the Second Advent (Second Coming at Armageddon—see Revelation 19:11). The twenty-one specific judgments of the scrolls, trumpets, and vials will have decimated this planet at the time of that glorious return with ten thousand of Christ's saints. God's wrath, Satan's rage, and man's gross sin and folly will have denuded the earth of, perhaps, three-fourths of human life. The radical environmentalists will see their dream come true–that of getting the planet's population to its bare minimum.

Rather than the utopian existence they anticipate, however, it will be hell on earth at the time Christ's foot touches down on the Mount of Olives upon His return. Remember—Jesus said that if He didn't come back at that time, there would be no flesh left alive on this devastated sphere (Matthew 24:21). The violence that has plagued mankind will reach its crescendo as Armageddon explodes in all of its fury in the Middle

East. And, the Bible indicates, no part of the globe will escape the effects of the seven-seals scroll found in Revelation chapters 6–19.

So, we look at Jesus' Luke 17 prophecy to discover why, exactly, I say I believe it is the most relevant foretelling for our time. We first must think on the characteristics of the time of Noah and Lot's days on earth. Again, that intervention has to be at a time when things culturally and societally are going along in a relatively normal fashion. Prophecy tells us elsewhere in the Scriptures that there will be a cry that peace and safety has arrived, when sudden destruction comes. Jesus' break-in on the world will be like the break-in of a thief in the night, according to His own words. It will be totally unexpected by the children of the night, we are told by the apostle Paul in 1 Thessalonians.

Point is, our present time frame seems to match up with another prophecy by the Lord Jesus that speaks to this business-as-usual profile. Again, we find the amazing words of Jesus Himself laying out specifically how things will be. He tells these future events within the framework of the Olivet Discourse. Read carefully what He says about what those attuned to the promise of His coming can expect. Particularly, look at the last verses of this prophecy.

> But of that day and hour knoweth no man,
> no, not the angels of heaven, but my Father only.
>
> But as the days of Noah were, so shall also
> the coming of the Son of man be.
>
> For as in the days that were before the flood they were
> eating and drinking, marrying and giving in marriage,
> until the day that Noah entered into the ark,
>
> And knew not until the flood came, and took them all away;
> so shall also the coming of the Son of man be.

Then shall two be in the field; the one shall be taken,
and the other left.

Two women shall be grinding at the mill;
the one shall be taken, and the other left.

Watch therefore: for ye know not what
hour your Lord doth come.

But know this, that if the goodman of the house had known in what
watch the thief would come, he would have watched, and would
not have suffered his house to be broken up.

Therefore be ye also ready: for in such an hour
as ye think not the Son of man cometh.

Matthew 24:36–44

Jesus was talking about the "think-not" generation that would be living at the time of the Rapture of His church. I know the seminary position has most often been that Christ was talking here about the time of His Second Advent. But, we just looked at why this isn't possible. Societal and cultural circumstances will not be business as usual at the time of Christ's return at Armageddon. These Scriptures can refer to none other than the calling of believers into the air to be with Him forever. (Read John 14:1–3; 1 Corinthians 15:51–55; 1 Thessalonians 4:13–18).

So, we consider further the days of Noah and of Lot. What is the most common characteristic—and there is one in particular—that marked those times as unmistakably similar to our current time? I believe we witnessed this characteristic in action just this past week. Next week's "Nearing Midnight" article will, I hope, provide an enlightening dissection of that characteristic.

AUGUST 2012

August 6, 2012
End-of-Days Violence—Part 2

Our question in this commentary is: What is the primary characteristic of our day that is like that which was prevalent during the days of Noah and of Lot? As I hope we saw in the last "Nearing Midnight" article, Jesus recounted those ancient times in prophetic terms, pointing out that times at some future date will be just like those days were when He next catastrophically intervenes in the affairs of mankind.

We looked at how Jesus was talking about the time He will come for His church in the Rapture. He was not prophesying about the Second Advent at the time when all flesh will be on the cusp of destruction.

The title of this commentary is, of course, "End-of-Days Violence," so, obviously, "violence" is the characteristic similarity prominent to both those ancient days and to our time, which I want us to examine.

There was much violence in the days of Lot—the days of the wicked cities of Sodom and of Gomorrah, to be sure. The violence was reported primarily through the sexual debauchery of that time. Homosexuality, in particular, pervaded society. While the days of those cities seemed almost civilized, the nights were filled with sexual violence and every sort of perversion.

We remember the angels were sought by the homosexuals of Sodom when heaven's messengers came to Lot's home. But, the reference to violence that I want us to examine here—of the sort given in Jesus' prophecy in Luke 17:26–30 and Matthew 24:32–44, as we looked at in last week's commentary—is found in the book of Genesis:

The earth also was corrupt before God,
and the earth was filled with violence.

And God looked upon the earth, and, behold,
it was corrupt; for all flesh had corrupted his way upon the earth.

And God said unto Noah, The end of all flesh is come before me;
for the earth is filled with violence through them;
and, behold, I will destroy them with the earth.

Genesis 6:11–13

While it can be said that violence perhaps hasn't reached the level of Noah's day, before the Flood, our present world can be called anything but nonviolent. The murders and woundings of the theatergoers a couple of weeks ago are proof that man is as violent as at any time in human history.

We sometimes gauge everything that happens culturally and societally upon what is happening in America. This is natural, because we have a news and entertainment media that seemingly relishes dwelling on horrors such as the shooting that took place during the showing of the latest Batman movie. It was nonstop punditry and interviews from every possible angle. It even knocked the political back-and-forth media war off the air, as both President Barack Obama and GOP candidate Mitt Romney put their campaigns on hold for a time.

The killings were heinous acts, to be certain. But, if this were the only such act of the sort that is called a mass murder, it would hardly constitute violence that warrants me equating our times with those of Noah and Lot. Even if we count all of the recent such mass killings found in that one small area of Colorado, from the Columbine murders to the theater massacre in Aurora, we can't necessarily make of that mayhem the equivalent of worldwide violence of prophetic significance. The millions upon millions of victims of war-making just since World War I is far greater evidence for Noah's day-type violence in our time.

But, there is something about such impersonal bloodshed as found in the spree killings that viscerally affect the soul, which grabs and shakes to society's core our foundations of pretend civility. These somehow bring to the surface of our time the sickness that proves to our collective minds that we are nearing the end of days—as secular journalists would term the prophesied end times.

And, despite some pundits in other parts of the world proclaiming that America is alone in this madness because we have such lax gun laws, a quick search of relatively recent history proves the violence is worldwide.

The following is based upon facts presented by Neil Cavuto in his weekday program for Fox News, "Your World Cavuto." The history was presented on the program "Gun Violence Isn't Unique to the U.S." Cavuto was exercised over the fact that many on the political left were trying to once again call for more gun control. He made the point that despite nations in Europe and elsewhere having some of the strictest gun laws on the planet, this sort of murderous activity isn't by any means restricted to the United States. I find the facts he presented to be proof that we live in a time as violent as any in history—including Noah's day. Cavuto said he found the accusations of America as being unique in the perpetration of gun violence as totally beyond truth, and unfair.

He said this:

> Because last time I checked, Norway has among the toughest gun laws on the planet, not to mention a reputation for having among the most peaceful citizens on the planet. But that didn't stop Anders Breivik from going on a rampage that left 77 dead—that's right, 77—in 2011. The same year Nordine Amrani murdered seven in Belgium. Or 17-year-old Tim Kretschmer walked into a German elementary school and killed 15 people in 2009. Or a 52-year-old British taxi driver named Derrick Bird butchered 12 and injured 11 others in a four-hour violent spree back in 2010. Barely a year after Ibrahim Shkupolli stabbed and killed his ex-girlfriend, he went on to a shopping mall in Finland to kill four others. The same otherwise

"peaceful" Finland, where only about a year earlier, a 22-year old culinary arts student walked into a school and killed 10 people. I could go on.

- the Birmingham, England man who killed three back in 2000.
- the Swiss kid who slaughtered 14 at the parliament in Zug in 2001.
- the 29-year-old who killed 11 and injured 6 in South Africa.
- the Slovakian man who killed 7 in a Netherlands shopping mall in 2011.
- or the 23-year-old Australian surfer named Martin Bryant, who shot dead 35 people at a popular tourist attraction there "just because he felt like it" that day.

My point is not to spread the blame but remind all, this kind of stuff isn't unique to us. It happens everywhere. Among peoples who are peaceful, and those who are not.

In countries with tough gun laws, and those without tough gun laws.

And it's been happening for a long time....

Like back in 1938, when Mutsuo Toi killed 30 in Japan.

Or in 1913, when Ernst August Wagner murdered 14 in Germany.[45]

Violence is exploding on a worldwide scale at the personal, one-on-one level to the mass and spree killings, to genocide perpetrated by the Saddam Husseins and Bashar al-Assads of the world. We are a violent race—racing, in fact, toward the Lord's sudden and catastrophic intervention. He will bring judgment because lost mankind is incorrigible without Jesus Christ's intervention.

God's Word calls all to repentance before that great and terrible Day of the Lord when God's judgment and wrath must fall. Jesus wants to take all who will accept His grace gift of salvation out of the time of that judgment, which is surely almost at the point of falling upon planet earth. Here's how to avoid being here for that devastating cleansing of this fallen world:

That if thou shalt confess with thy mouth the Lord Jesus,
and shalt believe in thine heart that God hath raised
him from the dead, thou shalt be saved.

For with the heart man believeth unto righteousness;
and with the mouth confession is made unto salvation.

Romans 10:9–10

August 13, 2012
Biting into the Apple

Stepping out of the Wellington Hotel on Seventh Avenue, my friend, Mike, and I traversed the concrete time after time until my now seventy-year-old legs hurt. I say "now seventy-year-old legs" because I was sixty-nine when we were in New York City only a couple of weeks ago, and I turned into a septuagenarian shortly upon returning home.

I really thought I was in the best of shape. That is, the best of shape for one who had just a year and a half earlier been clinically dead three times in the space of an hour, on Good Friday, April 22, 2011. My cardiac workouts over those months sense the heart "event," as I like to call it, took me on an hours-upon-hours ordeal of going nowhere on a treadmill with a vicious incline and speed of operation. Yet, I came back to the hotel room each time and lay with my legs draped over one of those large, round, tubular pillows that my wife tells me are really there just for decoration. Walking in the big city is much different than walking on the treadmill, I found out.

So, biting into the Big Apple was a painful experience physically, much as biting into the Edenic apple (or whichever fruit it was) was painful both physically and spiritually for Adam, Eve, and all of the rest of us. But take a bite out of the apple we did, and we are prayerfully hoping that the seeds planted during that visit will bear spiritual fruit.

Rapture Ready received a request for the interview some weeks ago. It was from a Canadian film company asking that Todd [Strandberg] or

I agree to answer some questions on camera about Bible prophecy. They particularly wanted to talk about the Rapture, after having visited www.raptureready.com and reading some of the thousands of articles on the topic posted there.

Todd and I have agreed that any on-camera interviews will be done by me, since I'm such a ham. Actually, that wasn't the reason we decided that I do the on-camera stuff, but the quip fits the jocular motif I wish to establish for the moment. Actually, there is some rather ironic humor in a blind guy doing all of the on-camera work—wouldn't you agree?

That said, the subject and our purpose in agreeing to the request is a most serious matter. Talking about God's prophetic timeline and the Rapture at this advanced stage of the Age of Grace is most critical for people around the world. The urgency made my answer to the producer's request the only one we could give the filmmakers.

Whether to do the interview in the city that has been called "Babylon on the Hudson" was a more serious twist of irony, as I considered and agreed to make the trip. I'm more than glad I did. I'm thankful for the opportunity to get the truth of where this generation stands at this crucial point in the nation's history before the eyes and ears of America and the world. I am even more thankful that we put that truth on film in the most influential city and in the most influential part of that city, in the view of the people of most of the Western world.

Every year, the New Year is celebrated as it arrives at Times Square in the heart of that great metropolis. As the big, glittering ball drops, the masses gathered there shout the countdown in unison and break into deafening cheering when the ball reaches the bottom. The Canadian film crew placed me directly in front of where the ball reaches bottom, framing the interview within the area where the big clock is positioned in the background.

The masses went about their many activities while I answered the producer's questions and the cameraman shot the film, occasionally stopping me to reload the cameras. The ambient noises in that great city are stunning, with people's voices in conversation or shouting, vehicles honking, sirens blaring, and all the other sounds that town generates. Times

Square is the center of the most frenetic activity, and although the producer stood near enough for me to hear his questions, my friend Mike and our friend Chris, a native New Yorker, said they couldn't hear either the questions or the responses. Fortunately, the microphone was attached to my tie, just beneath my chin, so my words were easily picked up by the recording devices connected to the cameras.

The first question was simply a request, something along the lines of, "Will you tell us about the Rapture, and talk about what happens from now until the Rapture?"

Interviewers, particularly those in secular media, are often naïve with their questions. They have little understanding of matters involved in the pretribulational view of the Rapture, for example. To answer questions such as this one requires much longer than these venues have time to include. So, trying to be precise and to the point is always the challenge.

I responded that there is nothing that must happen from that point until the Rapture, so far as Bible prophecy is concerned. That was precise enough. But, then, I felt it necessary to go into what is in fact going on right now that makes us know the Rapture is imminent. That line-up of current issues and events and what the future of the Middle East—for example—might hold, seemed to pique the producer's interest, and he wanted to know about what is the most important of these "signs of the end of days."

They always like that phrase, "the end of days."

My immediate, precise answer was, of course, that Israel is at the center of the world's spotlight, with a diplomatic proposal in process of attempting to force peace between Israel and its enemy neighbors—all surrounding Islamic countries. These things are exactly as God's prophetic Word says will be the case at the very end of the age.

Most important, the interview offered me the opportunity to give God's plan of salvation, which I hope I did to the Lord's satisfaction. It is up to Him to now make certain it survives the cutting room floor, once they begin putting the documentary and weekly program together. Let's all pray to that effect.

August 20, 2012
Buildup to Sudden Destruction

Rumors of war in the Middle East continue and grow by the day. We have heard of such Armageddon-like conflict that is coming for most of a decade. It's almost like the little boy who cried wolf, but not quite.

Anyone with any sense of the potential for conflagration in that volatile region that could bring worldwide war knows that the breaking point has now about been reached. Iran's nuclear weapons development project—or the fear that their nuclear program is for developing weapons of mass destruction—is, of course, the primary reason for the tensions involved.

Three observable factors are on the stepped-up agenda of potential war consideration: 1) Israel is in a top-alert configuration, talking more or less openly about its most advanced defensive capabilities; 2) Iran is expressing fear of imminent attack from Israel, and is hustling to protect its nuclear program; 3) The Israeli prime minister and his military have a strong sense that they must depend only on their own resolve, not that of their one-time staunch, superpower ally to defend the Jewish state.

Regarding point 1, the following news report indicates Israel's concern for its threatened citizenry:

> According to an unidentified official, new intelligence obtained by Israel, the United States, and other Western states shows that Iran's development of a nuclear weapon is progressing far beyond the scope reported by the International Atomic Energy Agency....
>
> Tehran has made significant progress towards assembling a nuclear warhead for a Shahab-3 missile, which has a range of nearly 1,000 miles, putting the whole of Israel, including the Dimona nuclear reactor in the southern Negev desert, within the Islamic republic's range....
>
> Benjamin Netanyahu, the prime minister, issued a public warning that Tehran must not be allowed to develop a nuclear bomb. "Every threat against the home front is dwarfed by one

> threat. Iran cannot be allowed to have a nuclear weapon," he told ministers at the start of the weekly cabinet meeting in Jerusalem.[46]

To punctuate the urgency, Israel's home front command, in a test run of alerting the populace, issued thousands of text messages to alert people when rockets are launched on specific areas of the country. Apparently, the test is ongoing, with the text messages being given in Hebrew, Arabic, English, and Russian.

Israel's increased national defense preparations were further reported:

> As testing began, Prime Minister Benjamin Netanyahu said Israel had chalked up "a significant improvement" in its home front defence capabilities, mentioning its highly-vaunted anti-missile systems such as Iron Dome and Arrow 2.
>
> "There has been a significant improvement in our level of defence capacity on the home front: with Iron Dome, with the Arrow, in terms of protection and shelters, in advanced warning systems and in other areas," he said.[47]

On point 2, reports grow about Iran's fears of attack by Israel, thus convincing them to deeply shelter its nuclear program at a quickening pace:

> Iran is disturbed by threats emanating from Israel to strike its nuclear sites and takes such threats seriously, a senior Iran expert told *The Jerusalem Post.* The past few days have been dominated by media headlines on a possible Israeli strike, with several reports claiming that a strike is imminent and could come within weeks. Iran has been busy fortifying its air defenses and moving parts of the uranium enrichment program to underground sites to make them immune to an Israeli strike.[48]

Regarding point 3, Israel's growing distrust for the American presidential administration's support is surfacing by the day. While Israel's government and military have presented evidence time after time that its most threatening enemy, Iran, is driving for a nuclear bomb, the U.S. intelligence services, obviously controlled by the Obama administration, say only that they suspect that the Iranian regime—although that regime has declared that it is committed to removing Israel from the earth—is seeking a weapons capability but that no decision has been taken on actually making one.

Such naïveté at best and willful disregard for the facts at worst is itself heightening the danger of all-out war in the Middle East, in my opinion. The buildup to such conflict continues apace—and increases by the hour. It is obvious that only the staying hand of God is holding back the inevitable. I am convinced that when the inevitable comes—the massive devastation that will involve the whole world—it will be the sudden destruction that will follow immediately the Rapture of the church, as indicated by Jesus' own words:

> But the same day that Lot went out of Sodom it rained fire
> and brimstone from heaven, and destroyed them all.
> Even thus shall it be in the day when the Son of man is revealed.
>
> Luke 17:29–30

August 27, 2012
Mideast Roman Empire—America's Future? Part 1

Two questions, among many, loom large among some within the ranks of those who believe we are at the very end of the Church Age (Age of Grace). I'm hearing about them every day by those who email, and in conversation.

The first matter involves the question of whether, based upon developments in the Middle East and the expansion of Islam into Europe and other places, those who hold to the Islamist Antichrist belief could be correct. Could those who hold to the Western leg of the Roman Empire being the geographical base from which the beast will come, after all of this time spent adhering to that view, be mistaken—having read the prophecy of Daniel 9:26–27 erroneously?

Certainly, for the Islamist or Eastern-leg Antichrist view to be brought up by those who are doing so is not heresy, as some dogmatists might have it. While I personally maintain that Daniel was given a definite heads-up that the "prince that shall come" will be from the people who comprised the heart of the Roman Empire (Western Europe), I can understand reasons for thinking—especially with developments taking place all around us—that a case might be made that Islam is the prophesied beast system, and that Antichrist will be from the people who made up the Eastern leg of the Roman Empire.

There is great quaking within the European Union at present, as there is in America, and we will examine some of these things, in view of the relatively new proclamations that the Antichrist will be a Muslim.

The Bible calls that future and last tyrant of the dispensation of earth's history before the Second Advent of Christ "the Assyrian." There's no question that the man, himself, will be of Middle Eastern extraction. Additionally, all geopolitical movement—both in biblically prophetic terms and in terms of what is happening today—is shifting back to the geographical lands surrounding God's touchstone city, Jerusalem. All attention is on that region, primarily because of its potential for producing nuclear conflict, which would engulf the whole world. An only slightly less powerful exigency that affects the entire world—particularly the Western world—is the influence petroleum exerts on geopolitics.

With the present presidential administration refusing to tap into Canada's vast quantities of oil, and with its determination to fight the development of America's own great reserves, the oil-rich Middle East is rapidly becoming even a more volatile point of potential conflict. It is, in my view, almost certainly the "spoil" which Ezekiel was told to prophesy will bring Gog and his Magog forces into the land of the Bible.

By the time of that attack, something catastrophic, apparently, will have happened to the United States. It is almost a guarantee that the economic powers that be—and they control all the world so far as geopolitical power is concerned—would never sit by idly and watch the great petroleum interests that fire the engines of their wealth-empire be taken over by a Russian leader and a swarm of Islamist Jew haters. But, according to the Ezekiel prophecy, the Western powers apparently send merely a note of diplomatic protest. Very strange…

It is as if the Western leadership knows that the forces of Gog-Magog will be unsuccessful. Of course, they will be more than merely unsuccessful. They will be utterly decimated, with all but one-sixth of them totally destroyed, God's Word tells us. Satan, of course, controls/influences all sides in humanism's war against God. He knows Bible prophecy. He believes all of it, I think, except the part that says he loses in the end. His man, Antichrist, will understand that if he just reserves his strength, he will have it for the really big takeover, after God, Himself, obliterates his Middle Eastern opposition. He will still have to contend with the forces from far-distant Asia, but in his arrogance, he will have confidence he can handle that problem when it must be faced.

All of that is just a scenario, as I'm convinced God's Word teaches it, with my postulations thrown in for good measure. So, it does nothing to prove that Antichrist will be either from the Western leg or from the Eastern leg. We will, of course, have to learn the truth about that after the fact—from the portals of heaven, for all who are born again into the family of God.

But, when looking at what Daniel the prophet was given to tell us about the "prince that shall come," we must consider who the people who destroyed the city and the sanctuary were. That is, who destroyed Jerusalem and the Jewish Temple atop Mt. Moriah?

The argument by the latecomer, bandwagon jumping, Eastern-leg proponents includes the claim that the forces that destroyed the city and sanctuary were comprised of people indigenous to the region, who made up the Roman legions assigned to control the area. While those of the Middle East did mingle with the Roman soldiers, they were under the very imposing thumb of Romans who dictated from the city of Rome.

General Titus, the son of Emperor Vespasian, was in charge. He and his father gave and saw to it that the put down of the Jewish insurrection was accomplished. Both were Romans in the Western-leg sense. They were head of the people of Rome—the Western leg—who destroyed Jerusalem and the Temple in AD 70.

We must remember that the Eastern leg of the empire wasn't established for another three centuries, when Constantinople (modern-day Istanbul) became the Roman Empire's Eastern capital in AD 330. Daniel's prophecy—later reflected upon by Jesus Christ, who gave it to the prophet in the first place—told of the Romans' destruction of Jerusalem and the Temple when there was no Eastern leg. Further, there was no Islam until more than six centuries later than the prophesied destruction. Thus, I conclude that any validity to the claim that Daniel—and Jesus—were referring to a "people" from the Middle East, Muslim world, who would produce "the prince that shall come" is untenable.

There are other reasons why the Eastern or Muslim Antichrist doesn't fit the prophecy, but I must move on. Next week, Lord willing, we will look at the second question I'm getting regularly that is involved in the quaking in Europe and America.

SEPTEMBER 2012

September 3, 2012
Mideast Roman Empire—America's future? Part 2

The questions continue about whether the revived Roman Empire predicted to produce the Antichrist will be from Rome or from the Eastern leg—which refers to the Middle East. In fact, there seems a more stringent insistence by the day that the beast of Revelation 13 will be a Muslim.

Developments taking place within the economic structures of Europe provide much of the fodder for the champions of the Mideast Antichrist theory. These proponents point to what they see as the unraveling of the European Union as indicative that it is losing, not gaining, power. One such development they point to is that Germany is reported to be printing money at a frenzied pace. It is printing deutsche mark notes, not euros. This is apparently because there is great fear that the eurozone sovereign debt crisis will end in a return to national currencies.

The following news item frames this feared collapse:

> [The]...British Foreign Office has issued warnings to embassies in the eurozone to prepare to handle the problems of its expatriates who may be unable to access local bank accounts and face rioting mobs. Perhaps this is only an example of highly developed countries planning for all eventualities but disaster planning always adds to fear as it shows that the previously unthinkable is now being contemplated: a break-up of the eurozone single currency.[49]

European officials continue to express their concerns about the fiscal turmoil that threatens what was once the most powerfully growing economic entity on the planet.

> "We have to face openly the possibility of a euro-break up," said Erkki Tuomioja, [Finland's] veteran foreign minister and a member of the Social Democratic Party, one of six that make up the country's coalition government.[50]

The powers that be in Europe, however, are not looking to simply allow all of the promise offered by Europe's once-burgeoning strength to simply atrophy into a second-rate force upon the world stage.

> "But let me add that the break-up of the euro does not mean the end of the European Union. It could make the EU function better," he said, describing the dash for monetary union in the 1990s as a vaulting political leap in defiance of economic gravity.[51]

Make no mistake: The European Union continues on its ascent and will soon be in position to be the superstructure from which Antichrist will launch his campaign to dominate the world and oppose everything of God. And this leads to the second question that I find predominant in the thinking of many today.

My ten-part series at the close of 2010 and the beginning of 2011, entitled "Scanning a Fearful Future," deals with this question in depth. So, I suggest the inquisitive reader look into that series. Basically put, the question is: What is ahead in America's future?

As of late, one of the primary news items that has made this question front and center involves U.S. government making strange preparations. For what? Well...that is the crux of the major expressions of concern I'm hearing. An article brought to my attention time after time by those who write involves the massive purchases of ammunition by government agencies that traditionally have had nothing to do with military or policing responsibilities. The questions are legitimate matters for investigation, I think.

One retired general of the U.S. Army wrote the following:

> The Social Security Administration (SSA) confirms that it is purchasing 174 thousand rounds of hollow point bullets to be delivered to 41 locations in major cities across the U.S. No one has yet said what the purpose of these purchases is, though we are led to believe that they will be used only in an emergency to counteract and control civil unrest. Those against whom the hollow point bullets are to be used—those causing the civil unrest—must be American citizens; since the SSA has never been used overseas to help foreign countries maintain control of their citizens.[52]

The general presents a legitimate question when he asks who would be the intended victims of these hollow-point bullets—ammunition, incidentally, that is outlawed by the Geneva Convention. These are outlawed on the field of battle because of their lethality. I know, I know—that seems like some sort of a schizophrenic rule. Isn't the purpose of war to kill? But, the hollow point is so devastating that even the war makers of the world want it outlawed because of the damage it does to living tissue upon impact. We won't debate the insanity of that matter here.

The retired general poses the question: "Potentially each hollow-nose bullet represents a dead American. If so, why would the U.S. government want the SSA to kill 174,000 of our citizens, even during a time of civil unrest?"[53]

He goes on to offer some rather frightening thoughts. What if the hollow-point bullets were, rather than for civilians, for military personnel who might oppose the administration ruling the nation at the time of severe crisis? What if that ammo was used to give power, instead, to forces loyal to and under the auspices of Homeland Security?

Whether this sort of dark scenario cogitation is warranted as we watch things deteriorate in our nation, I suggest it is at the heart of the questions being raised by those who watch the slumping of our society and culture toward Sodom and Gomorrah-type comportment. The Lord of heaven, I contend, still has His staying hand of control on matters in this nation, Europe, and around the planet. Otherwise all would have long since imploded.

I believe He will take His hand off, according to 2 Thessalonians 2, when the Holy Spirit withdraws from acting on the consciences of humanity. The greatest crisis of human history will then unfold. Perhaps we are seeing the preparations, unknowingly, by governments even now for that stunning moment when Jesus steps out on the clouds of Glory and shouts to His bride, the church, "Come up here!"

September 10, 2012
Restrainer at Work

In presenting this week's commentary, I must be careful to preface my thoughts. This is to make clear that I fully realize that the nation of which I am a citizen has no special, private, import, or status within God's prophetic dealing with mankind, so far as its people being a restraint against the influence of evil is concerned. I can say only that I believe America is very likely the nation in which the highest number of Christians reside.

By "Christians," I mean people who are "born again" in the sense of the words Jesus spoke on the matter of salvation as recorded in John

3:3–7. As a matter of fact, the United States has descended from being the most Christ-centered to, perhaps, the basest nation on the planet, in terms of exportation of the world's entertainment filth. With the constitutionally legalized murder of more than four thousand babies in the womb per day, we have spit in the face of the Almighty, telling Him that His love for the human race means nothing in view of expediency in the matter of lust for pleasure.

That established—that America is no longer the shining city on the hill to be admired—the United States still possesses the residual vestiges of greatness. The nation retains, I believe, remnants of the Christian ethic sufficient to be an influence in these closing days of the Age of Grace.

What I am saying—at least it is my intention to say—is that the born again within this nation do, indeed, have a special and private duty to perform in these times that look to be very near the first phase of Christ's Second Coming. Because of American Christians and their position within present history as the Church Age closes, I'm convinced that we can examine a specific prophetic section of God's Word and receive insight as to precisely where we stand as a generation on heaven's prophetic timeline. That specific prophetic section is found in the following verses:

> And now ye know what withholdeth that he might
> be revealed in his time.
>
> For the mystery of iniquity doth already work:
> only he who now letteth will let, until he be taken out of the way.
>
> And then shall that Wicked be revealed,
> whom the Lord shall consume with the spirit of his mouth,
> and shall destroy with the brightness of his coming.
>
> 2 Thessalonians 2:6–8

The reference "he who now letteth" in this passage is to God, the Holy Spirit—the third Person of the Trinity. The Holy Spirit, Paul is prophesying, has been and is acting as Restrainer of evil in the present world. God, the Holy Spirit, will continue to restrain the end-times evil until God removes from acting as the restraining influence during this Church-Age dispensation.

We who believe in the pretribulational, premillennial view of Bible prophecy hold that the Holy Spirit indwells each born-again (saved) person during this Age of Grace (Church Age). Christians are thus known, collectively, as the church. The church, indwelt by God the Holy Spirit, is the body of Christ, individually and corporately. It is this body of believers who act as salt and light for a world of corruptive evil that would otherwise bring about total decay, causing every area of human existence to implode.

The Holy Spirit will, therefore, the above prophecy informs, live within and exert influence through believers in Jesus Christ until the moment God no longer acts as Restrainer of this world's evil. This truth provides the answer to the question that is being asked prolifically in one form or another: When will all of the evil that is threatening America and the world bring civilization crashing down?

Some of that evil that looms threateningly over our daily lives brings worried glances from even the most ardent skeptics of Bible prophecy. An economic storm of unprecedented magnitude hangs angrily above America, with national debt that just turned $16 trillion as the Democrat Party—chief among contributors to the fiscal madness—began its convention the week just past. (The Republican Party, it must be said, contributed mightily to the staggering debt load as well.)

It amazes even the global gurus of finance as to why the world isn't already crushed by the impending economic crash. Iran's leaders tell Israeli leaders practically every day that they intend to wipe the Jewish state from the face of the earth. They do little to hide the fact that they are in the process of bringing into reality nuclear weapons that can make their destructive wishes a fait accompli.

With such an avowed, blood-thirsty enemy, missiles trained on Israel and, some believe, on the very brink of producing atomic weaponry, it astonishes many observers that the Israeli Defense Force hasn't already risked initiating all-out war by destroying Iran's nuclear production facilities.

Absolute evil pervades every strata of society. The days like those of Sodom and of the antediluvian times of Noah inflict debauchery and violence that only a decade ago would have seemed far distant. Islam is allowed to usurp, in some cases, the U.S. Constitution, favoring Sharia Law in order to show tolerance. At the same time, Christianity is pushed to the margins of society and held up as intolerant by the tolerance police—through the insane institutions many of the federal courts have become.

Yet, the world holds together, while seeming to be on the very cusp of *Implosion,* as the title of Joel Rosenberg's book would have it.

The Restrainer is at work. I believe that's the answer to why the implosion has not happened, bringing total devastation to this judgment-bound earth. When the Restrainer removes and the church is called to be with Christ, I'm convinced the impending horrors that have for so long engendered the questions about the end will fall instantly upon a Christ-rejecting world.

Are you Rapture ready?

September 17, 2012
Breaking the Bands

"If Obama is reelected the country is going to collapse, economically." These words by Rush Limbaugh on his talk show Monday, September 10, was a declaration that should cause all to take heed.

Many—those who dislike the talk-show host intensely—will declare this to be just political rhetoric from a conservative ideologue. That's a fair assessment by those who would disagree, I will concede. However, this declaration—the following statement that the nation is doomed, along with the foregoing declaration that the country is going to collapse—is something this particular conservative ideologue —Limbaugh—has not made, nor would make, if the handwriting wasn't plainly on the wall.

He said (I paraphrase): "We're doomed." Especially, he emphasized, "if Obama's policies on fossil fuel energy continue and his plans are implemented."

He said further, "That voluminous supply [of petroleum and other fossil resources] will remain off limits. We are sitting on energy independence [with North Dakota fracking potential] But, Obama won't let that potential be tapped."

Regardless of one's view of the vociferous Mr. Limbaugh, such a direct statement that the United States of America is in danger of being "doomed" and can never recover, as he plainly implied with the totality of his rant on the topic, is the type statement this particular radio host never issues. Always, there is a way out, politically, in his thinking. Genuine belief was reflected in his words that America is a goner, economically speaking, if the president is reelected.

I never cease to be amazed at the worldview of those who put their hopes for a brighter future, for a way out of troubles, into the political process—the power of economic manipulations and behind-the-scenes maneuverings. Rush, like everyone who invests in the political process—from the conservative side of the equation, at least—believes this is the most important election of our nation's history. I agree, but the reasons have only peripherally to do with politically massaged considerations.

At the same time, it is the process of moving through political machinations that lies at the heart of my point for this commentary. The true reason that this once-great nation and the nations and empires of all history have come to their terminus is found within the shenanigans demonstrated by the Democrat National Convention a couple of weeks ago. What happened there personifies why we have reached—as a generation upon this fallen planet—the end, or at least near the very end.

We all heard the voice vote on whether to continue to allow mention of God in the Democrat platform. There were a loud number of convention delegates who insisted that all mention of God be stricken from anything to do with the Democrat political platform. When word got out that the decision had been made to kick God out, there arose such a clatter from people around the country, through Internet blogs and from other forums, that the Democrat committee decided to get the changes they had made in kicking God out altered again to reflect a pro-God stance and back into the platform.

The DNC leadership didn't want to call for a secret ballot because they knew the vote to bring God back would fail—most likely overwhelmingly. This would be detrimental to Barack Obama's chances in November—to alienate a majority of people in America who still at least retain a form of godliness.

They chose to take a voice vote. We all heard the vote. The "Nos" were at least as loud as the "Yes" votes—probably louder. Yet the vote was ruled "Yes," and the God of heaven was put back in the Democrat platform as again mentionable. Surely, that pleased Him—to be reinstated within such an august body—along with the planks that contain same-sex marriage and murder of babies in the wombs of their mothers.

Then, another uproar—that which flared when the decision to consider taking out support for Jerusalem as the capital of Israel was made—brought another turn-about. Jerusalem, the powers that be within the DNC decided, will remain the rightful capital of the Jewish state. Thus, even though the head of their party, the president of the United States, has let it be known that he is neutral on the matter at best and against Jerusalem as capital of Israel at worst.

I must say that I saw developing, in microcosm, during that entire hubbub the prophecy that I believe is one of the key foretellings for this very time: "The kings of the earth set themselves, and the rulers take counsel together, against the LORD, and against his anointed, saying, Let us break their bands asunder, and cast away their cords from us" (Psalms 2:2–3).

It is clear to me, even if not to the Rush Limbaughs of our nation and world, that the leaders of this dying, decaying world system are determined to eventually kick the God of heaven out of the affairs of man. And, that reality is the nucleus of why there is little chance of either America or the world ever returning to things as they used to be.

There is little hope left other than the "blessed hope" of Titus 2:13, who is the One destined to make true the hope and change that politicians promise but always fail to deliver.

September 24, 2012
The Gog Equation

Anxiety of the first magnitude is again on the rise, involving feared impending military action by Israel against Iran and its nuclear development facilities.

Israeli Prime Minister Benjamin Netanyahu has made the now-familiar declaration that the international community cannot put red lights up to stop Israel from attacking Iran's atomic weapons factory if they won't support red lines beyond which Iran must not go in atomic weapons development. His implication is crystal clear, and, most diplomatic types think, aimed primarily at the U.S. administration. Israel will go it alone in doing what it must to protect itself, even risking world condemnation if necessary.

Iranian military has responded with war talk that approached seldom-reached levels.

> TEHRAN [Associated Press]—The top commander in Iran's powerful Revolutionary Guard warned Sunday that "nothing will remain" of Israel if it takes military action against Tehran over its controversial nuclear program.
>
> Gen. Mohammad Ali Jafari said Iran's response to any attack will begin near the Israeli border…Iran has in the past made reference to the destruction of Israel but his comments at a Tehran news conference were unusually strongly worded.[54]

As stated many times before in this column, the reports from many proven-to-be unreliable sources predicting imminent attack by Israel have reached my desk. All have been confirmed to be overblown and even downright made up. The current situation is different. There is obvious movement of major military naval assets by the international community in the region due to fears that the Iranians will make good on their threat to block the Straits of Hormuz if Israel assaults their nuclear laboratories.

> A dramatic show of naval power has assembled in the Persian Gulf. The force is constituted of far more than the minesweepers that might be expected to be present, in case the Iranians should mine the Straits. Battleships, aircraft carriers, minesweepers and submarines from 25 nations are converging on the strategically important Strait of Hormuz in an unprecedented show of force as Israel and Iran move towards the brink of war.[55]

Still, there seem to be more pressing matters than this tremendous build-up in the Persian Gulf—to those who gather and report news. It is puzzling to some extent as to why other Middle East exigencies are more central to coverage by media–although, as stated at first, there is a growing anxiety about when, not if, things explode over Iran's atomic weapons program.

It is as if the U.S. presidential election season keeps all other news of a critical nature from the top news spot. News media attention on how the proliferating hatred-filled demonstrations against America might impact the candidacies of Barack Obama and Mitt Romney has for the moment taken center-stage.

One thing sure: There is little attention being paid to these Middle East matters as they might involve Bible prophecy by anyone but a few watchmen—and that condemnation includes the Christian community in America. Yet, it is a time when some quite fascinating factors jump at the student of Bible prophecy.

Perhaps a relatively minor one of those factors, but one which nonetheless signals plainly where this generation finds itself on God's prophetic timeline, jumps at me from a report about recent attacks in Afghanistan:

> Kabul, Afghanistan (CNN)—An insurgent group close to the Taliban said its attack Tuesday that killed 12 in Afghanistan was revenge for an anti-Islam film that has angered the Muslim world. Eight of the dead were South Africans, a government spokesman confirmed, all working for international flight provider Air

Charter Services, some of them as pilots. Three of the dead were Afghan civilians, and another was a citizen of Kyrgyzstan, Afghan President Hamid Karzai's office said in a statement. The South Africans were ethnic Caucasians, said Clayson Monyela from South Africa's International Relations Department, who suggested they could have been mistaken for Westerners associated with U.S. or NATO military powers.[56]

These Middle East wars and rumors of wars are based almost exclusively on religious and ethnic (racial) factors. No matter how the pundits and the terrorists want to couch the excuses for the terrorism and threats, the bottom line is that they stem from the very thing Jesus Himself prophesied in His Olivet Discourse:

And ye shall hear of wars and rumours of wars:
see that ye be not troubled:
for all these things must come to pass,
but the end is not yet.

For nation shall rise against nation,
and kingdom against kingdom.
Matthew 24:6–7a

Jesus spoke here of "nation"—*ethnos*, the Greek term for our English word "ethnic"—in prophesying what would be at the heart of the end-times violence between peoples of planet earth. The news from the region makes it clear that the terrorist murders of the South Africans were likely because they mistook their victims for American Caucasians.

Another most fascinating factor is that Jesus said that the end wasn't yet, when those who hear His prophecy see wars and hear of great military conflicts to come. Again, I think this is a primary indicator of the end of the age, where I'm convinced we find ourselves today. And, now, I'll stretch out my neck with the hope it doesn't get my head lopped off.

My question is once again one involving the one called Gog by the prophet Ezekiel. Is the Gog spirit inhabiting the region, like the Bible tells us the Prince of Persia is inhabiting the area we know as Iran, at present controlling the leadership of Russia?

That wicked minion of Satan—Gog—will at some point put together the thought—a hook in the jaws given him by God Himself, apparently—inducing him to want to attack Israel to the south. Persia—Iran—will be the Russian leader's chief ally in that attacking coalition, the prophecy tells us. Iran could do that prophetic Russian leader no good if Israel's IDF had earlier destroyed that country's ability to mount a military force. There seems to be no use of nuclear weapons by those forces as they storm southward toward Jerusalem—although there seems to be a possibility of such weapons falling elsewhere—in the coastlands, for example.

More importantly, however, the real assault against Israel seems to be a surprise attack by a cunning Russian leader who has gathered his coalition after his specific "evil thought." Iran bringing the kind of chaos to the region, as it threatens to do if its nuclear program is attacked, it seems to me, would change the configuration for quite some time in the region.

Realizing that there are a thousand factors that could alter the geopolitical dynamics of the region and world, I'm just again wondering if Russia isn't working behind the scenes, even now, to bring this standoff with Israel and the whole international community to a temporary resolution. Might Vladimir Putin convince the Islamist leadership for the time being to step back from their nuclear program, thus to fight another day, in a different way, against God's chosen people?

Much in the same way that a global economic disaster continues to loom precipitously, the Iran-and-Muslim-world-vs.-Israel standoff continues to hang ominously over the Middle East for some inexplicable reason.

OCTOBER 2012

October 1, 2012
Crises and Antichrist

While doing my own version of athletic endeavor—walk-jogging on a treadmill—I finally had enough. Not of the jog-walk on the treadmill, but of talk about the apparently most pressing crisis of our time.

"Please, let's listen to something else," I pleaded with the exercise physiologist (EP) who runs the heart clinic's cardiovascular workout center. (I said "let's listen" because I'm blind and can't "watch" the TV while we work out.) I was sick of hearing ESPN pundits saying over and over, in as many ways as it could be said, that the replacement referees for the National Football League (NFL) are destroying the game.

When our EP, Zach, acquiesced to my plea and began going through the channels, there it was again, wherever he turned. Commentators were practically in tears, agonizing over the blown calls from the previous Sunday and Monday that were just beyond all calamities. This was a crisis of monumental magnitude, and someone—maybe President Obama—needed to step in and resolve the union referees vs. the NFL and get some sanity back into pro football.

But, on two of the channels that weren't hosting meltdowns over the referee crisis, the television audio blared mostly two other matters, specifically. Alas, Mr. Obama was taking care of more important business, speaking with the intellectual titans of societal voyeurism in America—the ladies of *The View.* He was preoccupied with that and addressing the United Nations General Assembly on other sorts of crises. However, thankfully, this, the number-one crisis in the nation—and apparently the universe—has since been resolved.

Much in the way that born-again believers in Jesus Christ for salvation are apathetic about the spiritual condition of America and the world and are doing anything and everything except looking for "the blessed hope" (Titus 2:13), the American populace for the most part is caught up in such cataclysmic problems as the aforementioned replacement referee situation, and doesn't, as a whole, have the slightest clue of the apocalyptic crises lurking just beyond the present hour.

It will be crises that will bring the great humanistic savior to the stage of world history. We might just be almost there, because no matter which way one looks on the geopolitical horizon, there is crisis, as we continually bring to your attention through these commentaries and through our news/article forums.

It is one thing to point the finger of blame at the apathetic American people in general. However, such condemnation of God's people is something far more profound to contemplate. This "think-not" generation that comprises the church, when considered alongside Jesus' prophecy about the very end of the age, must almost certainly be that generation to which He was referring:

> Watch therefore: for ye know not what hour your Lord doth come.
>
> But know this, that if the goodman of the house had known in what watch the thief would come, he would have watched, and would not have suffered his house to be broken up.
>
> Therefore be ye also ready: for in such an hour as ye think not the Son of man cometh.
>
> Matthew 24:42–44

Jesus gave in-depth forewarnings of the crises that would usher in the time of the beast of Revelation chapter 13. And, it was Jesus who told John the revelator of the coming judgment of rebellious, humanistic endeavor and of this man of sin, as is pointed out in the very first chapter of that, the greatest of all prophetic books of the Bible.

> The Revelation of Jesus Christ, which God gave unto him, to shew
> unto his servants things which must shortly come to pass;
> and he sent and signified it by his angel unto his servant John:
>
> Who bare record of the word of God, and of the testimony
> of Jesus Christ, and of all things that he saw.
>
> Revelation 1:1-2

This same Jesus told John—and us—of the two beasts who will appear at the time when God's judgment will fall upon mankind (read Revelation 13). The one called "the prince that shall come" by Daniel the prophet (Daniel 9:26–27), "the son of perdition" by the apostle Paul (2 Thessalonians 2:3), and "the beast" and "Antichrist" (2 John 2:18) by John will come to power at a time of unprecedented crises upon planet earth.

War looms in the Middle East, more portentous than at any time in history, because of the threat of igniting World War III. Every nation of earth faces coming economic collapse that experts say will be the worst ever experienced on the planet. Breakdown of culture and society at every level threatens civilization. Even nature is feared to be on a course that will bring world-rending catastrophe, while humankind moves deliberately as far from their Creator as they can get.

Jesus said it would be just this way as the time of His intervention into history draws near. He said that His people are to "watch" (Mark 13:37) and to "look up" when these things begin to come to pass (Luke 21:28), because He is on His way to rescue them.

The launching pad for the one called Antichrist continues to be constructed for the time that world crises reach the point of imploding the building bubble of impending doom we are currently witnessing. When Jesus calls His church to be with Him (John 14:1–3; Revelation 4:1–2), the beast will step forward with answers that people will be duped into believing will resolve their problems and bring peace and prosperity.

That reviving Roman Empire launching pad is front and center in the news—news that the church and the world ignore in favor of, for instance, news of the NFL referee crisis. Greece and Spain are in crisis over threatened austerity cuts to welfare and bureaucratic retirement programs, with rioting building daily. Greece threatens to pull out of the European Union (E.U.) if funds to rescue the country's imploding economy aren't forthcoming. The E.U. itself is in dramatic flux that is of great concern to economists who worry about preservation of Western democracies and world financial stability.

The new push for a European Union federation, complete with its own head of state and army, is the "final phase" of the destruction of democracy and the nation state, the president of the Czech Republic has warned.

> In an interview with *The Sunday Telegraph*, Václav Klaus warns that "two-faced" politicians, including the Conservatives, have opened the door to an EU superstate by giving up on democracy, in a flight from accountability and responsibility to their voters.
>
> "We need to think about how to restore our statehood and our sovereignty. That is impossible in a federation. The EU should move in an opposite direction," he said.
>
> Last week, Germany, France and nine other of Europe's largest countries called for an end to national vetoes over defense policy as Guido Westerwelle, the German foreign minister, urged the creation of a directly elected EU president "who personally appoints the members of his European government."[57]

Once again, the swiftly approaching, ultimate crisis for planet earth impresses my spirit. For the Christian, it will be not crises, but Christ, that will instantaneously be in view:

> For the Lord himself shall descend from heaven with a shout,
> with the voice of the archangel, and with the trump of God:
> and the dead in Christ shall rise first:

Then we which are alive and remain shall be caught up together with them in the clouds, to meet the Lord in the air: and so shall we ever be with the Lord.

Wherefore comfort one another with these words.

1 Thessalonians 4:16–18

October 8, 2012
Global Economic Gulag

One can feel the noose tightening, even though freedom of movement—in America, at least—seems as unfettered as ever for the most part. While people plan for the next week, month, and year—whether considering purchases of homes, cars, or other big-ticket items like college education for children, or whether planning vacations to places near or far—economic rumblings from Europe and from within our own nation engender uncertainty and uneasiness among those truly paying attention.

The mainstream media is complicit in helping the government keep the actual statistics of employment from coming to light. They fudge the figures to show that unemployment is slightly under 8 percent, while economists in the know will tell you it could be, in actuality, as high as 15–16 percent, and growing.

What both the media conglomerate and the bureaucracy-laden federal government don't want you to get clear in your mind is that a class of U.S. citizenry has been created that is enslaved within a gulag environment out of which no people so enslaved have ever escaped. It is a system out of which no empire on earth that has come to the point at which the United States now finds itself has ever escaped.

Presidential candidate Mitt Romney merely mentioned this "47-percent" class of gulag-bound citizenry. The mainstream media, echoing his opponents' attack, descended upon him like Serengeti scavengers and carrion upon the prey left by a pride of lions when finished feeding on the carcass. The fact was not changed. Romney is correct. There is a gulag class that will never vote for anyone or any system that might take away their chains of poverty and release them to begin doing work that would rebuild an economy that would restore their ability to earn their way through life. Rather, they prefer to be fed by the state like the prisoners they are. This is because sloth–again speaking of those who can but don't want to work—is a baser element of the fallen nature. They simply don't agree with God's Word on the matter that if one does not work, neither should he eat (2 Thessalonians 3:10).

It is true that a small percentage caught up within that incentive-killing class warfare created by vote-voracious politicians and bureaucrats (that include both major parties, incidentally) would much prefer to work, but for legitimate reasons can't. This is not to denigrate these. Nor is it meant to denigrate those who have been locked generationally into this imprisonment that is as much slavery as was the slavery over which this nation suffers guilt-obsession, fed by that same media and governmental system, to perpetuate the voting bloc they must have to stay in power.

So, America, shackled with and to the slaves of entitlement is, as my friend Jack Kinsella has put it, "headed toward an economic abyss." As soon as austerity is seriously mentioned as the beginning of the way to try and avoid the crash—as it surely will be not long after this election cycle—the nation will experience inner turmoil that will perhaps even eclipse the rage fomented by the Civil War.

Freedom as we have known it will be, as a necessity to quell the rage, lost to this once-great experiment in republican democracy. We are indeed headed for economic gulag, both nationally and globally.

News from Europe, with the impending financial cataclysm that looms over Greece and Spain, presages America's own approach to the precipice of economic abyss. The following report contrasts Switzerland and Sweden—which still hangs onto fiscal sanity—with the ticking time-bomb the European Union has become.

> STOCKHOLM, Sweden—As headlines continue to trumpet the economic tsunami swamping much of Europe, there are at least

two countries that are weathering the storm better than the rest: Switzerland and Sweden.

[Reasons] why the Swiss and Swedish economies are doing so well relative to the European Union: economic freedom, national currencies, work ethic, and more.

Other governments could learn something.

The largely free Swiss economy is performing the best by far, but even Sweden, after a decade of market reforms, is doing very well compared to the rest of Europe. Both economies are still growing even as the eurozone contracts.

In Switzerland, the unemployment rate is hovering at about 2.7 percent. Sweden, even with its nightmarish regulatory regime over the labor market, has a stable unemployment level of about 7 percent.

By comparison, in socialist Portugal, the number is over 15 percent and climbing fast. With 25 percent unemployment, socialist Greece and Spain are doing even worse.

The average in Europe is about 11 percent if official figures are to be believed....

The Role of Economic Freedom:

To attribute the relatively strong performance of the Swiss and Swedish economies to any one factor would be overly simplistic.... Instead, there are multiple reasons for their successes.

Among the most commonly cited are high levels of economic freedom compared to other countries, low government debt levels, strong work ethic among the Swiss and Swedish populations, and the fact that neither country adopted the controversial euro.

According to the Heritage Foundation's Index of Economic Freedom, Switzerland has the freest economy in Europe. It placed fifth globally—well above the United States.

Well-secured property rights, low levels of corruption, strong respect for the rule of law, an efficient legal system, openness to foreign trade, and other factors all contributed to Switzerland's designation as one of the freest economies in the world....

> Part of the reason that the Swiss have managed to maintain such a high degree of economic freedom is a uniquely decentralized political system—a confederation with a Constitution under a weak central government—where most issues are decided locally. Voters always get the final say.[58]

America's government continues to become more centralized by the day. Executive orders and federal court intervention in overturning voters' decisions, and socialistic regulations that are choking every aspect of private enterprise, assure that we are going the way of the Europeans—Switzerland and Sweden apparently excepted—as they look for the strong man that can give them the kind of high wage, low work hours they desire.

Such a man is on the way. He will bring with him the most horrendous form of global gulag imaginable. He will enslave every man, woman and child. That's the world's future as foretold in Revelation 13:16–18.

The fast track of financial enslavement upon which this generation finds itself is a prime indicator that Christ's intervention into human history can't be far in the future.

October 15, 2012
October Surprise Surfacing?

American presidential politics are more powerful in their impact than at any time in history. The nation's future has never been more precarious.

While it can be legitimately argued that nothing can be done to change that future, from the perspective of Bible prophecy, we live in the flesh-and-blood reality of the present and have decisions to make. Things are on the fast track to the Tribulation hour, as most who watch for Christ's return firmly believe. We move and operate within the minutes and hours of everyday life, however, and must address those increments of time as they approach, then become the present.

The term "October surprise" has long been linked to presidential politics. This means that the administration, defending its incumbency, usually saves something under its capability to influence votes until the last moment in order to interject into the campaign process during the October immediately preceding the election month of November. Never has an "October surprise" been more likely than with this presidency. At least, that is my opinion and the opinion of almost every pundit I've heard on the national scene.

This is a close and tightening presidential race. Anything can happen to break the virtual tie. We are at the midpoint of October, which means the surprise—if one is to happen—might have occurred by the time of this commentary's posting. The anxiety inherent in all this is the fear that such a surprise might cause uncontrollable ramifications. This is because the many dynamics currently interplaying within building crises around the nation and world consist of elements that present X factors—that is, unknown possibilities for triggering catastrophe.

My commentary, here, is merely to present a hypothesis as follow-up to a scenario I have proposed in past articles. The subject is Iran's ongoing nuclear development program and the longer-term threat it poses to Israel and the world. It involves, too, of course, the more immediate threat of direct confrontation with Israel, the Jewish state that must perhaps take preemptive action to eliminate the Iranian nuclear threat. The risk is all-out war with Israel's Islamist enemies in the Middle East.

One opinion piece this week piqued my interest with regard to these matters. Although it is purely punditry slanted against the president's reelection, the hypothetical it proposes evokes concerns that it might have some degree of credibility. And, in an odd sort of way, it fits some of my own postulation, thus intrigues me. I'll try to explain momentarily.

The article said in part:

> A former CIA operative and spy in Iran's Revolutionary Guard is reporting that a deal has been struck between Barack Obama and Iranian Supreme Leader Ayatollah Ali Khamenei. According to Reza Kahlili, "Iran could announce a temporary halt to uranium enrichment before next month's U.S. election in a move to save Barack Obama's presidency." Kahlili's source for this story

> reports that a 3-member team of negotiators representing President Obama met this week with a Khamenei representative in Qatar. They asked that the Iranian leader "announce a halt to enrichment, even if temporary, before the Nov. 6 election." In return, Obama promised to suspend some of the sanctions that have effectively crippled the Iranian economy.[59]

My own speculations on the Israel-vs.-Iran nuclear standoff come more into focus for me when considering the suggestions implicit within the above opinion piece.

One who reads this column regularly might recall that I've wondered aloud whether the Gog spirit of the Ezekiel 38–39 Gog-Magog prophecy might be presently at work in the mind of Vladimir Putin. Far-fetched? Well, maybe the answer to that is still "yes." However, the "yes" seems to be morphing more into a "maybe" or "maybe not."

To refresh, I wondered whether the Russian president might convince the Iranian leadership to pull back from its nuclear program, thus to avert a preemptive attack by Israel.

Follow me in this...

This would: 1) make Putin and the Iranian leadership look like good guys and peacemakers, while 2) making Israel look like bullies without a cause. They could keep their powder dry, so to speak, in order to deal with Israel at a future time when prospects for destroying the Jewish state are more advantageous.

Now, enter the present speculation, beginning with that now-infamous incident in which President Obama was heard to whisper—through an open microphone thought silenced—to Russian President Dmitry Medvedev to tell Vladimir (the then president-elect of Russia) to just be patient about America's willingness to come to the table of nuclear disarmament. That—President Obama said—will happen once he, Obama, is re-elected and no longer has to contend with campaigning for the office.

Now, the scuttlebutt is that a deal has been struck between the leading ayatollah and the Obama administration to announce that they have agreed to halt the enrichment of uranium, based upon negotiations by the very one who was given the Nobel Peace Prize before he had even sat down in the big desk chair in the Oval Office.

Voila! The October surprise!

Such would fit the scenario that Putin's influence is working behind the scene, while proving that Obama's words to Medvedev had indeed been relayed to ol' Vlad.

Ah, well...perhaps just my long vent-up aspirations to become the next Ian Fleming...

There is, however, surely coming an October surprise of some description. We shall see what it is, together. Most I've heard from recently through email and in conversation want it to be the greatest of all surprises—the Rapture!

October 22, 2012
The Issues According to God

This time of October always reminds me of the issues of life and death. My dad died near this date in 1992. My pain from his passing from this life, while diminished over the twenty years since, continues to evoke a sense of emptiness, a void that nothing can fill.

Jesus, while on earth in the flesh, the Bible tells us, experienced in His Spirit every human emotion that involves suffering:

> For we have not an high priest which cannot be touched
> with the feeling of our infirmities;
> but was in all points tempted like as we are, yet without sin.
> Hebrews 4:15

Where death of a loved one is concerned, we can be assured our pain is understood by God Himself, because Jesus wept over the death of His friend Lazarus (John 11:33–35). Life and death, then, constitute an issue very close to the heart of the Creator of all things, the Heavenly Father.

More than any other matters involved in the issues of this presidential election, I believe it is life and death that are most important to consider in exercising not just our right, but our duty, to vote. I believe with all that is within me that America's slide toward national oblivion began in earnest with the imposition of abortion as a legally sanctioned death style by the Supreme Court decision in *Roe v. Wade* in 1973. Since that time, a holocaust of immense magnitude has brought the deaths—the murder—of 53 million human beings in the wombs of their mothers. Abortion is the nucleus of the national sin around which this all-important issue involving life and death revolves.

However, the gravity created by many corollary aspects within life and death as an issue also contributes to sucking the American soul ever more deeply into the quicksand of decay. As a result, the removal of the protective hand of Almighty God from our nation can, I believe, be easily observed taking place on a daily basis.

Sociologists who compile such statistical information report that America has a homosexual population of no more than 5 percent. Yet, the gay agenda has overtaken American society and culture as if gays constitute the 95 percent majority of our population, instead of the other way around. Since the days of the Moral Majority's efforts to stem the tide of national immorality, there has been so little such organized opposition to the roughshod overrunning of America's social structure as to make opposition virtually nonexistent.

These two issues, abortion and homosexuality, represent ways diametrically opposed to life. They are devoted to death. They are directly devoted to rebellion against the Giver of life.

Abortion is outright murder of the innocent (the shedding of innocent blood, as God's Word puts it [Proverbs 6:16–19]). Homosexuality, when carried to its ultimate outcome, means the elimination of human life from the earth. Rebellion against the God who created us—manifest most egregiously in our culture through these two great sins—is the cause for all of the other problems resident within the issues that so trouble us, individually and governmentally. Whether talking about the sins of fornication and adultery within our heterosexual numbers or any other anti-God transgression one can list, rebellion—doing what is right in our own eyes—festers at the heart of humanity's death wish. And, a death wish fallen man indeed has, because there is no sign of let-up in the march down the broad way to perdition.

Rebellion brings loss of common sense at some point. It produces a reprobate mind (Romans 1:26–27), the Scripture informs. We are witnessing the insanity in handling the problems that are proliferating, thus the meltdown of social, economic, and all other elements within human affairs in these troubling times. We face, as a nation and as a world, certain destruction because of our refusal to follow the prescription for life offered by God's love letter to mankind, the Bible.

> For the wages of sin is death.
>
> Romans 6:23a

The moral issues, then, most directly affect our lives, according to God's own Word. Of course, in thinking upon this presidential election, I realize that those lost in rebellion-transgression can never recognize that the moral issues are most directly relevant to our well-being as a nation.

> But the natural man receiveth not the things of the Spirit of God: for they are foolishness unto him: neither can he know them, because they are spiritually discerned.
>
> 1 Corinthians 2:14

Sadly, tragically, much of God's own family have become so blinded to the lies fed them by the social architects and engineers who say man can build heaven on earth that they miss what truly matters as we approach the voting booths this November.

I will not be so arrogant as to tell the readers of this commentary who to vote for as president or for any other office in this or any election. But, I will suggest that you weigh carefully what each of the candidates claims is his position, according to party platforms and/or stated positions on these matters that are so close to the very heart of our God.

America has always presented voters with choices on the issues that affect our quality of life. The Founding Fathers saturated their writings with Judeo-Christian principles while formulating this great experiment in liberty. They intended for "we the people" to stand upon solid moral ground. Christians should seek that solid ground in this and every election, even when faced with having to vote in many cases for and against spiritually fallen individuals as candidates.

Although eroded and under constant assault, our process still produces Judeo-Christian options that offer the quality of life—i.e., options that are not in opposition to biblical principles. Such is the case in this election. We can be assured that we will be held accountable for the options we choose when we—and I believe it could be soon—stand before Christ at the judgment seat.

October 29, 2012
Startling Starting Over?

Rumor has it that the politicians and the money powers that be, nationally and globally, have a plan that would eliminate all debt and intend to put it in place and restart under a totally changed economic system. Things are so chaotic within the fiscal world that such is the only solution.

Absolutely ludicrous, unthinkable, you say? Well, I thought so, too, until the rumor began taking on more and more legitimacy just this past week.

Rush Limbaugh made a special point of the fact that it came to his attention that the planners of the Obama administration were rumored to be considering such an option immediately, or not long after beginning a second term. All debt would be written off with a stroke of the presidential pen, and a new monetary regime, excluding the old dollar, would be put into place.

He didn't give details, but who could possibly give details on what such a change would take—and would mean? Such rearrangement would have incalculable ramifications and consequences.

So, I pushed that to the back of the cogitations of my gray matter. Then, I began seeing stories appearing talking about such possibilities as wiping out debt and replacing the system with something...exactly what, who knows?

One such article, in particular, I've excerpted here.

> So there is a magic wand after all. A revolutionary paper by the International Monetary Fund claims that one could eliminate the net public debt of the US at a stroke, and by implication do the same for Britain, Germany, Italy, or Japan. The IMF reports say the conjuring trick is to replace our system of private bank-created money.
>
> One could slash private debt by 100pc of GDP, boost growth, stabilize prices, and dethrone bankers all at the same time. It could be done cleanly and painlessly, by legislative command, far more quickly than anybody imagined.
>
> The conjuring trick is to replace our system of private bank-created money—roughly 97pc of the money supply—with state-created money. We return to the historical norm, before Charles II placed control of the money supply in private hands with the English Free Coinage Act of 1666.
>
> Specifically, it means an assault on "fractional reserve banking." If lenders are forced to put up 100pc reserve backing for deposits, they lose the exorbitant privilege of creating money out of thin air.
>
> The nation regains sovereign control over the money supply. There are no more banks runs, and fewer boom-bust credit cycles. Accounting legerdemain will do the rest. That at least is the argument.[60]

All one has to do to imagine the upheaval such a thing as writing off all debt and beginning again would bring is to think of one word—China. Imagine that the U.S. says to China, "We are writing off all we owe you. Hope you will understand."

Now, I'm no economist, and I realize all of the above is so shallow in its pondering as to probably make yours truly appear a simpleton to those with acumen within and great knowledge of global economics. But, I do know that the Chinese leadership would not take kindly to our saying: "We've decided to just not pay you back. Now, won't you please join us in this new monetary experiment?"

That brings me to the point that such an undertaking as writing off debt and beginning again could never be as simple as a stroke of the pen. We have contemplated often that there is no way out of the economic morass in which this nation and the world are now imprisoned. We have considered often that either something must be done or the U.S. and the world face catastrophic implosion.

Love of money is the root of all kinds of evil, Paul tells us through divine inspiration (1 Timothy 6:10). So, it is fitting that this world of rebels has made its own bed and now must climb into it.

That rebellious world will still be the same in its comportment following this presidential election. No matter who wins, America and virtually all other nations face the prospect of stark change or total implosion. And that is just considering the economic circumstance. Throw into the mix the Middle East rumors of war and the myriad potentially devastating problems on the horizon, and to paraphrase the late Sen. Everett Dirksen regarding billions of dollars in spending the government was already doing, pretty soon you're talking some real problems.

Whoever is the president after the next inauguration, the task is not to be envied. However, I'm convinced that Christians can continue to look forward to the brightest of all futures, because God's most devastating judgment is reserved for the time when Jesus intervenes and brings His bride, the church—all born-again believers—into His presence and takes them to the Father's house (John 14:1–3).

We are in the end times the Lord described as like the days of Noah and the days of Lot. The same day those men and their families were removed from their judgment-bound environments, judgment fell. That's why the total implosion of the economy continues to loom rather than occur.

When the Lord calls as recorded in 1 Thessalonians 4:16–17, the crash so feared will cascade upon this doomed world:

For the Lord himself shall descend from heaven with a shout,
with the voice of the archangel, and with the trump of God:
and the dead in Christ shall rise first:

Then we which are alive and remain shall be caught up together
with them in the clouds, to meet the Lord in the air:
and so shall we ever be with the Lord.

Now, that will truly be a startling starting over!

When writing the "Nearing Midnight" commentary for October 15, "October Surprise Surfacing," I wrote: "There is, however, surely coming an October surprise of some description. We shall see."

That "October surprise" is upon us, and it is from God, not from either political party in the presidential race. However, it isn't the ultimate October surprise—the Rapture—for which so many emailers expressed to me that they had been hoping. But, we aren't at election day yet, I guess it is good to remind.

This storm is certainly hyped like none other I can remember. Hurricane Irene in 2011 came forth and threatened much of the East Coast of America. But, its teeth were removed to some extent before landfall, and the region was mercifully spared from what might have been.

Hurricane Sandy looks to be one whose teeth are getting sharper as it joins with advancing storms from the north and west to create a "perfect storm," as the 1991 East Coast monster was dubbed. It is more than coincidence—because there is no such thing as coincidence within God's economy—that the storm is coming at this time, with this intensity and into such a heavily populated region so central to the governing of this nation. How it might affect voting on Tuesday of next week is a matter most intriguing.

An October surprise it is, indeed!

NOVEMBER 2012

November 5, 2012
Harbinger Storm

> Israel was unique among nations in that it was conceived and dedicated at its foundation for the purposes of God.... But there was one other—a civilization also conceived and dedicated to the will of God from its conception, America.

The above passage of dialogue from *The Harbinger,* the huge best seller by Jonathan Cahn, is at the heart of the criticism the author received for his book—unduly so, in my view.

The harsh words of condemnation flowed from some I respect. Nonetheless, the criticism was wrong, and I am quite disappointed in them and question their discernment in leveling the charges, because they should be much more aware of exactly what Cahn was saying than they demonstrated. The critics clearly had not read his book in its entirety. The author's words, as well as his book in its entirety, pointed out that America was, like Israel, dedicated at its birth to godly principles.

Please understand the difference in the relationship the two nations have to the Almighty. Cahn was saying through his protagonist that America, like Israel, was "dedicated" to godly principles at its foundation—not that America was brought into a covenant relationship with God in the sense that Israel is in covenant with God.

While it is stated in *The Harbinger* that America's founders considered the founding like a covenant, Cahn made it clear that the American republic was meant by George Washington, John Adams, Thomas Jefferson, Benjamin Franklin, and most others involved in founding the country to be devoted to the high moral principles of life found in the Holy Bible. *The Harbinger's* author did not mean in any sense that God had covenanted with those Founding Fathers of America in the way He did with Abraham, Isaac, and Jacob.

That is all preface to the points I hope to make with regard to America's disposition at this late hour of human history. I say "late hour" because I am convinced the unfolding of events presents overwhelming evidence that we are at the very end of the age—at the terminus of the Age of Grace.

There should be little doubt in the minds of anyone who reads American history and honestly assesses all things from the time of America's founding until today that God's hand has been on this nation. Facts are legendary surrounding the war fought by a ragtag army of civilians against, at the time, the most powerful nation on earth. The many times divine intervention appears to have occurred are on the historical record for all to see.

Despite the fact that many, particularly of the progressive mindset, would disagree, all indicators point to a very special relationship between the God of heaven and the United States of America. Israel is the nation God chose to be the people on the planet through which to demonstrate His blueprint for how peoples everywhere—all nations—should live and interact. There should also be little doubt that God has purposed to form a very special relationship between Israel and the American republic.

America acted as midwife at the rebirth of Israel into modernity in 1948. This nation has stepped to the forefront many times since to stand behind modern Israel as that Jewish state faced threats—literally—to its very existence. And this returns my thinking to *The Harbinger* and brings into focus in my mind the storm that has so devastated America's northeast.

Mr. Cahn's book was intended to do one thing. I know, because I've personally corresponded with him on matters involved. His book was given him by the Holy Spirit to call this most blessed nation to repentance. The book is, as its title indicates, a harbinger of judgment to come, if the people of America do not turn from our wicked ways to God, asking His forgiveness for our national sinfulness.

The author gave through his fictional account a nonetheless absolutely true picture of how God punished Israel for its wicked rebellion. He, using absolute biblical truth, demonstrated precisely how America's condemnation and judgment is building, in eerie similarity to how the Lord dealt with His chosen nation in history long past. Cahn used the city of New York in his novel to lay out the call to repentance.

Again, he used the facts, particularly about matters attendant to the 9/11 terrorist attacks on New York City, to show where America might be on God's timeline for judgment. An astonishing lineup in similar arrangement to judgments that brought Israel to its proverbial knees millennia ago fits the American landscape today. We are going down that same pathway to destruction.

Israel's God—the only God—consistently and incrementally forewarned His people throughout their history. He brought increasingly intensive measures of punishment to forewarn them to turn from wickedness, rid themselves of their idols, and instead turn to Him in repentance. He brought "harbingers" of things to come if repentance was not forthcoming from the people He loved and had blessed so mightily with His great protection and material, as well as spiritual wealth.

We have covered many times in these "Nearing Midnight" and other commentaries and articles the Lord's dealing with the world in forewarnings. We have indeed detailed the birth pangs we believe are happening, based upon Christ's Olivet Discourse, and the prophets of the Old and New Testaments. Birth pangs are coming with greater frequency and intensity, we believe it is obvious. Hurricane Sandy and the super storm into which it morphed is the latest of these end-times indicators that Christ's return must be very near.

This latest harbinger of things to come means the birth of a new dispensation is even nearer than before Hurricane Sandy exploded upon this nation at the time of perhaps its most crucial presidential election. The millennial reign of the King of all Kings is on the cusp of God's restoration to fellowship of mankind with Himself.

First, however, there must develop the painful throes of Tribulation, much of which is delineated in the Olivet Discourse and the book of Revelation. Todd Strandberg's "Nearing Midnight" accounting of the convulsions leading to the birth of restoration details the frequency and intensity of the process of the Second Advent of the Lord Jesus Christ.

To avoid that coming apocalyptic storm, you must be born again. That is, you must accept God's grace offer as given here:

> That if thou shalt confess with thy mouth the Lord Jesus,
> and shalt believe in thine heart that God hath raised him
> from the dead, thou shalt be saved.
>
> For with the heart man believeth unto righteousness;
> and with the mouth confession is made unto salvation.
>
> Romans 10:9-10

November 12, 2012
Your Future—What Next?

My series of articles I called "Scanning a Fearful Future," written in the closing months of 2010 and the beginning of 2011, was prompted by an emailer. The writer asked my opinion on whether martyr-level persecution of Christians in America had to be very near. He asked for my thoughts, he indicated, because Christians were becoming more isolated due to their support for Israel, according to what Hal Lindsey had stated.

Answering his question, I wrote how the then-Fox Network show host, Glenn Beck, was proclaiming that the powers that be, such as billionaire George Soros and others of his globalist mindset, were pushing the United States toward a completely changed economic order. We would awaken one morning, Beck said, and our nation will have been changed forever—unrecognizable as what the Founding Fathers had given to us.

Well, the metamorphosis is incomplete as of the moment, but Beck's nightmare scenario is playing out. Rather than awakening in his one-morning scenario and finding America fundamentally changed forever, we have just witnessed the nation being moved toward a massive shift prior to our going to bed on election night.

Our country is, at its very core, forever changed, in my view. We have reached the tipping point about which we were forewarned by Alexis de Tocqueville in 1835.

> A democracy cannot exist as a permanent form of government. It can only exist until the voters discover that they can vote themselves largesse from the public treasury. From that moment on, the majority always votes for the candidates promising the most benefits from the public treasury with the result that a democracy always collapses over loose fiscal policy, always followed by a dictatorship. The average age of the world's greatest civilizations has been 200 years.

America was 236 years old on July 4 just past.

I'm aware that many hate Rush Limbaugh for whatever reasons, and his arch conservatism can make him too abrasive to many. But, his comment summed very well the root humanistic cause for the national election results. The remark is, however, in keeping with de Tocqueville's profound forewarning. Limbaugh said: "Many of those who voted in the majority in this election voted for Santa Claus."

It is the same humanistic core value system that now has Spain, Greece, Portugal, and, indeed, the entire European Union on the verge of fiscal collapse. It is the road we're now headed down—and it is a steep incline that ends at an economic cliff leading to devastation. The brakes have failed, and those in the driver's seat are inebriated with political power, which Henry Kissinger once said is the ultimate aphrodisiac: the power to take from the working haves and give to the nonworking have-nots. It is the formula for the ruination of any people, culture, or civilization.

But, it isn't the humanistic, real-world aspects of what has just happened in the political process in America that most troubles the spirits of Christians who love this once great country. It is the ever-darkening slide of immorality toward oblivion that most distresses the soul.

The delusion of 2 Thessalonians 2:11–12 has invaded and infected America and the world. The evidence is everywhere one looks on the humanistic horizon. A reprobate mindset has become evident even among those within true Christianity; that is the most troubling fact within the matters involved.

I'm not referring only to Democrats and/or Republicans. The reprobate mindset today crosses all lines, political and otherwise.

Every rubric of what makes for inevitable political change—such as, for example, high unemployment, threat of high taxation, and in the case of this president, the highly unpopular Obamacare health program—pointed to the Obama administration being turned out of office, according to traditional, observational methodology. I don't wish to go into those individually, because there isn't space at this time, and they are, in my view, much less important than the following realities that make this truly a catastrophic decision by the American electorate. I also won't present the issues of gay marriage or abortion, as we've covered these so many times in these commentaries.

Here are the heaviest issues that loom in the forefront of things to consider in days, weeks, and months of the immediate future:

- The Obama administration's promise of sequestration—to bring the U.S. military down to levels near those of World War I. This, when we face the most ambitious, terroristic enemies in our history.
- The Obama promise given to Dmitri Medvedev (then president of Russia) to pass along to Vladimir Putin that he, Obama, would

make a good deal in getting rid of American nuclear weapons once the problem of the election was over.

- Mr. Obama's telling France's Nicolas Sarkozy that he agreed with Sarkozy that Israeli Prime Minister Benjamin Netanyahu is a pain to deal with, saying, "Think of me, I have to deal with him regularly." Obama's saying on occasion that he wants to put "light" (distance) between America and Israel is perhaps his most dangerous attitude.
- Mr. Obama blocking at every possible juncture the drilling for oil and gas within our reserves—among the most plentiful on earth. Refusal to allow pipelines from Canada into the U.S. to deliver petroleum and gas that could help greatly lessen dependence on Middle East oil.
- Obama's cap-and-trade philosophy that wants to make costs for operating outside of the international (U.N.-global model) super confiscatory in order to destroy the American, free enterprise model of doing business. At the same time, the president wants to sign on to carbon tax protocols in the global warming scam. All of those are actions that would immensely raise transportation and home energy costs for every American.
- The Obama administration constantly threatening to attempt to dilute the Second Amendment right to bear arms, particularly by entering treaties with internationalists that would require congressional action to combat the threat, lest it become, in effect, legally binding.
- President Obama's apparently proudly international stated and implied thoughts that America is no longer a Christian nation (expressing his belief , incidentally, in which he states the truth—America isn't a "Christian nation"). What does this portend for the individual Christian and for the nation? Mr. Obama's constant reaching out to the Muslim world in apology, while having his Department of Justice imprison American citizens—specifically, the filmmaker ludicrously accused of sparking the riot with

his anti-Mohammed, YouTube video in the Libyan terrorists' murder of America's ambassador.

- The administration's profligate printing, borrowing, taxing, and spending money in ways that has raised the national debt to a level that makes it impossible to ever repay—more than $16.3 trillion to this point. The so-called fiscal cliff looms just ahead.
- The administration's constant erosion of rights to privacy and of freedom of speech through executive orders as part of Homeland Security. Admittedly, this is a massive expansion of things begun in the Bush administration after 9/11. It is likely only a matter of time until private communications, particularly involving the Internet, will come under assault through federal regulatory "reform." Increasing surveillance upon citizenry, through ever-advancing technologies, continues apace.

There has never been a more critical time for God's watchmen on the wall to come together in understanding the times and seasons. Christians, in particular, face a problematic future.

November 19, 2012
The Gates of Hell

A great number of those who name the name of Christ believe this season of presidential politics in America represents cumulative proof that satanic darkness is descending at a pace that makes coming judgment unstoppable. Every social issue involving morality that the born again hold dear has, they believe, observably been steamrolled by a juggernaut from the darkest regions forewarned of by the Bible. There seems little, if any, hope of culture as it has been known in this nation surviving the next four years.

Such is the general sense among those who were on the losing side in this election—not just among Christians. We can know this, because all fifty states have growing numbers of quite worried, unhappy citizens signing petitions to have their respective states secede from these United States.

While secession isn't going to happen—and should not happen—the strong sentiment for doing so, rampant and growing, makes it clear that we are a nation divided. We remember that Abraham Lincoln—another president facing the United States' split down the middle, invoking the truth spoken by Jesus about a house divided—stated that a nation divided cannot stand. It is clear that it has been Satan's desire to so divide America since its inception. What we face now in the coming months, and perhaps years, just might be as close as America has come to the devil achieving his goal.

Lucifer's quest got well underway in this country back in the time of slavery, of course. Although economic and other exigencies of the time divided Americans one from another, it was the matter of the horrors of slavery versus abolition that generated the division to the point of producing civil war. However, the division actually raised its serpent-like head at the time the Founding Fathers were trying to form a constitution that would be suitable to frame the republic they envisioned. According to historical letters between early American citizens, the Constitutional Convention, during the time of formulating the document that would govern the United States, was rife with anger and division. It seemed impossible that any conciliation was to be forthcoming. This nation, so obviously put together by Providence, was coming unglued at its core beginning. Satan was at work to prevent any influence by the God of heaven.

Fast forward to 1963. The United States' history to that point proved God's mighty hand had guided the American ship of state through the troubled waters of its conception, its battle with the British, at that time the greatest of all powers on earth.

There was in the American Revolution a supernatural energy that superseded that earthly, British power. It was an unlikely Founding Father who convinced the members of the Constitutional Congress to appropriate that supernatural influence so the nation could survive and thrive. The gentleman claimed by many to be the deist—the existentialist within the group who was thought to believe that God put the world in motion before sitting back with arms folded to only observe—made a recommendation that astounded the gathering. He first analyzed the situation. Each representative had his own provincial interest that was blocking the coming together for the good of the fledgling nation. He recommended that they depart for three days to reflect and consider what was in their hearts and minds, and what needed to be accomplished.

Dr. Benjamin Franklin said to George Washington and the others in that gathering, before they left to follow his advice:

> Before I sit down, Mr. President, I will suggest another matter; and I am really surprised that it has not been proposed by some other member at an earlier period of our deliberations. I will suggest, Mr. President, that propriety of nominating and appointing, before we separate, a chaplain to this Convention, whose duty it shall be uniformly to assemble with us, and introduce the business of each day by and address to the Creator of the universe, and the Governor of all nations, beseeching Him to preside in our council, enlighten our minds with a portion of heavenly wisdom, influence our hearts with a love of truth and justice, and crown our labors with complete and abundant success![61]

Back to 1963

Progressive thinkers decided by the eventful year of 1963 that invoking the help of the Almighty, which was adopted with great reverence by those at that foundational congress, was no longer appropriate for America's children in public schools. Even though the founders had looked with disdain at Alexander Hamilton's angry objection to the appointing of a chaplain and of opening with prayer, the Supreme Court in 1963 readily ruled that God was to be removed from the classrooms. That has been the case ever since, and the results have been devastating.

America finds itself in a slide toward oblivion. The populace has been dumbed down through values clarification that proposes no moral absolutes be applied to situational ethics. This hellish philosophical inculcation has been inflicted upon children at the most formative levels for fifty years. Moral clarity has been replaced by the reprobate mindset, about which God's Word forewarns:

> And even as they did not like to retain God in their knowledge, God gave them over to a reprobate mind.
>
> Romans 1:28a

That brings us to November 2012 and the presidential election just concluded. America has just said "yes" to humanism's "no moral absolutes," and "stay out of our business" to the Creator of all things who has said that the shedding of innocent blood is a sin of monumental magnitude.

The world is going full throttle down the broad way that leads to destruction. It is movement through a gaping opening the Lord terms "the gates of hell." A great division is coming that will forever codify God's opinion of humanism's deadly rebelliousness. The born again, who are the salt and light of the earth and of this nation, will soon be removed in the Rapture, and judgment will begin. Jesus said He would build His church upon Himself, "and the gates of hell shall not prevail against it" (Matthew 16:18c).

> Choose you this day whom ye will serve.
>
> Joshua 24:15b

November 26, 2007
Israel Always the Problem

Often I use the line: No matter which way the cameras and microphones of the world media are focused, they will always turn back to the Middle East, and to Israel and Jerusalem in particular.

This has again been proven correct. The most turbulent presidential election in U.S. history, taking place in the middle of one of the most horrific storms to hit a highly populated area of the country, was front and center for news coverage. Almost as if those things never happened, the microphones and cameras as well as the international diplomatic community's attention are again turned squarely on the tiny Jewish state.

The interim event—the Al-Qaeda murder of the American ambassador to Libya and three others at the consulate in Benghazi—began the swing of media cameras and mikes back in the direction of the Middle East, a movement mainstream news organizations did all within their power to avoid covering while the presidential election was going on. They have had no such reservation getting back to doing their jobs in throwing light on Israel's threat to invade Hamas-infected Gaza because of the incessant rocket attacks Israel has suffered.

The emphasis they chose—as always—was on Israel, not its attackers, being the problem. For example, mainstream news outlets zeroed in on and seem to relish in dwelling on comments about who is the culprit in the death and destruction taking place in the region. They all readily reported, with little explanation of the facts, the words of the Turkish leader, who continues to take his nation farther away from a working relationship with Israeli leaders.

> WASHINGTON—A top Turkish official has claimed that Israel is committing acts of terrorism by bombing Hamas targets in Gaza.
>
> Turkish Prime Minister Tayyip Erdogan told the Eurasian Islamic Council conference in Istanbul that the Jewish state is systematically mass-killing Muslims. "Those who associate Islam with terrorism close their eyes in the face of mass killing of Muslims, turn their heads from the massacre of children in Gaza," Erdogan said, according to Reuters. "For this reason, I say that Israel is a terrorist state, and its acts are terrorist acts."[62]

Those same journalists—if they can honestly be termed as such after the bias they continue to display—imply with cynical speculation that Israel secretly wanted to engage in the military action against Hamas for reasons other than to stop the rocket attacks, or at least to engage in the action for reasons more important than merely to defend against the attacks from Gaza.

Some of the Sunday major network programs had "experts" as guests who speculated that the Israeli Defense Force (IDF) welcomed the military interaction in order to prepare for missile fire that would ultimately come from Lebanon and points north. All of the Hamas activity is, some of these experts offered, a welcome action against an Iranian proxy war surrogate.

Washington Post defense writer David Ignatius suggested Sunday, November 18, on *Face the Nation* that Israel's purpose was to test its air strike capabilities for "a likely war with Iran." He said further: "Some people think...Israel [is] testing the rockets that would be fired against [Iran] from Gaza, next from Lebanon." Ignatius said during a roundtable discussion, "So we may see something with Lebanon soon because it's a preliminary; this is a, kind of, warm-up round for the real conflagration that's ahead that involves Iran."

While it is totally within reason to expect any military brain trust to learn from battlefield action in regard to dealing with future contingencies, the unified tone of the mainstream news media seemed bent toward assigning the darkest of intentions to Israeli thinking. That Israel is always the problem is consistently the tenor of mainstream journalistic analysis.

One encouraging bit of news in this latest round of attacks on Israel is that the newly re-elected American president, at least for the moment, has spoken with Israeli Prime Minister Benjamin Netanyahu, and has indicated that the U.S. stands with Israel. U.S. Secretary of State Hillary Clinton was dispatched to the region to offer an American presence in striving for a cease-fire.

> The Obama administration has firmly supported Israel's right to self-defense, saying only that the U.S. ally should seek to avoid civilian casualties. And the U.S. can only hope to exert influence over Hamas by proxy, because it considers the group a terror-

ist organization and doesn't allow contacts between its members and American officials. For that reason, it is relying on countries such as Egypt, Turkey and Qatar to deliver its message to Gaza's rulers.[63]

On the not-so-bright side of things, some key players within the European Union, as well as within the Israel-hating majority of the United Nations body, have joined turkey's Prime Minister Tayyip Erdogan in classifying Israel as a terrorist state for its determination to defend itself. Zechariah the prophet had it right (Zechariah 12:1–3). At the wrap-up of human history, Israel will be the problem in the eyes of the world. One day, however, God's prototype nation will be considered a blessing to all nations, when this raging, satanic, sin fever that infects the world of nation-states has run its course and the King of all Kings reigns from Jerusalem.

December 10, 2012
Damascus and Doomsday

Here we are approaching the middle of December 2012, and prophetic possibilities are popping all around us. Israel is in the middle of being pressured—as part of dealing with the attacks by Hamas—to divide God's land, meaning that Joel 3:2 is on the cusp of coming to pass. The "covenant made with death and hell" of Isaiah chapter 28 might not be far distant in the making.

Paul's "perilous times" (2 Timothy 3:1–5) words describe American culture and society to a *T*. The "days of Noah" are here, with God's message of repentance being mocked by rebels of a judgment-bound world.

Debased human behavior like in the days of Lot proliferates, so that it now seems to be more the norm than the aberrant.

Many within the ranks of those who are antagonistic to or who ignore the God of heaven seem to instinctively sense something ominous is brewing. Something isn't right, and a visceral fear streams just beneath the surface of civility. The behavior of mankind—especially in America—demands correction of some sort, although neither the problem nor the correction can be discerned. A reprobate mind like that forewarned in Romans 1 prevents clear analysis in trying to understand the matters involved.

Ominous predictions like the prophecies of the long-dead French seer Nostradamus pique the interest of many every time his name is mentioned. The "prophecies" of the long-extinct Mayan shamans grab at the fearful wonderment of many, while the date of December 21, 2012, grows ever nearer. In the minds of some, at least, a nebulous justice of some sort must demand a penalty for the base things infecting this generation. Guilt feelings fester in the collective consciousness to a degree.

Things going on in the Middle East trouble these who are unsure about the source and the reason for their uneasiness. Israel is most often given by mainstream press outlets as the number-one culprit in fomenting hostilities in that incendiary part of the world. However, the usually-pointed-at Israel doesn't seem an underlying cause of things taking place in Syria, with the massacring of his fellow Syrians by dictator Bashar al-Assad.

There is good reason for fear of things developing in Damascus. It is a city of biblically prophetic import like only two others. Jerusalem is slated for both great turmoil and magnificent glorification, according to Bible prophecy. Babylon—whether the actual city within Iraq or whether figurative, as given in Revelation chapter 18—will suffer destruction as none other in history.

Damascus is prophetically scheduled for similar devastation. With all other signs of the return of Jesus Christ on the end-times horizon, the current developments in this, the oldest occupied city on the planet, is most relevant for those who are "watchmen on the wall." The fate of the Syrian capital just might be nearly the top indicator of how near the Rapture of the church is.

The verse of great interest among those who watch for Christ's return is, of course, the following:

> The burden of Damascus. Behold, Damascus is taken away from being a city, and it shall be a ruinous heap.
>
> Isaiah 17:1

According to the signals given in prophetic Scripture, the present generation of earth dwellers looks to be in the last of the last days before the first phase of Christ's Second Coming—the removal of all born-again believers from the earth. This prophetic utterance by the prophet Isaiah has recently and dramatically arisen to prominence amid all of the other indicators pointing to the end of days. Damascus' destruction fits somewhere within the general time frame of the very end of the age. Whether we have reached that parenthesis in God's prophetic program is the question, when considering news of the current tumult in Syria.

The Syrian dictator, President Bashar al-Assad, it is thought by some, senses that his time is about up. He will soon go the way of, at worst, Saddam Hussein and Moammar Gadhafi, and at best, Hosni Mubarak. Many of the "experts" believe al-Assad will choose to bring the entire Syrian people down with him rather than abdicate rulership or flee to escape his comeuppance.

The international community powers that be view warily al-Assad's activities within his capital city and nation. He is feared to have had weapons of mass destruction, particularly chemical weapons, stockpiled for years—his armory the beneficiary, for example, of much of Saddam Hussein's chemical arsenal, once that dictator realized he was about finished as Iraq's evil tormentor.

White House spokesman Jay Carney weighed in on behalf of the Obama administration with regard to how Bashar al-Assad is making troubling moves as his demise seems to be closing in: "We believe that with the regime's grip on power loosening with its failure to put down the opposition through conventional means, we have an increased concern about the possibility of the regime taking the desperate act of using its chemical weapons," he said.[64]

Al-Assad has certainly witnessed what happens to former tyrants in his part of the world in recent times. The question is not without merit. Might the Syrian dictator himself invoke his own Samson Option, of sorts, and become the instrument of prophecy in making Damascus the "ruinous heap" it is destined to become?

December 17, 2012
World Without End

The end of the world is scheduled for this Friday, December 21, 2012, according to the Mayan calendar, as analyzed by some. Many scenarios of what supposedly will happen on that date have for months—even years—been predicted by the purveyors of doom for planet earth. The Mayan "prophecy" goes basically as follows.

The Mayan civilization was extremely advanced in mathematics, engineering, and astronomy. They also had an incredible understanding of time and space. Various calendars were in use to track time in linear progressions within cycles. The "Great Cycle" of the "Long Count" calendar equates to 5,125.36 years. The current Great Cycle is due to be completed on the winter solstice of 2012—December 21. So, it has been interpreted that on this day, the Great Cycle ends, time ends, so the earth must end as well.[65]

The Mayan Long Count concludes on the very day the sun lines up with the center of the Milky Way galaxy. It is said that this stellar event occurs every 25,800 years. The end-of-the-worlders predict that a number of cataclysmic things will occur at 11:11 p.m. Eastern Standard Time (I think) on December 21, 2012.

A polar shift of the earth will occur, bringing about every sort of tectonic plate shift imaginable, thus oceans washing over all the land masses and perhaps the earth, itself, ripping apart in some way. This is the direst of the predictions, I suppose.

Well, not exactly, on second thought. There is some sort of planet that has been hidden from view by our sun, according to some who hold to the December 21, 2012, date with destruction. It might suddenly be in a direct collision course with the big blue marble on the Mayan prophecy date in question. Such a collision would eclipse even the polar reversal in terms of the severity of impact upon life on earth. I'll have to check with the experts on the dynamics of such collisions to determine whether an impact like that would be more catastrophic than a mere polar reversal.

Either way, you get the seriousness of the matters involved.

There are many who are preparing for such an eventuality as predicted. Some are buying/building underground shelters and doing many other things to survive. I'm missing something, in their thinking, I'm afraid. How does one survive an earth-size, even moon-size, object colliding with earth? Or for that matter, how in the world—pardon the pun—does one survive when the big ball on which we live suddenly turns upside down? Oh, well, I'm sure there are the experts who will chide such an ignorant perspective as mine as completely not understanding the physics of such a thing, should it happen.

They would be right. I don't even come close to comprehending what would be the chances of survival in such an event. I am dumbfounded over those who will believe a Mayan prophecy—or any other such soothsaying of a now-extinct civilization. I am as perplexed over their believing such "prophecies" as many of those doomsday believers are berating and not accepting Bible prophecy. To most of these, Nostradamus, or even Rasputin, is given almost mesmerized validation, while Jeremiah, Isaiah, Daniel, and Ezekiel—and especially Jesus Christ—are pushed to the back of the line with regard to credence given to those considered to be prophets.

To determine which of the prophets should be given the label of the true prophet, one need only consider history of the Jews. The Jews—the nation Israel—exist despite millennia of attempts to scour their likes from the planet's surface. That attempt continues. Yet, the nation Israel—the

Jewish race—is at the center of attention, a blessing to all of mankind, while being hounded and hunted throughout the eras of human history.

Biblical prophets have both chronicled this traversing of history by the eternal Jew and have foretold their place at the very end of the age and beyond. In every instance, the foretellings can be traceable as 100 percent on the mark, right to the present moment.

Here's what a couple of God's prophets, one an Old Testament prophet and the other a New Testament prophet, have to say about the earth and its longevity:

> But Israel shall be saved in the LORD with an everlasting salvation:
> ye shall not be ashamed nor confounded world without end.
> For thus saith the LORD that created the heavens;
> God himself that formed the earth and made it;
> he hath established it, he created it not in vain, he formed it
> to be inhabited: I am the LORD; and there is none else.
>
> Isaiah 45:17–18

> Now unto him that is able to do exceeding abundantly above
> all that we ask or think, according to the power that worketh in us,
> Unto him be glory in the church by Christ Jesus throughout all ages,
> world without end. Amen.
>
> Ephesians 3:20–21

Get it? It is a world that will never end! It will be changed; it will be transformed at some future point. But, it is a world without end!

December 24, 2012
No Peace on Earth

How I wish I could put forth the usual message of good tidings of great joy we hear presented every year at this time. But there is no peace on earth. Rather, there is decreasing exhortation for Christmas cheer to be issued to men of goodwill in this darkening time in the nation and around the world. As a matter of fact, there are fewer and fewer men of goodwill, as the Christmas message traditionally proclaims.

Christmas is, in fact, in the process of being outlawed through the national insanity known as political correctness.

Heart-wrenching report after report coming from Newtown, Connecticut, continues to make the point. Just as the apostle Paul prophesied long ago:

> Evil men and seducers will grow worse and worse.
>
> 2 Timothy 3:13a

We are living that predicted nightmare.

Rather than men of goodwill looking at the horrendous act of a crazed product of our anti-God culture/society and rationally analyzing the cesspool-like environmental factors that have brought us to this murderous rampage, politicians, quick to want to make their political points, rush to the microphones, putting the blame on guns. Those who want to garner power while eliminating opposition to their own ideas and demands desperately have desired to vilify firearms for decades—thus to take them from the hands of patriots who would defend against oppressive government, should it raise its head, as has happened in every civilization upon this sin-fallen sphere.

The national news and entertainment media conglomerate has joined in a diatribe against Second- Amendment rights like at no time I can remember. It is done in a soft, reverential tone, calling for us all to sit and reason together. It is done with sophistry that pretends compassion for the children slaughtered by the evil of that horrendous attack. But, it is a luciferic mantra; make no mistake. They want to disarm America, even though they don't fully realize—indeed, cannot even know why—the passion within themselves wants to take away our right to bear arms.

This is why they have no comprehension of the potential for enslavement madness they propose.

> But the natural man receiveth not the things of the Spirit of God: for they are foolishness unto him: neither can he know them, because they are spiritually discerned.
>
> 1 Corinthians 2:14

America and the world face, at this darkening time of evil, men growing worse and worse as part of a spiritual battle of such proportion that even those who have the sound mind of God cannot fathom it. Thus there is a spirit of fear even among God's people—the born again, despite the words given the apostle Paul to set those who are the Lord's at ease while we watch these end-times prophecies unveiling before our eyes minute by minute.

> For God hath not given us the spirit of fear; but of power, and of love, and of a sound mind.
>
> 2 Timothy 1:7

That assurance is just as true as it has ever been, but the majority of the people of God choose to go deeper into the attention diversions of our time rather than heed God's words of comfort. Churches themselves have become Laodicean-like bastions of diversion from the reality of these evil times. These present instead entertainment centers that keep the flock from seeing the true reason for the heinous acts like the one that took the lives of those precious little ones and the adults who were victims.

There is no peace on earth at this bleak moment in the end of this debauched, humanistic age, because Jesus Christ has been progressively pushed to the perimeters of this nation's life stream. Thus, the satanic influence that is at the center of Ephesians 6:12 has for the moment taken an ever-increasing position of dominance over the fallen minds of men, women, and children.

> For we wrestle not against flesh and blood, but against principalities, against powers, against the rulers of the darkness of this world, against spiritual wickedness in high places.

This is why the twenty-year-old man did what he did in Newtown, Connecticut, on December 14.

Neither assault weapons nor any other inanimate objects are the cause of peace having been kept from this generation. The peace Jesus offers to all men is constantly under assault by the devil and his minions. Mankind murders mankind for the same reasons Cain killed Abel—and with something other than a firearm, I might add. The human "heart is deceitful above all things, and desperately wicked" (Jeremiah 17:9).

Only Jesus Christ, the reason we are supposed to celebrate Christmas, can restore the peace that is so needed in this dying, decaying world. Thankfully, He is coming back soon for that very purpose.

January 7, 2013
Violence at Genesis 6 Levels

My last column for 2012 presented my opinion that there was no peace on earth as we celebrated the birth of the Prince of Peace. Earth's history is replete with proof that nature abhors a vacuum. Existence in this dimension must fill with something in the absence of another. In the case of human nature, the absence of peace means violence rushes to fill the vacancy.

As we enter this new year of 2013, the murders of the children and others at the Connecticut kindergarten is one most visible case of such proof. There is much evidence that violence is gushing into every vacuum created by humanity's deliberate refusal to accept God's moral counsel. One such instance of unchecked, global, sexual violence is presented in the following excerpt:

> Doctors have announced that a young Indian woman who was gang raped and severely beaten on a bus in India's capital, New Delhi, has died at their Singapore hospital. A statement by Singapore's Mount Elizabeth Hospital where the 23-year-old victim was being treated said she "died peacefully" early on Saturday....
>
> The horrific ordeal of the woman galvanised Indians, who have held almost daily demonstrations to demand greater protection from sexual violence, from groping to rape, that impacts thousands of women every day, but which often goes unreported. The victim and a male friend were traveling in a public bus on December 16 night when they were attacked by six men who raped her and beat them both. They also...stripped both naked and threw them off the bus on a road. Police have arrested the six attackers.[66]

I intentionally left out some graphic details of the horrendous acts done to this young woman.

Again, violence rushes in where there is an absence of true peace—that which is only available through the Prince of Peace.

Certainly, this generation cries out for peace. Most conspicuous in this regard is the global outcry for a cessation of hostilities between Israel and its Palestinian neighbors. The hue and cry for peace, however, can be heard from every quarter on earth. From nations in conflict with each other, from ethnic groups warring one against another, from communities experiencing ever-increasing violence, from families in turmoil, from individuals who murder and maim each other, every hour of every day:

> They cry peace, peace! when there is no peace.
>
> Jeremiah 6:14, 8:11

This generation seeks to calm the rage, but does so through anything and everything but the one and only source of true peace, Jesus Christ. An example of the Son of God being pushed out of American culture was the announcement by the president general of the Daughters of the American Revolution (DAR) this week just past that the name of Jesus Christ cannot be used in closing prayers given at DAR meetings, but that a more generic form of closure must be used. His Holy Name is being expunged by the organization's headquarters in Washington, D.C., from DAR literature in many cases, according to a Fox News report on Thursday, January 3.

Often, in discussions involving the state of the world, it is said that societies such as the most brutal regimes upon the planet have no regard for human life. Such accusations imply that America and Western Europe are the truly civilized societies and cultures of planet earth. However, with more than one million children legally murdered while still in their mothers' wombs every year in the United States, the assertion that America honors life more than do the barbarous nations of Asia or Africa is hypocrisy. The hypocrisy is magnified many times over when we consider that this nation has had God's grace shed upon it in ways no other nation, with the possible exception of Israel, has ever experienced.

Darkness has not come upon America because of wicked regimes suppressing gospel truth. Darkness is engulfing us because we, as a people, are turning our backs on God. We are deliberately and methodically turning off God's light so that we can do our sinful deeds under cover of darkness. American money has inscribed on it "In God We Trust." Today, it would be more accurate to say that our slogan is "In Money We Trust."

Growing numbers of men are following the "if it feels good, do it" tenets taught by humanism and vividly portrayed by Hollywood. Divorce rates continue to climb, the majority of divorces due to men leaving wives and children to pursue relationships that require of them little or no responsibility. This is not to say that women are not culpable as well. Statistics show a growing number of women are deserting husbands and children for the same self-centered reasons.

Why get married? That is another attitude that pervades American culture today. Single mothers who have never been married constitute a rising tide of irresponsible behavior that has resulted in great societal, cultural, and fiscal tumult. Federal welfare entitlements, rather than help lessen or eliminate the resultant cultural insanity, feed the proliferation of illegitimacy. Gangs of youth without fathers to nurture and discipline them cling to each other and rage against a society that neither understands nor seems to care except when crimes committed by the gang members on occasion directly touch our lives.

Abortion proponents give unwanted children (such as those who end up in gangs and who might predictably produce future gang members) as good reasons for ending pregnancies. Such children, if allowed to be born, they say, will only suffer the abuse of America's gang culture or worse. The truth is, however, that abortion imprints upon the minds of our children—and everyone else—the idea that human life is a commodity like any other commodity and can be discarded without a second thought. Man, not God, it is implied, has authority over life and death. The message clearly has gotten through to the young gang members who slaughter each other each night across America.

Although fighting in the streets of this nation has so far been confined to youth gangs sporadically shooting it out in our larger cities, troubling reports of increased drug dealings and other criminal activities in suburban and even rural areas should serve as a wake-up call. Rumors of wars threaten to turn into actual wars if peace is not forthcoming.

So-called gangbangers—inner-city youth gang members—sometimes now receive something akin to diplomatic recognition by city officials and other leaders who desperately wish to negotiate an end to gang crime and gang war. Although such overtures to these juvenile thugs are well-intentioned, they serve to give gang leaders and the gangs themselves increased prestige, power, and authority, thus making the gang life more attractive to youngsters. Rarely is peace made, and never is peace maintained through these "summit" negotiations.

The apostle Paul wrote in 2 Timothy 3 that in the last days, perilous times will come. He wrote that many people will be fierce in those closing moments of human history. Death dealing carried on by the gangs and the drug dealers who rove our streets late at night and make thousands of new gang members through death threats and thousands of new customers through addictions indeed prove that we live in a time when a growing number among us are of fierce demeanor. How long can it continue at the present rate of increasing ferocity until every street in America becomes a battle zone like those streets in so many Third-World countries?

Violence is on the rise while labor unions across America sense that right-to-work laws are beginning to catch on in many places. Gangster-like thugs among the union memberships use violence against those who want to work without paying dues to those unions. Several top leaders of unions have even threatened—on camera—that blood will flow as a result of the right-to-work legislation being passed around the nation.

Jesus, the greatest of all prophets, foretold that conditions within human interaction will be as they were in the days of Noah, at the time of His next intervention into human history. We read of those conditions:

> The earth also was corrupt before God,
> and the earth was filled with violence.
>
> Genesis 6:11

According to our minute-by-minute news headlines, it seems violence might be very near Genesis 6 levels.

January 14, 2013
Future Is Now

Having just returned from Future Congress II at Dallas, a number of things about what was discussed/learned while there are firing in the synapses. Chief among them are Hal Lindsey's words spoken during the Saturday evening session. *The Late, Great, Planet Earth* author and *The Hal Lindsey Report* anchor said the following: "The Bible says the United States must fall. And it is falling. We've passed the point of no return. America as we know it isn't going. It is already gone."

My reaction upon hearing his words was to say in a whisper to myself: "It is true."

Like Jack Kinsella noted in his *Omega Letter* of Wednesday, January 9, the reaction to Dr. Lindsey's stunning declaration was absolute silence.

It was as if everyone in the audience was so accustomed to believing the statement's factuality that it failed to register on their concern seismographs. Most all indicators point to the reality that the United States of America has been weighed in the balance and found to be unworthy to continue, like Babylonian King Belshazzar as presented in Daniel 5:22–28.

Those who study Bible prophecy and consider current issues and events in that light frequently speculate about just how much time might be left for America and the world before God's hand of judgment begins to fall. I fear we all too often do disservice to the Lord's commission to be watchmen on the wall when we present the mindset that things aren't yet at the point of incorrigibility. We are often remiss in speaking up when it is stated that there will be the mythical "revival" about which we hear, but which is found nowhere in the Bible for the end of the Church Age.

Can there be revival? Of course, the answer is yes. God calls all sinners to repentance; therefore, there remains the option open for repentance so long as God calls. However—again—there is no mention in Bible prophecy of revival for the end of the Church Age (Age of Grace). As a matter of fact, Paul, the apostle and prophet, tells us that "evil men and seducers" will grow "worse and worse, deceiving, and being deceived" (2 Timothy 3:13). He points out as recorded in the "perilous times" verses of 2 Timothy 3 that the end times will bring about anything but revival.

Perhaps no other symptom of the age has struck me in a more profound way than the report published by Planned Parenthood, the organization that presides at the center of one of America's most egregious sins—the annual murder of millions of babies in the wombs of their mothers, the shelters where they should be most safe from the horrors of this world.

The report gave the following facts about the infanticide, and it is indeed infanticide, because God's Word indicates He considers people as individual human beings from the moment of conception.

Planned Parenthood's annual report from the 2012 fiscal year reveals a record number of taxpayer contributions and abortions performed. During the twelve-month period, Planned Parenthood received $542 million in taxpayer money. These funds came to the organization through Medicaid reimbursements and government contracts and grants. The amount of government money received accounts for nearly half of Planned Parenthood's operating expenses for the year. The annual report also revealed that the organization performed 334,000 abortions, which, according to previous reports, is a record number.[67] Marjorie Dannenfelser, president of Susan B. Anthony List, stated the following, giving her opinion that reflects many who see abortion as a national sin against the God of heaven:

> While government subsidies to Planned Parenthood have reached an all time high, so too has the number of lives ended by this profit-driven abortion business. Destroying nearly one million children in three years is not health care and does not reflect a concern for vulnerable women and girls.[68]

Franklin Graham, son of evangelist Billy Graham, recently put his finger on the direction the nation is taking and upon the only hope for a cure for America's ills:

> For far too long, as a nation we have neglected—and even rejected—the Word of God and His commands. Yet the Scriptures are mighty, able to penetrate even the most hardened and darkened hearts with convicting, life-giving power.... This is the only cure for a sin-sickened country that is about to slip into a moral abyss, and it is why we must proclaim the Good News.[69]

Graham wrote further that America's financial problems "are nothing compared to the spiritual and moral cliff that is far more destructive to our nation than any economic concerns."[70]

The time when Jesus returns will be the worst in human history is the theme that runs throughout Bible prophecy for the last of the last days. We are there. The future is now. According to our minute-by-minute news headlines, it seems violence might be very near Genesis 6 levels.

January 21, 2013
Israel's Prophetic Positioning

Israeli Prime Minister Benjamin Netanyahu is, amazingly, being viewed as a moderate in the politically right-oriented Likud party these days. This fact shouldn't go without considerable notice by those who look at Bible prophecy from the futurist viewpoint. Eschatologically speaking, this otherwise strange development as of late makes sense. Here's what I mean.

Israel must somehow—for now—be kept in the world diplomatic loop. The Jewish state cannot afford to be totally marginalized to the point that the nation has no one with whom to negotiate, or at least to talk with, on the negotiating front. At the same time, elements within the present make-up of the Knesset and the government as a whole have reached the point that they, in order to show resolve, have to adhere to a hard-line approach to Israel's enemies, who pressure them to give in at every point of the international community's demands. This resolve translates into intransigence in the thinking of most Israel-hating diplomats of the U.N.—i.e., Israel's resolve is propagandized by diplomats and the world's mainstream journalists as deliberately disruptive stubbornness in doing harm to the peace process.

Netanyahu currently wears his moderate, right-winger, actor's mask effectively. This is to keep the channels open in dealing with the world's anti-Semite predators, most of whom want Israel gone from the land of which they are occupiers in the majority opinion of today's U.N. constituency. The Israeli prime minister, as I have written on many occasions, has, I believe, learned to play the game made famous by Yasser Arafat during the Palestinian Liberation Organization (PLO) terrorist-in-chief's brutal reign.

The PLO tyrant became a master of playing to the microphones and cameras of the world news outlets, always offering to sit down and negotiate with Israeli leadership. But, when it came down to actually doing so, he always found a way to push away from the negotiating table. The journalists somehow always saw and reported it as the Israeli negotiators being at fault for the burnoose-wearing Arafat's last minute withdrawals from talks.

Benjamin Netanyahu has recently said all the right things about wanting to negotiate. He talks about the possibility of stopping the building of the new developments in Judea and Samaria. But, he never seems to get around to the actual negotiating table. Thus, he has managed to take on the appearance of a moderate among an increasingly hard-line Knesset. He keeps the lines of communication open for all the world to see in this way, assuring all the while that there is less and less chance his government will ever agree to giving in to dividing Jerusalem in the way Israel's would-be destroyers desire. The idea is to play for time—never getting to the final "no" to the nations of the world's demand that Israel give up part of its capital city to those enemies blood-vowed to wipe all Jews off the map.

One Israeli pundit wrote about the hard-right shift that has taken place just recently. The ideological reason for the shift is quite interesting.

> This is a different Israeli right, almost certainly helming and setting the tone for our different Israel. This is an Israeli right whose soaring political force is Naftali Bennett, an ex-IDF commando, former head of the Council of Settlements and previous top aide to Netanyahu, who brushes aside the notion of a Palestinian state anywhere in the biblical Land of Israel. It's just not going to happen, he declares, with a confidence born of his party's [The Jewish Home (Habayit)] Hayehudi dizzying rise, from three seats in the last parliament to what the polls indicate will be well over a dozen this time.[71]

The ideological shift is theological, actually. The new Israel sports the face represented in the kippa-wearing Bennett, who champions religious Zionism. The right of the nation of Israel to Jerusalem is God-given, and nothing will change in his and his like-minded compatriots' passion for the Jewish state. U.S. President Barack Obama said repeatedly recently that Israel does not know what its own best interests are, according to *The Atlantic's* Jeffrey Goldberg, writing in *Bloomberg View*. Goldberg wrote that when he was told about the Israeli decision to approve construction plans in Jerusalem's E1 area:

> Obama, who has a famously contentious relationship with the prime minister, didn't even bother getting angry.... He told several people that this sort of behavior on Netanyahu's part is what he has come to expect, and he suggested that he has become inured to what he sees as self-defeating policies of his Israeli counterpart.[72]

Goldberg wrote further:

> With each new settlement announcement, in Obama's view, Netanyahu is moving his country down a path toward near-total isolation.[73]

There is increasing concern among Israel watchers that the Obama administration privately more and more veers from its public position of support for Israel's right to decide whether to continue construction in this, the most potentially volatile city on the planet. How long Netanyahu can keep up the pretense that he yet holds open the possibility of negotiations regarding the status of the settlements of Jerusalem is the question of greatest interest.

The Israeli prime minister is known to be holding private prayer sessions and Scripture readings these days. Something has definitely changed, and the change almost certainly portends increasing isolation for the tiny Jewish nation. Israel is rapidly positioning itself to become the burdensome stone and cup of trembling Zechariah the prophet foretold Israel and Jerusalem will become at the very end of the age. This generation is indeed nearing the midnight hour on God's prophetic timeline. The Rapture of the church has never seemed more imminent!

January 28, 2013
The Real Crisis

Crises and potential crises surround us during every waking moment. Except for those who are oblivious to what's going on in this nation and world today, the cultural and societal pathway ahead disappears into the anxiety-laden darkness of the unknown. Rather than take on the entire world and its problems in this regard, I will, for our purposes in this commentary, stick to analyzing the fearful future of this nation I love.

Most in America—and sadly, in the church (born-again believers)—fall into that category of the oblivious. Therefore, the crises, from their perspective, don't exist. All the forewarnings of coming disaster seem issued to ears that will never hear and presented to eyes that will never see. Yet, at the same time, the crises, themselves, do create undercurrents of worry. Even the otherwise diverted masses notice, at least for fleeting moments, when societal dangers disrupt their world of shopping and entertainment—for example, the murder of the children at Sandy Hook Elementary School in Newtown, Connecticut. Then, it is back to buying, selling, building, marrying, and giving in marriage, and the thousand and one other things that matter most to them.

Crises dominate the horizon politically, economically, and morally. As a matter of fact, they intertwine in such convolution as to now be inseparable so far as discerning where one aspect begins and the others end. There has developed, because of the incessant progression of assaults by evil actions, desensitization that affects the masses like a venomous bite by a deadly serpent.

The analogy is more than coincidental. It is a precise description of what has happened. The serpent of Genesis 3 has successfully injected much of America's population with the same sort of morality-paralyzing toxin that separated man from God those many millennia ago. We have indeed reached the point of becoming a people like those at whom Isaiah the prophet pointed the finger of condemnation:

> Woe unto them that call evil good, and good evil;
> that put darkness for light, and light for darkness;
> that put bitter for sweet, and sweet for bitter!
> Isaiah 5:20

This crisis of moral decay was brought home to me as I listened to the minister who was selected by the forty-fourth president to read a prayer during the Obama inauguration on January 21. He, we are supposed to presume, prayed to the God of heaven, asking Him to bless the gay lifestyle in that prayer for inclusiveness and tolerance in America.

This is the same administration that has made homosexuality and those who fight for the right to openly display the debased, debauched activities of that community in a very public way as the equivalent of the black community crusading for civil rights. This is the same political entity that will pull all the levers of governmental power at their disposal to protect the young of wildlife, thus to impose as much control as possible over individuals and businesses, under the guise of environmental concerns. These will, at the same time, do everything within that power to facilitate the murder of babies in their mothers' wombs for the sake of placating a voter base that desires to expediently get rid of the unwanted fruits of their pleasure-seeking indiscretions.

While America sleeps, liberties are eroded one at a time, and the powers that be viciously seek to marginalize all who would disagree with their seizing by "executive action" constitutional powers the Founding Fathers built into the nation's safeguards through checks and balances. Even those who have until recently adamantly opposed such a power grab seem now to be shrugging shoulders and going along with the mainstream media mantra that it is just the new norm.

But the dumbing down of the American public and apparently, too, many of those constitutionally elected to represent it, in convincing that the new norm is just the hope and change that is the natural progression of such an advanced, sophisticated culture—thus the moral implosion that continues to take its toll—isn't the real crisis.

"The real crisis is wrapped up in the following: The church in this crucial hour is asleep, and if there is no preacher, how will they hear?" (Romans 10:14).

The Lord of heaven might have just about reached the limits of His patience with a nation peopled by a populace that has lived the most materially—and even spiritually—blessed existence in the history of mankind. Proof that we might be near the outer limits of God's tolerance for national rebellion is the fact that there seems a collective mindset now developed like that forewarned by the apostle Paul.

Please consider with all gravity the Word of the living God. I believe it is the equivalent of Isaiah's finger pointed at my beloved United States of America:

> Because that, when they knew God, they glorified him not as God,
> neither were thankful; but became vain in their imaginations,
> and their foolish heart was darkened.
>
> Professing themselves to be wise, they became fools,
>
> And changed the glory of the uncorruptible God into an image
> made like to corruptible man, and to birds,
> and fourfooted beasts, and creeping things.
>
> Wherefore God also gave them up to uncleanness
> through the lusts of their own hearts, to dishonour their own
> bodies between themselves:
>
> Who changed the truth of God into a lie,
> and worshipped and served the creature more than the Creator,
> who is blessed forever. Amen.
>
> For this cause God gave them up unto vile affections:
> for even their women did change the natural use
> into that which is against nature:

And likewise also the men, leaving the natural use of the woman,
burned in their lust one toward another; men with men working
that which is unseemly, and receiving in themselves that
recompence of their error which was meet.

And even as they did not like to retain God in their knowledge,
God gave them over to a reprobate mind,
to do those things which are not convenient;

Being filled with all unrighteousness, fornication,
wickedness, covetousness, maliciousness; full of envy, murder,
debate, deceit, malignity; whisperers,

Backbiters, haters of God, despiteful, proud, boasters,
inventors of evil things, disobedient to parents,

Without understanding, covenantbreakers, without natural
affection, implacable, unmerciful:

Who knowing the judgment of God, that they which commit such
things are worthy of death, not only do the same,
but have pleasure in them that do them.

Romans 1:21-32

FEBRUARY 2013

February 4, 2013
Dawn's Early Light

This week's commentary is a reminder for those who believe in Jesus Christ as defined by the following scriptural description of the term "Christian":

> That if thou shalt confess with thy mouth the Lord Jesus,
> and shalt believe in thine heart that God hath raised him
> from the dead, thou shalt be saved.
>
> Romans 10:9

Tragically, to the reader who hasn't genuinely confessed sin and asked forgiveness of the God of heaven, and adopted this faith prescription from God's Word, this essay cannot apply. Thankfully, all people everywhere are invited to come to belief in the Son of God, who came to earth the first time specifically to die so that anyone who accepts His shed-blood antidote for sin's deadly venom will be saved from the eternal fires of hell, and will instead live forever with the Father in heaven. My prayer is that the reader, if you haven't done so, will do so right now—for this is the only moment guaranteed to you. You might not have a follow-up second of life. Your last heartbeat might come before you finish reading.

Paul the apostle reported God's words on the tenuous nature of life and the importance of immediately making the decision in the matter of salvation:

> For he saith, I have heard thee in a time accepted,
> and in the day of salvation have I succoured thee: behold,
> now is the accepted time; behold, now is the day of salvation.
>
> 2 Corinthians 6:2

With the gospel message offered, as the Holy Spirit draws, we will proceed with additional good news, something that some accuse is a rarity for a "Nearing Midnight" commentary. The name of this section for our Rapture Ready website conjures in the imagination darkness and foreboding—a very bleak outlook for America and the planet we call earth. When considering the troubling course we see narrowing in the distance, while we examine today's issues and events under the microscope of God's prophetic Word, we must be truthful and faithful in giving the forewarnings of the watchman (Mark 13: 37).

But, while nearing midnight, the world keeps turning. There is coming a moment after the gore and terrible dangers of the battle at twilight's last gleaming—like Francis Scott Key wrote—the dawn's early light. The flag of the United States of America is under attack, and the nation is staggering. It might well fall this time, unlike during the time of its birth as given in the "Star Spangled Banner."

But, as much as we all love this nation, we look toward a heavenly home, built by the Lord Himself (see 2 Corinthians 5:1; John 14:1–3) and a world without end (Ephesians 3:21). The matters to think upon for you and me as God's children involve a glorious dawning of unimaginable things to come. Paul the apostle puts it this way, as we have all read many times:

> But as it is written, Eye hath not seen, nor ear heard,
> neither have entered into the heart of man,
> the things which God hath prepared for them that love him.
>
> 1 Corinthians 2:9

While I often express in this column frustration over the fact that the majority of Christians are today inward turned, not at all thinking of things of God, and are asleep in the pews because they get only pabulum from the pastors in the pulpits for the most part, I am of the conviction that this is a malaise that is an important indicator of exactly where we are on God's prophetic timeline. Jesus said the following:

Nevertheless when the Son of man cometh,
shall he find faith on the earth?
Luke 18:8b

This said, each child of God—whether on fire for the Lord, or living life oblivious to the things of God—needs to know that when Christ's call "come up hither" (Revelation 4:1) is heard, every truly born-again (John 3:3) believer will go instantaneously to be with the Lord. He will then take us to the home He has been preparing for us (John 14:1–3).

Even those who have not been watching for His coming for them in the clouds—in the Rapture—will go in that stupendous atomos of time to be with Him, forever!

I know the foregoing will be angrily disputed by many. There is an erroneous visceral belief among many who know the pretribulational view of prophecy to be truth from the Bible. That mistaken belief purports that the watchful Christians will go to be with Christ when He calls, and the slothful, earth-minded Christians will stay behind to—well, I'm not sure what.

Those holding this view just cannot accept the full scope of what the Bible says about God's love for His family. Christ did it all on the cross at Calvary, so what can we do to make ourselves more secure in Christ?

Paul said in 1 Corinthians 15 and 1 Thessalonians 4 that ALL will go in that twinkling of an eye. The Word of God didn't say that some will stay and some will go. Here's the thing: God knows who is and is not His child; we, His children, are not privy to that knowledge.

My friend, Dr. Dave Breese, used to say that the Lord Jesus will not leave part of His bride, the church, here on earth to be bloodied and bruised during the most horrendous time of human history. He will take a perfected bride home to the Father's house. Jesus did the cleaning up when He shed His precious blood at Calvary two millennia ago. He cried "It is finished!" —and, it was! The translation—the transformation from mortal to immortal—that will take place in that stunning, glorious, split second will make every one of us worthy and acceptable in the heavenly city!

Now, let me say that the child of God living like the devil, with unrepented-of sin, will pay a tremendous price at the bema (judgment seat of Christ). Make no mistake: There will be an eternal instant when all will look into those eyes of absolute love and understand their Lord's disappointment. We will at that moment want more than anything we've ever wanted to hear Jesus say, "Well done, good, faithful servant."

The dawn's early light will one day shine its rays of glory. It will happen as Christ breaks through the dark, death-decaying clouds at Armageddon (Revelation 19: 11). He will defeat all of His—and our—foes. Antichrist will be thrown in the lake of fire, with the False Prophet. Satan will be chained for one thousand years. Jesus will clean up planet earth.

But, that's not the really good news for you and me. Just consider: You and I are here at this strange time, and in this foreign land, for purposes the Lord, Himself, has determined. We could have been placed here at any time in history. But, He chose us to serve Him, and now, while all around us break the most stunning prophetic possibilities imaginable. For example, no other generation has seen Israel reborn and as hated by the entire world of nations as has our generation—exactly as prophesied. Something is up, and it is big!

We will see the "dawn" at the close of Armageddon described above as we descend on gleaming, white, heavenly steeds as Christ leads the way.

However, for believers of this Age of Grace, "dawn's early light" is scheduled to break brilliantly and instantaneously much earlier—during this darkening hour we presently face. We do not have to wait at least seven years for that other "dawn" as Christ returns at the end of the Tribulation. The Rapture is very near! Serve Him as if He could call in the next second. He just might! Take heart!

February 11, 2013
Monetary Magicians and 2014

I don't like "I told you so's" any more than you do. However, I did write things that we see developing now in a number of "Nearing Midnight" commentaries, so will take the credit—or blame—for doing so here.

I wrote that I suspected things would start looking up in the short term for the economy—for America and for the world. But, I also said that it will all be the proverbial smoke and mirrors, sleight-of- hand wizardry by the controlling powers that be. The mantra is on by the Obama administration and its collective mouthpiece, the mainstream media. The mantra is that if the opposition would just get out of the way and let them work their magic, there will be no stopping the march not only to recovery, but to a utopian, national construction of some sort.

My friend, economic expert Wilfred Hahn, pointed out the specious nature of the arguments for supposed glowing recovery regurgitated by the above-described administration propaganda machine. Similar sophistry about almost-miraculous recovery is gushing from reportage in other parts of the world. Hahn writes in the February 1, 2013, issue of his newsletter, *Eternal Value Review*, the following:

> The drumbeats are again starting up. Surely good times are coming. Everything is coming up roses. That's the new sentiment at the start of the year 2013.74
>
> This past year, we have observed some remarkable—and, we would even say, earth-shaking—worldwide developments....
>
> At the very least, another major turning point is evident. All of the world's largest central banks have crossed the so-called "Rubicon." They have gone past the point of no return. They knowingly and willingly have chosen to brazenly "steal and thieve." It is awe-striking to witness.
>
> What signifies this turning point...a new defining moment in the slide to global financial bedlam? Recently, some unorthodox new policies were announced by a number of major central banks around the globe...both European bond and stock markets soared, thinking that no matter how severe the financial state of the Eurozone, the central bank could be relied upon to eventually bail everyone out.
>
> A few weeks later, the U.S. Federal Reserve Board (FRB) also demonstrated its resolve to print unlimited money....

> It announced QE3 (Quantitative Easing #3), a third program to flood the economy with money deposits. Ben Bernanke, the head of the FRB, stated that he would do so "without limit" and assured financial markets that ZIRP (zero interest rate policy) would extend into the year 2015.[75]

This past week, President Obama told reporters that his administration had overseen the creation of more than six million jobs. The truth is that there have been more than eight million jobs lost (jobs no longer available to American workers) in the past several years. No one calls the president on such statistical bait-and-switch gobbledygook. He indeed paints a rosy picture of recovery at every opportunity, as does his spokesman, Jay Carney, and others who propagandize for this administration. This is politics in America, and I am fully aware that this is the way it's done in the process of bamboozling the voting public, a large percentage of which has no idea—some not even caring—that they are being lied to.

My problem with the politicians' spin process at this time is that no one in the major news media will question the overtly obvious misinformation and deliberately false reporting of the figures. No president in American history has been given this sort of slavish acquiescence. Such adoration as is daily given Mr. Obama by ABC, CBS, NBC, the *New York Times*, the *Washington Post*, and practically all others that constitute mainstream news journalism is nothing short of dangerous to assuring a free, well-informed populace. Such sycophantic obeisance is the kind of stuff of which dictatorships of every variety are made.

One must wonder whether this idolization of America's first black president—making him the equivalent of a cult figure, a celebrity icon worthy of Hollywood in its heyday—might be setting up in the minds of some the possibility of attempting a most disturbing constitutional change. As a matter of fact, there are growing rumors to that effect. The rosy picture being painted, cooking the books, and just downright lying about the economy roaring back, when in actuality it is headed in the opposite direction, are an attempt to set up certain outcomes for the 2014 midterm elections. Might it be, it is conjectured, that creating the illusion of a robust economy is desired by the president's slavish press in order to enhance chances for winning a greater majority in the senate, and to win back the House of Representatives for the Democrat party in the midterm elections—thus to begin dismantling certain constitutional restrictions with a majority in both houses of Congress?

Many harbor the concern that getting rid of the Twenty-Second Amendment to the U.S. Constitution—or at least to change it—might be the objective of the president and his political handlers. Might a third Obama presidential term be a part of the monetary magicians' blueprint for America's future?

If getting the president a third term or even more, through the constitutionally prescribed political process, could be legitimately accomplished, there is really no reasonable argument that can be made to say it is wrong. The key here is the word "legitimately." Lying to the American people—even if many of them are willing dupes—is the epitome of lawlessness. The Constitution is law by which we the people are to comport ourselves. The Founding Fathers drew from God's Word to construct much of that national legal document.

Here's what that Bible says about things that are contrary to law genuinely designed to see to it that people live safely and peaceably:

> Knowing this, that the law is not made for a righteous man,
> but for the lawless and disobedient, for the ungodly
> and for sinners, for unholy and profane, for murderers
> of fathers and murderers of mothers, for manslayers,
>
> For whoremongers, for them that defile themselves with mankind,
> for men stealers, for liars, for perjured persons, and if there be any
> other thing that is contrary to sound doctrine.
>
> 1 Timothy 1:9–10

Lawlessness is a deadly matter. It destroys people. Antichrist will, through devilish wizardry, come to wield, through lawlessness, absolute power.

> And he shall speak great words against the most High, and shall wear out the saints of the most High, and think to change times and laws: and they shall be given into his hand until a time and times and the dividing of time.
>
> Daniel 7:25

February 18, 2013
Roman Road of Prophecy

Many who are Christians are at least somewhat familiar with one particular scriptural formula for coming to Christ in becoming a believer. It is known as the "Roman Road to Salvation."

It has often been used for many years to show those who haven't heard the reason salvation is needed, and how it is obtained. The following is that scriptural road map:

Romans 3:10: "As it is written, There is none righteous, no not one."

Romans 3:23: "For all have sinned and come short of the glory of God."

Romans 5:8: "But God commendeth his love toward us, in that, while we were yet sinners, Christ died for us."

Romans 6:23: "For the wages of sin is death; but the gift of God is eternal life through Jesus Christ our Lord."

Romans 10:13: "For whosoever shall call upon the name of the Lord shall be saved."

These Scriptures mean that none of us is worthy, nor can we earn the right to go to heaven when we die. But Jesus loved us so much that He died for us to pay the price for our sin so that we can be with Him forever. All we have to do is ask Jesus to come into our hearts and be our Lord and Savior, and then follow Him.

In similar fashion—but, perhaps somewhat more circuitously—I believe there is a "Roman Road of Prophecy" that can help the student of Bible prophecy receive understanding of things involved with some recent developments.

With the announcement on Monday, February 11, by Pope Benedict

XVI that he is resigning as pope effective February 28, has come considerable concern and curiosity about what it might mean, prophetically. Most who email me, of course, are vitally interested in Bible prophecy. They know, to one degree or another, about the supposition that the next pope will be the last pontiff.

This prediction comes from the twelfth-century Irish Catholic bishop, St. Malachy, who was said to have had a vision in the year 1139, in which he received foreknowledge of the 112 popes who would reign in the line of papal succession from that point until the final pope. Although some aspects of the names of the popes from that time until now have been somewhat nebulous in terms of accuracy, they have in many cases been considered to be close enough to the "prophesied" names to validate St. Malachy's prognostications. The last forty-five popes, I'm told the research shows, have been almost precise in their accuracy.

So, we await the installation of the next pope to see if the Malachy "vision" that the last pope is to be Petrus Romanus ("Peter the Roman") will prove to indeed be the case. We shouldn't have long to wait.

While preparing for being a guest on a nationwide radio program, the program host and I discussed a number of things in our preliminary phone conversations. As part of our talking through the pope and end-times matters before doing the program, we agreed that we couldn't be absolutely dogmatic about whether Rome was the city about which the prophecies in Revelation chapter 17 foretell. The Vatican, headquarters of the Roman Catholic Church, as everyone knows, sits upon the "seven hills of Rome." Therein resides the almost universal belief among Bible prophecy students that the Catholic Church will be a major player in the last days.

That prophecy about the end-times city that will play a profoundly deleterious role in the consummation of the age states:

> And here is the mind which hath wisdom.
> The seven heads are seven mountains,
> on which the woman sitteth.
>
> Revelation 17:9

Although I still maintain that we can't be absolutely dogmatic that the city referred to is Rome, I remain personally convinced that this is the case. I believe there is a scriptural road map of sorts that we can explore that might present strong evidence that the city given in Revelation 17: 9 is Rome. Therefore, let's look at what I term the "Roman Road of Prophecy":

Daniel 9:26–27 and the ties to Rome: The wind-up of this Age of Grace (Church Age) is encapsulated in the prophecy given Daniel as recorded in this passage. The great prophet was told to write that the "prince that shall come" would confirm the covenant (agreement of peace between Israel and its enemies) for seven years. This prince would come out of the people who would destroy the city (Jerusalem) and the sanctuary (the Jewish Temple). These were the Romans. Regardless of their regional makeup, they were Romans, whose leaders were Emperor Vespasian and his son, General Titus—of Rome. Romans fulfilled part of this end-times prophecy in AD 70, beginning earlier, around AD 33 with the "cutting off of Messiah" (Daniel 9:26). All of human history, from the confirming of the covenant by this Roman prince (the Beast of Revelation 13) through Christ's return, would, the Daniel 9:26–27prophecy indicates, conclude in almost total devastation for planet earth. This prophetic area of Scripture puts the city of Rome at ground zero for the wind-up of human history.

Luke 2:1–3: Rome holds sway over the world. During the prophesied time of Israel's Messiah being born, Rome was the power center of the then-known world.

> And it came to pass in those days,
> that there went out a decree from Caesar Augustus,
> that the entire world should be taxed.
>
> [And this taxing was first made when
> Cyrenius was governor of Syria.]
>
> And all went to be taxed, every one into his own city.

> And Joseph also went up from Galilee, out of the city of Nazareth, into Judaea, unto the city of David, which is called Bethlehem [because he was of the house and lineage of David];
>
> To be taxed with Mary his espoused wife, being great with child.
>
> Luke 2:1-5

Again, Rome is in the prophetic spotlight while the Savior of the world makes His appearance in the flesh upon a judgment-bound planet.

Revelation 17:15–18: Rome represents the focus of God's judgment at the wind-up of the age. God's Word uses a drunken, debauched prostitute as symbol for the end-times religious system that is located—you guessed it—in Rome, whose tyrant regime had exiled John the apostle and prophet to Patmos. There, John was given the Revelation:

> And he saith unto me, The waters which thou sawest, where the whore sitteth, are peoples, and multitudes, and nations, and tongues.
>
> And the ten horns which thou sawest upon the beast, these shall hate the whore, and shall make her desolate and naked, and shall eat her flesh, and burn her with fire.
>
> For God hath put in their hearts to fulfill his will, and to agree, and give their kingdom unto the beast, until the words of God shall be fulfilled. And the woman which thou sawest is that great city, which reigneth over the kings of the earth.
>
> Revelation 17:15-18

Can there be much doubt that Rome was the city that reigned over the whole earth at the time of John's exile? Bible prophecy tells us in these passages that Rome will be at the center of world rebellion "until the words of God shall be fulfilled." A corrupt religious system will be prominently ensconced atop the seven mountains.

Make no mistake: With its expansive reach and influence, the doings of the Roman Catholic Church in the coming months are worth watching for the observer of Bible prophecy.

February 25, 2013
Why Islam Might Buckle

An interesting email appeared in my in box the other day. It set me to exploring in a slightly different direction things that look to constitute a major quandary in trying to understand certain prophecies, juxtaposed against realities of these strange times.

The emailer—Dan—put his queries this way:

> I do have one question that I have asked many, but to date no answer. I am still wondering how under the New World Order, led by the revived Roman Empire, [is the rising of the Islamic threat to Israel and the rest of the world going to be squelched]? Is this part of the "covenant" that the Beast will confirm after the Rapture, or does a PS 83-type war need to take place first?

A couple of very good and relevant questions, to be sure.

We have only to think about how Islam has made inroads into Western Europe—and, in fact, into this nation—to understand the seeming insurmountable problem the world faces with that religion, as implicit within Dan's email queries. Only twelve short years ago America was viciously attacked by the same religious zeal that over the years since has set our hourly news headlines ablaze. More than three thousand people, the majority of them U.S. citizens, were forced to jump or be burned alive in the towering infernos, or die where they were on the hijacked planes and in the Pentagon, when nineteen Muslims carried out the orders of Osama bin Laden on America's most tragic day in history.

Yet Islam is like a protected species adopted by the leftist do-gooders of the eco-freak sorts who think humankind should—except for them,

I suppose—be eliminated, so that Mother Earth can return to her pristine condition. It is the same perverted, intolerant mindset that says it is right to marginalize Christianity because Christians are intolerant, while embracing a religion whose "holy" book demands that all who will not bow the knee to Allah are legitimate targets for elimination by the most heinous methodologies available.

The Obama administration and its slavish mainstream media—both news and entertainment—have done all they can to try to convince us that Islam is a "religion of peace." We have seen the president and his underlings go to extreme absurdities to blame anyone and everyone except Islamist terrorists for their dastardly deeds. Most recently, the Benghazi murder of the American ambassador and some genuine American heroes, and the totally disproved claim by the White House and State Department that it was an anti-Mohammed YouTube video that caused a spontaneous riot, thus incited the good people of the area to commit the murders, serves as prime example.

An insanity pervades the minds of those who continue to insist that Islam presents no threat to civilization, and that if we just embrace that religion, whose adherents refuse to assimilate, and who rather create enclaves within our own republic ruled by sharia law, they will love and accept us as fellow Americans and live at peace with the world. The truth is that the best thing one can say about that belief system is that at least you have a choice: Bow the knee to Allah or die.

So, let's get back to my emailer's question as to how, under the New World Order led by the revived Roman Empire, the rising of the Islamic threat to Israel and the rest of the world is going to be squelched—and whether it is part of the agreement the Beast will confirm after the Rapture. The title of this commentary is "Why Islam Might Buckle." Therefore, one can correctly presume that I infer that this unyielding religious system, which harbors at its spiritually black center the murderous terrorism with which we are all too familiar, will succumb either to outside forces or to implosion. It appears that such a thing as Islam buckling to any sort of pressure short of being defeated in war is nearly an impossibility. It is on the march across the Middle East, and around the world. The very civilization it wants to behead if its victims don't bow the knee seems blind to the dangers of the scimitar-wielding juggernaut.

Will it be a Psalms 83 war that will cause Islam to buckle—to cease to be a threat? My own thoughts include the belief that Psalms 83 is an imprecatory prayer, not a prophesied war. It is a plea by the chosen people for the Lord to vanquish their immediately surrounding enemies (enemies within the Mideast region). It is a plea that I believe will be answered by God when He destroys all but one-sixth of the Gog-Magog forces who attack, according to Ezekiel, chapters 38–39.

I know all of the arguments presented by the growing numbers who believe Psalms 83 will be an actual war. If I'm wrong, I will profusely apologize for not seeing it coming. I have considered all of the thinking by those such as my good friend Bill Salus—who is an absolutely brilliant thinker and writer, in my estimation. However, I must listen to the inner voice speaking to my own spirit. I simply can't see Psalms 83 as a war, but as a prayer that will soon be answered when God decimates Russia, Iran, and "many people with thee" (Ezekiel 38:6).

That said, I do believe that the Gog-Magog war will effectively eliminate Islam as any future threat—will take it off the table of war-making.

But, there is one other thought I would like to interject that could, in my thinking, cause Islam to buckle. God will send "strong delusion," He says (2 Thessalonians 2). This will happen post-Rapture. The Holy Spirit will withdraw as Restrainer of evil. The minds of mankind—of all races and belief systems—will be open to unimaginable influences from Satan and his minions during that most horrible of times in history.

It is my belief that Islamists will be "deluded," if you want to term it as such. That is, even the minds of Satan's own religious deception will be profoundly affected by the delusion of 2 Thessalonians 2, thus will be easily persuaded to go along with Antichrist and allow the rebuilding of the Jewish Temple atop Mt. Moriah.

Certainly, anything that could change the mindset of the imams of Islam would necessitate supernatural action of the most profound sort.

God's prophetic Word says that just such profound, supernatural action is forthcoming!

One thing sure...Islam will one day buckle.

MARCH 2013

March 4, 2013
Rush Limbaugh's Low IQ

Pointing to individuals still alive, when trying to comment on pertinent matters as we do in this column, is not my usual method. We prefer to analyze issues and events of the times as they might involve prophetic import, while including individuals only obliquely when possible.

What I mean is that we often do include the names of those who are at the center of the news-oriented things we analyze/report. But, almost never do we hold a particular person up as primary example of being at the center of problematic symptoms of these end times.

I will make an exception with this article.

Rush Limbaugh, who needs no introduction, has been for quite some time now on a radio crusade to point out that Barack Obama was elected in the 2012 presidential election by what he terms the "low-information" voters. By this, he doesn't mean those voters were/are unintelligent. He says he means that those in the majority of voters were/are ill informed because they get their information from media that provides vastly inferior information, or just outright lies.

Limbaugh is talking about CBS, NBC, ABC, CNN, MSNBC, the *New York Times*, the *Los Angeles Times*, the *Washington Post,* and all of the liberal, mainstream news outlets in the U.S. Of course, he includes in that group of "low-information" purveyors outlets around the world such as Reuters, etc.

Included in the grouping of those who deliberately seek to dumb down the voting public, in Rush's almost daily expressed view, are the many venues within the American and world entertainment media. From *Saturday Night Live* to *David Letterman* and a hundred and one other such programs and shows politically antagonistic to the traditional American way of life, these foment a cultural revolution that is flushing this once great nation into the cesspool in which the rest of the world has long been swimming.

The "low-information" voter, Rush says, believes—because of the sycophantic media just mentioned—that Mr. Obama is fighting with all his might to restore lost wages and lost jobs in order to bring the economy back. These malinformed voters totally go along with Obama, who blames the Republican Party, the so-called Tea Party, and all who don't go along with Obama's plans, his ideology, as being the real problem. This, Limbaugh says—correctly, in my opinion—is exactly the opposite of what is happening.

It is the Obama administration and the ideology of ruling by presidential order and deliberately trying at every turn to grab power at the expense of liberty—while, through manufactured, fear-inducing crises that tug America toward European-style socialism and a global order—that is at the heart of what is destroying this nation. The "low-information" voter, the conservative talk show host proclaims during practically all three hours of his show daily, would rather, in effect, just veg on the lies and entertainment nonsense provided by the incessant show biz stuff. They prefer to not think about the unpleasantness of all of this—to not seriously consider the disastrous consequences that lie in the future if the power grabbers in Washington, D.C., aren't brought to account for taking the path of least resistance when it comes to facing down the president and making corrections necessary to getting America's financial house in order.

With all of that as a prelude, I must now state an even more troubling fact than those matters that Rush Limbaugh correctly dissects. Each and every day, Rush demonstrates that his own "low IQ" presents an issue even more troubling than all of the things against which he rants. His malady is the reason the nation has no chance of coming out of the swiftly descending, out-of-control, freefall that will most likely answer the question once and for all: Why isn't America mentioned anywhere in Bible prophecy?

Now, I'm not talking about Limbaugh's "intelligence quotient." He has a quite fertile mind—as he is fond of frequently (and, I believe, tongue-in-cheek) reminding his listeners. There is nothing wrong with this IQ in that regard. The area in which he does have a problem is infinitely more troubling than that wrapped up in his ability or inability to reason, to muster rationale.

Therein is the reason I believe it is necessary to hold Rush up as being at the heart of everything that is fatally flawed about America's hopes of proceeding into the future as a viable country of significance. Rush's problem infects, almost without exception, every political thinker in government, be that person liberal, conservative, or moderate.

Rush suffers from a "low-information quotient," if I may borrow from what we usually think of as IQ. Just as the "low-information" voter suffers from a dearth of accurate truth in making decisions at the voting booth, Rush—and most every political leader or thinker of influence in this nation—suffers from "low-information quotient" in the desire to govern the rest of us.

"Low-information quotient" means, in my vernacular creation, that Rush and the others haven't a clue about things necessary to correct what is wrong in this nation and world. They will never understand—nor do they want to understand—that Jesus Christ must reign, or else all things fly apart. That is, all things humanistic come unglued, because they are not held together by the Creator of all things.

The humanist thinkers' constant pulling against the traces of governance God put in the minds and spirits of the Founding Fathers have brought us to this point of no return. The refusal to integrate information about Jesus Christ into their thinking and refusing Him His rightful place within the human condition prevent the attainment of peace the diplomatic would-be saviors of the world proclaim they want so badly.

Rush has implied on his program that he, as did his own father before him, believes that the book of Revelation should not have been included in the canon of Scripture. It simply should not be there.

Here's what God says about such thinking:

> For I testify unto every man that heareth the words of the prophecy
> of this book, If any man shall add unto these things,
> God shall add unto him the plagues that are written in this book:
>
> And if any man shall take away from the words of the book
> of this prophecy, God shall take away his part out of
> the book of life, and out of the holy city,
> and from the things which are written in this book.
>
> Revelation 22:18–19

One of the primary things that can be construed as a plague from the prophecies of God's Word is that people who deliberately go in direction opposite of God will be given up to reprobate minds. No matter how brilliant, or of what political ideological persuasion, that does not bode well for the humanist thinkers of today's America and world who have low IQs.

Listen up, El Rushbo! Better untie that other half of your brain that's behind your back. Jesus is about to intervene catastrophically into the twisted affairs of mankind. We prayerfully hope your IQ and that of many others improves markedly before that stunning moment.

March 11, 2013
Time Again for a Reality Check

A number of emails have invaded my inbox of late. They involve concerns—even hysterical-level fear—that a system is about to be instituted that calls for all Americans to be implanted with computer chips. And, it will be done or at least begun by March 23. That is this month!

Now, dear reader, it is time for us to have yet another reality check in light of this and other things making the speculation circuit in these closing days of this swiftly fleeting age. First, let's consider the most recent of the chip implant frights that is currently making the rounds. There are blog conversations running the gamut from declarations that each of us in this nation will be required to go into government centers and submit to implantation of the computer chips to the proposition that government agents will be somehow anesthetizing us while we sleep and sending agents into our homes to secretly inject the chips while we are asleep/unconscious.

Some bloggers say those are crazy who believe such things, while other bloggers answer that this is the same thing people were saying about Adolf Hitler's rise to power, thus were dragged under the terror of the Nazi regime before they recognized that they were victims of der Führer.

Some who believe the federal government plans to do this within just two weeks or less proclaim that this is the mark-and-numbering system that will doom the soul of anyone who takes the chip. Others say that no politician in his right mind would propose, much less implement, such a thing and that the claim that this is a real threat is lunacy.

There are those who claim they discovered during the 2012 presidential election that all Americans will be forced to be implanted by a trackable RFID (radiofrequency identification) microchip by March 23 of this year. This, they claim, is written into the Patient Protection and Affordable Care Act, known by most now as Obamacare.

These claim that the Medchip, as it is termed, is given authorization in the healthcare reform law by the following language:

> The Secretary shall establish a national medical device registry (in this subsection referred to as the "registry") to facilitate analysis of postmarket safety and outcomes data on each device that—(A) is or has been used in or on a patient; and (B) is a class III device; or (ii) a class II device that is implantable.

Two areas of thought to consider are important in the effort to validate the claims that we will all begin being microchipped within a couple of weeks.

Authorities who refute the claim by those who propose that it is a 666 device say that upon close examination:

1) The legislative wording that supposedly indicates that all Americans will be required to accept an RFID chip doesn't in actuality say anything with regard to creating a massive RFID implantation program. The process would create a system for the evaluation of the safety and effectiveness of particularly stipulated medical devices, including those that are implantable.

2) The legislative language, they say, isn't actually in the Patient Protection and Affordable Care Act. These invite those concerned to "search the text of the law yourself. You won't find any mention of a national medical device registry."

While I agree that it is beyond reasonable to believe that we will all be forced to begin receiving the RFID microchip by March 23, I am not exactly comforted by the fact that policy has been bent toward allowing for future such implementation of such instrumentalities.

Like so many things in process today, this troubling trend of laying groundwork for a system of control through the burgeoning tracking technologies is but another indicator of this generation being prepared for the fulfillment of Bible prophecy.

Be assured: We are not yet in the time of the 666 marks-and-number system that Antichrist will utilize to, through economic mastery, control and subject the world of those left behind following Christ's call to His church. However, the technology developing at such a blistering pace is one more solid indicator of just how very near must be the exhilarating moment of that stunning Rapture event.

March 18, 2013
Peace Arrangements for Coming Desolation

A spirit of accommodation is wafting about in and around Jerusalem during these increasingly strange times. Israel seems—if Israeli President Shimon Peres is speaking from his heart—to be in agreement that a peace arrangement is all but a done deal.

> President Shimon Peres has commented on the peace process in his speech before the European Parliament plenum: "The peace process with the Palestinians already has an agreed beginning and an agreed solution. Two states for two nations. An Arab state—Palestine. A Jewish state—Israel—living in peace, security and economic cooperation." Peres added: "Peace for Israel is not just a strategic choice. It is a moral call which stems from the depth of our heritage."[76]

It is becoming more apparent by the day that a number of members of the Israeli government harbor not the spirit of King David, a man after God's own heart, but another spirit—perhaps the spirit of Antichrist, which observably infects the humanistic, diplomatic world as condemned in Psalms 2:

> The kings of the earth set themselves, and the rulers take counsel together, against the LORD, and against his anointed, saying, Let us break their bands asunder, and cast away their cords from us.
>
> Psalm 2:2-3

While Peres' words, understandably, reflect the sentiments of the dovish elements within the coalition that Israeli Prime Minister Benjamin Netanyahu is struggling to hold together, it cannot be ignored that Netanyahu's silence on the matters of a two-state proposition is deafening. We might just be very near the time when a peace covenant is cobbled that will bring to front and center the prophecy that leads to the consummation of the age. That covenant, well known by most Bible prophecy students, is given by the prophet Daniel:

> And after threescore and two weeks shall Messiah be cut off, but
> not for himself: and the people of the prince that shall
> come shall destroy the city and the sanctuary;
> and the end thereof shall be with a flood,
> and unto the end of the war desolations are determined.

> And he shall confirm the covenant with many for one week: and in the midst of the week he shall cause the sacrifice and the oblation to cease, and for the overspreading of abominations he shall make it desolate, even until the consummation, and that determined shall be poured upon the desolate.
>
> Daniel 9: 26-27

Like many observers of the times who hold to a pre-trib view of Bible prophecy propose, we understand that there must be a covenant in place when the "prince that shall come," Antichrist, steps forward as a world leader from the area of the European Union (E.U.). Although such building material for a covenant has for some time been in place as a backdrop—a proposed foundational bed of understanding that a two-state solution (a nation of Israel and a nation of Palestine) will eventually be confirmed—the implementation of such a solution has been unreachable. There are too many reasons that this has been so to go into in this commentary. But, suffice it to say that the chasm separating the two sides has been one seemingly impossible to span. There has been almost complete intransigence on the part of those negotiating from the so-called Palestinian side. And, until the statement by Peres, there seemed only a cat and mouse-type hinting that the Benjamin Netanyahu government was toying around with the idea of eventually sitting down to talk with the inheritors of Yasser Arafat's hatred for Israel.

Now, Shimon Peres declares, "Peace for Israel is not just a strategic choice. It is a moral call, which stems from the depth of our heritage." He thus blatantly equates Israel's refusal to agree to giving up God-given land for a Satan-inspired peace in a two-state solution as being immoral. This is precisely what the Israel-hating majority in the United Nations and in the diplomatic world, not to mention the entire Arab world, have been declaring for years. Israel is the occupier...

Benjamin Netanyahu seems in a severe bind. He is desperately trying to hold on to a very tenuous coalition, one that is ready to make a covenant made with death and hell (read Isaiah 28:15, 18). It will be fascinating to observe the goings on at Jerusalem, if and when President Obama goes there to work on the peace everyone is clamoring for these days.

Daniel foretold that there is coming a peace agreement that "destroy many." It will produce a flood of catastrophe that will make the region and world desolate until the very consummation of the age.

All other signals point to the fact that this generation is on the brink of something most ominous. But Jesus, Himself, said that when we see these things begin to come to pass, we are to look up—our redemption draws near! (see Luke 21:28).

March 25, 2013
Are You Vexed, Yet?

Biblical language when extracted from the King James Version (KJV) has on occasion amused me—like when it was said that David was "sore afraid" (1 Samuel 21:12), or when Saul was "sore afraid" (1 Samuel 28:20).

I once heard a comedian extrapolate on this term "sore afraid." He said that when you are "sore afraid," you're "flat scared."

David and Saul, in their situations, had every right to be thus, as have many other people in their various situations throughout the Bible as it recounted the dire situations in which those folks found themselves.

Now, I'm not meaning to be irreverent. I just find the language, not the dire circumstances of David, Saul, and the others, amusing. It was certainly no laughing matter to those who were "sore afraid."

Another rather antiquated expression from the KJV amuses me, and again, I don't mean to be irreverent. I had better view the term in question with great reverence, because I can't think of a more relevant word for Bible-believing Christians of these increasingly troubled times.

The term is wrapped up in the apostle Peter's description of Lot, who, of course, lived in Sodom at the time of that wicked city's impending judgment from God. Peter tells of how the Lord looked down into Lot's situation:

And delivered just Lot, vexed with the filthy conversation
of the wicked: (For that righteous man dwelling among them,
in seeing and hearing, vexed his righteous soul
from day to day with their unlawful deeds).

2 Peter 2:7–8

The first thing that stands out in this condemnation of the citizens of Sodom (and its twin sister city, Gomorrah) was that the conversation was "filthy."

Lot was vexed by the cesspool language that surrounded him.

There is a direct parallel today in this nation we call home, in that even professing Christians are caught up in using the same filthy language that was obviously repugnant to the Lord then—and is undeniably so today. God does not change, His Word tells us. Certainly, the conversation that spews from the mouths of many of His professing children must grieve Him greatly.

Here's what James, the apostle, has to say about this sinful language that must be a sorely vexing sound in the holy ears of our Heavenly Father:

But the tongue can no man tame;
it is an unruly evil, full of deadly poison.

Therewith bless we God, even the Father; and therewith
curse we men, which are made after the similitude of God.

Out of the same mouth proceedeth blessing and cursing.
My brethren, these things ought not so to be.

Doth a fountain send forth at the same
place sweet water and bitter?

Can the fig tree, my brethren, bear olive berries? Either a vine, figs?
So can no fountain both yield salt water and fresh.

> Who is a wise man and endued with knowledge among you? Let him shew out of a good conversation his works with meekness of wisdom.
>
> James 3:8-13

Vexing, too, is the deterioration of American culture and society. I wrote years ago for one of my books a chapter titled, "Days of Our Lives, as the World Turns." I found upon revisiting that chapter that much of what was written there is even more a part of the scene today:

> Powerful forces are at work beneath the relative tranquility that masks the true state of our nation and the world. Ours is a society that boils with turbulence beneath a veneer of sophistication. It is a society mirrored by television soap operas and hedonistic movies, which have in turn mesmerized much of the American public. Life has indeed imitated art, while year after year morals have degenerated and the very concept of morality has been turned upside-down and inside out. We are a people given a thrill-a-minute fix to satisfy our insatiable cravings for instant gratification. We are a people all the while descending deeper and deeper into depravity.
>
> Gleam and glitter and unparalleled technological gadgetry have procured for the American public hours upon hours of time for pleasure seeking, and it is more than abundantly obvious, for mischief making. While it is true that the moguls of science provide great benefits for human health, wealth, and achievement within the sphere of human potential, to see the direction in which all of this is truly sweeping us, one has only to consider any given local evening news broadcast. We are not as a society every day and in every way getting better and better, like the New Age evolutionary thinkers would have us believe. Feeding our voracious appetites for more exciting thrills and greater pleasures has served only to generate phenomenal growth in criminal activity.

Those who perceive themselves to be the "have nots" ravenously desire those material things which the American propagandists flash before their lusting eyes. Because Big Brother government has, in effect, destroyed work ethic through give-away welfare programs, but can in no way give this dependent class the shimmering lifestyle it lusts after. The rip in the fabric of society worsens daily as the ungovernable elements engage in the only occupation they believe can secure for them the thrills and pleasures they seek [the crime that grips our inner-cities, in particular].

Can there be any doubt that conditions and activities which God's Word predicts will be prevalent while the end of the age approaches are now being played out before our very eyes? The similarities between the biblical descriptions and the reports we witness on our nightly newscasts are stunningly evident. Man's atrocities against his fellow man are pandemic. Stories of debased human behavior are so numerous that items that would have formerly been front-page headlines now are relegated to pages farther back because even more heinous stories overshadow them.

Jesus Himself prophesied about the generation that would inhabit planet earth at the time of His Second Advent:

> But as the days of Noah were,
> so shall also the coming of the Son of man be.
> Matthew 24:37

Jesus Christ, who is God Himself, gave with that reference an unmistakable characterization of the generation alive at the time of His Second Advent. Like was written about the days of Lot, we can say with conviction that it is all truly vexing. Christ's call to His church must indeed be near!

APRIL 2013

April 1, 2013
"Seas Roaring" and the "Gog" Factor

I've found it always a good thing to do when striving to serve as a watchman on the wall: Always look at Jesus' prophetic words when examining these times of omega signs. The best place to start is in the Gospels that record the Lord's Olivet Discourse.

It was thus when I began thinking on what is most pertinent in the news this past week. Something in particular jumps out of the pages of the Lord's recorded foretelling:

> And there shall be signs in the sun, and in the moon, and in the stars; and upon the earth distress of nations, with perplexity; the sea and the waves roaring.
>
> Luke 21:25

Earlier, I had been "watching" a news program, listening to a correspondent shouting to be heard over the noise of an angry mob. The network then cut to several other scenes of irate crowds shouting in unison words I couldn't make out. The correspondent was saying the roaring of the crowds in the various locations shown was all about the decision by the Eurogroup to "haircut" depositors of the banks of Cypress. At the time, the Eurogroup, which was responsible for insuring deposits of the banks involved, had decided to grab money from the accounts of most everyone. Later, the Eurozone powers that be decided on a less draconian action. They determined not to take as much from the accounts of the depositors with lower euro amounts in their banks. Thus the noise—the "roaring" in the streets—has lessened, if not completely abated.

I admit up front that I don't fully understand everything involved in the economic abyss into which Cypress has plunged, and into which, it is feared, much of Europe, such as Greece, France, Italy, Spain, and others might plunge. However, I do understand, as should anyone who has ever deposited hard-earned money into their bank, that for someone in government—or anyone else—to reach in and rob one's bank account is the stuff of which riots are likely to be fueled.

Kind of makes you mad just thinking about it happening to you, doesn't it?

And that sentiment was explored throughout the financial expert community this week just past. One of my favorite economic experts weighed in with a thought along these lines:

> The decision of the government in Cyprus to simply take money out of people's bank accounts there sent shock waves around the world. People far removed from that small island nation had to wonder: "Can this happen here?"[77]

Exactly...

Is this a test to see how the masses will react to such overt robbery by those in authority? I've gotten that question many times over this week, and have asked it myself. Call it conspiracy "kookdom," but the powers did start in the smallest of venues in their—shall we call it—experiment?

They quickly decided to take a milder tact. However, the robbery will still take place. They just will reduce the size of their haul in their need for money to fix the horrible mess they've made of managing fiscal matters. Absolute power has indeed corrupted absolutely in Europe, as Lord John Edward Acton would have it. The United States mess is infinitely bigger in terms of the amount of indebtedness. The only saving grace is that America is so gargantuan in its influences and so intricate in its linkages in monetary affairs worldwide that the powers that be will keep it propped up at all costs—at least until some unforeseen circumstance or deliberate action for purposes of serving the globalist banksters' lust and greed becomes feasible to institute.

In either case, it will take a crisis of major magnitude to bring the U.S., thus all the world, down in one gigantic collapse into chaos. When that happens, there will indeed be a roaring of ear-shattering decibel. I am convinced that the roaring will be worldwide in its scope.

The economic morass that gets more quicksand-like by the day not only causes the sea of humanity to roar in distress, but draws other foretold end-times elements into the quagmire. Thus, the student of Bible prophecy attuned to Holy Spirit enlightenment can begin to understand how the last-days puzzle fits together.

I cite as example Russia's growing involvement in the fiscal turmoil now swirling about to America's east.

The Russians were particularly hard hit by the financial goings-on in Cypress, it was at first surmised, because many Russians, particularly those with considerable funds, had placed money in that country's banks for tax shelter purposes. It is rumored that the Russian underworld—the Russian Mafia-types—particularly would be given the proverbial "haircuts" by the Eurozone's actions.

Russian President Vladimir Putin at first was threatening in his repudiation of the Eurozone's actions, but for some reason changed his mind and spoke more conciliatorily about the action taken. This has puzzled many observers. His spokesman, Dmitry Peskov, said:

> Considering the decisions adopted by the Eurogroup, Putin considers it possible to support the efforts of the president of Cyprus and the European Commission aimed at overcoming the crisis in the banking system of this island state.[78]

One has to ask, knowing the former KGB head's modus operandi: What's in it for Vlad?

It is conjectured by some apparently in the know that Putin and others in Russia likely were given a heads-up on the coming seizures of depositor assets. It's hard to fathom what other intrigues might have been at work to change the mind of this hard-nosed Russian dictator-to-be.

As a student of Bible prophecy, one must consider the words of Ezekiel the prophet. He said that a group of leaders that sounds an awful lot like the current diplomatic lot of America and Europe will one day ask Gog, who almost certainly will be a future Russian leader:

> Art thou come to take a spoil?
> hast thou gathered thy company to take a prey?
> to carry away silver and gold, to take away cattle and goods,
> to take a great spoil?
>
> Ezekiel 38:13

Economic matters will be, from now until the return of Jesus Christ as King of Kings and Lord of Lords, the catalyst that will cause the seas of humanity to roar in tumult and, finally, produce a war that will threaten to extinguish all life on the planet. Jesus has promised to intervene before that destruction can fully play out.

Again, I'm convinced it will be the Rapture of the church that will burst the building bubble and bring the financial structure of this fallen world crashing down around all who are left behind. Jesus is the blessed hope (Titus 2:13). Accept His offer of salvation this very moment, and escape the carnage to come.

April 8, 2013
The Jesus Haters

"We must all be tolerant of other religions!" So goes the mantra constantly hammering us from the progressive, cultural watchdogs. Even beyond that, we must, according to the loving, liberal, politically correct give special "hands-off" status to a religion that harbors at its core hatred for all who don't accept its tenets and condones murder of whom they term infidels.

Although case after case can be made that Islam as a whole is—by its silence if not by its actions—approving of the militants among its ranks who murder and terrorize all who don't bow the knee to Allah, we in America are supposed to smile and accept that it is a religion of love, as the guardians of political correctness demand. Sharia law, which gives women less of a place within society than animals, and which approves of family honor killings for stepping one foot outside the bounds of the Muslim prescription for living, is given preference, it seems, over the U.S. Constitution and local laws in America in places such as Dearborn, Michigan. This sharia malignancy is metastasizing and little is being done to slow its spread.

All religious thought must be respected and tolerated, the political correctness police demand—all, except the tenets of one particular religion. True Christianity is fair game, and the politically correct crowd of Christianity-haters doesn't just look the other way when true Christianity is attacked; it joins in the fun. These people attack at every opportunity and are never condemned for their hate diatribes; rather, they are joined by the priesthood of the entertainment world at the center of their ranks.

Eyebrows are no doubt raised at the use of my term "true Christianity." I make no apologies for the use of the term. There are a number of counterfeit forms of Christianity, and more are coming into existence each day as strange winds of doctrine blow across our nation and the world. There is but one true Christianity. It is found throughout the pages of God's Word. If I could choose only one Scripture to encapsulate true Christianity, it would be these words spoken by Jesus to His disciple:

> Jesus saith unto him, I am the way, the truth,
> and the life: no man cometh unto the Father, but by me.
>
> John 14:6

And therein lays the anti-Christian diatribe. That is why all other religions are acceptable—are tolerated—except true Christianity.

But, wait! Islam claims Allah, Mohammed's creation, is the only way, and will even slaughter those who don't believe or accept that religion's god. Yet the diatribe never goes against Islam; rather, it always goes against true Christianity's claim the Jesus is the only way to heaven and salvation. The hatred for Christianity runs the gamut of artistic blasphemy, such as, we remember, the crucifix submerged in urine, and, later, the actress, who upon winning an award held it up and shouted for Jesus to "**** this!" The increasing hostility becomes more blatant by the hour, with cultural crucifixion of Christ on the rise, as this excerpt of a recently reported story attests:

> Last month, it was reported at various online outlets that Ryan Rotela, a junior at FAU, was suspended for refusing to participate in a class assignment from a textbook for an Intercultural Communications class titled *Intercultural Communication: A Contextual Approach*, 5th Edition. The assignment called for students to write the name "Jesus" on a piece of paper, put the paper on the ground, and stomp on it. Rotela told local media that he went to school officials to protest the assignment.[79]

The school announced that the teacher who gave the assignment has been put on leave, but not for the blasphemous assignment. He was put on leave out of fear for his safety. The school administration obviously has true Christianity mixed up with mainstream Islam, which puts bounty on the heads of those who blaspheme the prophet Mohammed. Jesus told that culture and society would react this way to His name:

> If the world hate you, ye know that it hated me before it hated you.
>
> If ye were of the world, the world would love his own: but because ye are not of the world, but I have chosen you out of the world, therefore the world hateth you.
>
> Remember the word that I said unto you,
> The servant is not greater than his lord.
> If they have persecuted me, they will also persecute you;
> if they have kept my saying, they will keep yours also.
>
> But all these things will they do unto you for my name's sake,
> because they know not him that sent me.

If I had not come and spoken unto them, they had not had sin: but now they have no cloke for their sin.

He that hateth me hateth my Father also.

If I had not done among them the works which none other man did, they had not had sin: but now have they both seen and hated both me and my Father.

But this cometh to pass, that the word might be fulfilled that is written in their law, They hated me without a cause.

John 15:18-25

Yet, God loves even the Jesus-haters of this world, and is not willing that any should perish, but that all should come to repentance (2 Peter 3:9). We who are Christ's are commanded to love sinners, as does our Lord. Let us in these closing days of the dispensation of grace lift the name of Jesus at every opportunity so that men, women, and children will be given gospel light by which to come to saving knowledge of the only begotten Son of God (John 3:16).

April 15, 2013
Satan's Mindset Prevailing

Last week I presented the essay entitled "The Jesus Haters." Jesus' own words foretold that such hatred for Him and for His followers would grow intensively down through the generations as time progresses toward the climax of human history and Christ's return at Armageddon.

Paul, as prophet, gave the characteristics of end-times man in his perilous times enumeration as recorded in 2 Timothy 3:1–5. Paul, as Christ's faithful apostle, gave parallel analysis of that prophetic end-times generation as recorded in Romans, listing what will be the results of evil men and seducers growing worse and worse while writing God out of their cultures and societies:

And even as they did not like to retain God in their knowledge,
God gave them over to a reprobate mind,
to do those things which are not convenient;

Being filled with all unrighteousness, fornication,
wickedness, covetousness, maliciousness;
full of envy, murder, debate, deceit, malignity; whisperers,

Backbiters, haters of God, despiteful, proud, boasters,
inventors of evil things, disobedient to parents,

Without understanding, covenant breakers,
without natural affection, implacable, unmerciful:

Who, knowing the judgment of God, that they which commit
such things are worthy of death, not only do the same,
but have pleasure in them that do them.

Romans 1:28-32

How many times have you heard—or said yourself: "This world has gone crazy," or something similar? Paul was predicting that the people of the world would indeed go crazy as the end of the dispensation of grace nears. People would be allowed to have the reprobate—satanic—mindset they desired. They would, in the final rush to throw off the shackles of God's restraining influence (Psalms 2:2–3), exchange in their thinking processes good for evil and evil for good (Isaiah 5:20).

The satanic mindset is upon us, with evil these days being called good and good being called evil. There is but one good, and His Name is Jesus. He is the only person who has been born in human flesh who has not sinned. That is why God, His Heavenly Father, offered Jesus—His only begotten (sired by Him personally) Son—as the Lamb that takes away the sins of the world.

It is the perfection of Jesus Christ that God accepts as the only payment for the sins of mankind. The righteousness of Christ provides the only way to heaven. As I mentioned in last week's article, this is why Jesus is hated. It is the satanic mindset that infects the fallen minds of the world and enlists them to come against the only good there is in the world.

Now, lest the enemies of Christ take that previous statement and proclaim that I'm saying Christians are without sin, thus better than those who aren't Christians—as human beings—I will endeavor to explain. Christians are fallen creatures just like all of humanity. But they have been redeemed by Jesus Christ, the sinless Lamb of God that takes away the sins of the world.

Because believers in Christ are born again into the family of God (John 3:3), the Heavenly Father sees them as pure and righteous—through the prism of His Son Jesus, who died on Calvary for them. They have chosen the only way to God the Father and heaven for eternity (John 14:6).

This "only way" to Heaven—to God—enrages the satanic mindset. Such satanic rage was made obvious in a news item this past week.

> The U.S. military has been told in a training briefing that evangelical Christians are the number-one extremist threat to America—ahead of groups like the Muslim Brotherhood, the KKK, the Nation of Islam, al-Qaida, Hamas, and others.... The briefing, which was given to an Army reserve unit in Pennsylvania, came from a U.S. Army Reserve Equal Opportunity training brief titled "Extremism an Extremist Organization." A slide titled "Religious Extremism" lists multiple organizations such as the Muslim Brotherhood, al-Qaida, Hamas, the Nation of Islam, the Ku Klux Klan and the Christian Identity movement as examples of extremist groups.... However, the first group on the list is evangelical Christianity.[80]

Again, Jesus forewarned about the satanic mindset and how it would act to impact His followers—Christians of the last days:

> But all these things will they do unto you for my name's sake, because they know not him that sent me.

> If I had not come and spoken unto them, they had not had sin:
> but now they have no cloak for their sin.
>
> He that hateth me hateth my Father also.
>
> If I had not done among them the works which none
> other man did, they had not had sin: but now have they
> both seen and hated both me and my Father.
>
> John 15:21-24

The only thing the Lord Jesus has done to "offend" the world—the satanic mindset—is to love the world of sinners so much that He died for each and every one of us. He is the only being who has ever lived who can offer the world the peace that has been so desperately sought throughout the millennia.

Despite the satanic mindset that opposes at every turn, we who are Christians are to serve with all our might as royal ambassadors to present God's peace offering to mankind.

April 22, 2013
Tears in Heaven

Losing those we love is the deepest emotional hurt we can suffer, I believe most will agree. Those whose spouse, boyfriend, girlfriend, or best friend betrays the relationship and rejects us leaves us devastated. Even more terrible is the loss through death of someone dear to us.

When those we love die, the break is final. We will never look upon their likes again in this earthly life. The ache eats at our very core; their every remembrance gnaws at our soul, even if the memories are among the best of our ability to recall.

It's not manly to love felines is the general rubric of understanding between the males of our species. It's okay to love canines if you are a guy, but it's not okay to love a cat.

I lost Stanley the other day when he was hit in the street in front of our home. Stanley came to us probably a year and a half ago. Somehow, this yellow and white, half-grown cat knew that I'm blind. He instinctively knew...he would hurry to get in front of me, from no matter where he had been, and would position himself in front of my left leg, making me bump against him all the way down the hallway.

He always led me into the bedroom—every time.

There was a food bowl in the bedroom, and he would always reward himself with a face full of cat chow at the end of his mission. It was a self-administered, Pavlovian response, no doubt.

This was still going on the last day of his life. We were amused and amazed. He did this for/to no other of the family, just me. I loved Stanley. I'm still hurting, and thinking about the many nuances of our relationship. I have his name on the tip of my tongue and just say "Stanley," to try to assuage the hurting, I guess. I don't know why the Lord so obviously put Stanley with me, then so abruptly took him. I do know that God knows why, and all will be made perfectly clear some eternal day. I'm comforted by that assurance.

Now, I'm writing to perhaps thousands in Rapture Ready's vast audience who have lost those very close to them. The loss of an animal seems ridiculously superfluous to those whose mother, father, or perhaps child is near death or has just passed away. "There is no comparison" will be the response—and I will agree—to my experience with this little yellow feline.

I'm coming to the point of this essay, so bear with me. Jesus knows our every hurt. He experienced them all during His short time on this planet. He wept over the death of Lazarus, feeling the depth of the kind of hurting you and I experience when a loved one dies. Our loved ones who die, whether human beings we love or the pets many love dearly, all have names. We have them on the tips of our tongues and only the passing of time pushes their cherished memories to somewhere in the middle of our very spirit. The Heavenly Father, however, thinks without ceasing about every creature He creates—even the sparrows, we are told.

Those of us who constitute fallen mankind, on the other hand, are more often than not substantially unmoved by the loss of those who aren't directly, or at least indirectly, linked to us, individually. We have no attachments to those who don't directly relate to our lives; we make no place for their names in our cerebral or emotional centers of concern. Of course, I realize that this is the nature of the human condition.

This fact of life—that we can't find or make time to concern ourselves beyond our own orbit—we justify by pointing to our torrid pace in America today. But, no excuse justifies the incomprehensible blind eye turned from the horror of the abortion industry which the news, finally, brought to our attention this past week.

America's greatest sin should burst with convicting fire into the concern center of every person made aware of the story. There are reasons, however, that the horrific information needed to prick the consciences of every American will not be forthcoming. The reasons are summed up in two words: mainstream media.

This unbelievably reprehensible lack of accountability for what has been going on can be laid at the feet of the nation's news organizations. The reason they've gotten away with such journalistic malfeasance can be laid at the feet of the American public. Fifty-plus million abortions that have anesthetized U.S. citizens to the reality and horror of this holocaust have been willfully accepted with only moderate resistance since the Supreme Court decision in *Roe vs. Wade* on January 22, 1973.

The nameless children who have been murdered in their mothers' wombs by the multiplied millions are screaming in deafening silence. Now it is learned just how heinous have been the murders of the aborted little ones outside their mothers' wombs as well as inside. Still, mainstream media remain silent for the most part about this infanticide that has taken place under their supposedly superior reportorial investigative noses.

The grisly abortion activities of Dr. Kermit Gosnell in his Philadelphia, Pennsylvania, abortion horror chamber—which, incidentally, has been known since 2011—have finally reached the trial stage, thus is forcing some degree of reporting by reluctant news media organizations. Gosnell is charged with the murder of one woman and seven born infants, in which he allegedly "snipped" with scissors the babies' spinal cords once they were outside their mothers' wombs.

The liberal champions of the woman's right to choose are hard pressed to look upon the things being uncovered in that horrendous murder factory. All the agenda-driven pundits on the left can come up with is that Gosnell's unsanitary, nonprofessional clinic shows all the more reason for increased federal funds and regulations to assure clean, "safe" abortions.

The above is almost precisely what I heard Alan Colmes, the liberal pundit for Fox News, say in response to Gosnell's trial. Here's what one angry journalist against legalized murder of babies had to say in regard to Gosnell and the reporting of the atrocities involved.

> Thus far, Gosnell's wretched clinic, with its filthy speculums, jars filled with severed baby feet, and photos of female genitalia, has had a hard time piquing the interest of major news outlets. After all, racy, sexy murderess Jodi Arias is much more intriguing than some twisted biracial abortionist carrying out Margaret Sanger's eugenic ministry on vulnerable people of color. Isn't she?[81]

So, the big-time news men and women are being dragged kicking and screaming into covering this vile representation of the industry of infanticide they so fervently champion.

The little ones who have died since *Roe vs. Wade* have no names. They have been treated as inconsequential refuse to be flushed or sent to the garbage dumps of America. But, just as I have the name of my little Stanley forever etched in my memory, and each of you who has lost loved ones have their names stamped indelibly upon your hearts, the God of heaven has a name for each of the little ones who are now safely with Him carved in His omniscient memory.

While the Word of God tells us that tears will one eternal day be wiped from every eye in heaven, the Heavenly Father must at the present time shed tears of sadness for what continues to be the most severe child abuse possible: abortion. More than that, He must have hot tears of anger as He watches this nation He blessed so mightily shed innocent blood by more than 3,700 babies per day—something those who sacrificed their children to Molech in ancient times came nowhere near matching. Jesus made it inescapably clear what would be the fate of those who dealt so egregiously with little ones:

> But whoso shall offend one of these little ones which believe in me, it were better for him that a millstone were hanged about his neck, and that he were drowned in the depth of the sea.
>
> Matthew 18:6

April 29, 2013
The Peace and Security Rant

Israel, in the opinion of most of us who write, teach, broadcast, and pontificate on the last days from the pretrib perspective, is the number-one signal that gives indication of where this generation stands on God's prophetic timeline. It is among the very tiniest of countries, yet no nation in history has ever drawn the attention of the whole world as does that little Jewish state.

Lest you think that is an overreach, I remind that at no time in history has the world had the global, instantaneous news coverage, as has been the case since Israel's rebirth into modernity in 1948. That fact, alone, has made Israel the focus of interest. Add to the 24/7 coverage of the never-sleeping-media conglomerate today, the petroleum that drives the machinery of the world, and the prospects for all-out war in the region at any moment, and Israel as a focal point becomes all the more riveting.

In my presentations on Bible prophecy, I can't help but always say something like: "No matter which way the microphones and cameras of the world's news media turn to catch other issues and events, they always end up focused again on Israel—and upon Jerusalem, in particular. As a matter of fact, there are cameras that have the Temple Mount live via satellite at all times, for everyone on the planet to view.

This, in itself, brings to mind the two witnesses scheduled to prophesy and preach to those left behind after the Rapture. These Jewish thorns in the side of Antichrist will make his life and the lives of his regime miserable as they point the prophetic finger of accusation and warnings at those rebellious earth-dwellers. We are told that everyone on earth will see these two witnesses killed and lying dead in the street in Jerusalem.

> And when they shall have finished their testimony, the beast that ascendeth out of the bottomless pit shall make war against them, and shall overcome them, and kill them.
>
> And their dead bodies shall lie in the street of the great city, which spiritually is called Sodom and Egypt, where also our Lord was crucified.
>
> And they of the people and kindreds and tongues and nations shall see their dead bodies three days and an half, and shall not suffer their dead bodies to be put in graves.
>
> And they that dwell upon the earth shall rejoice over them, and make merry, and shall send gifts one to another; because these two prophets tormented them that dwelt on the earth.
>
> And after three days and an half the Spirit of life from God entered into them, and they stood upon their feet; and great fear fell upon them which saw them.
>
> And they heard a great voice from heaven saying unto them, Come up hither. And they ascended up to heaven in a cloud; and their enemies beheld them.
>
> Revelation 11:7–12

Perhaps it will be the very cameras now focused on the Temple Mount around the clock that will capture this for the initially jubilant, but instantly terrified, anti-God rebels of the Tribulation. Just as Israel is the number-one signal of where this generation stands on God's prophetic timeline, the second most glaring signal is the ongoing Mideast peace process: "The Roadmap to Peace," as it is termed.

We have witnessed over the past decades the many secretaries of state for the United States shuttle back and forth to that most volatile region of the world in search of peace. From Henry Kissinger to Hillary Clinton and John Kerry, who has now taken the baton as peace emissary for earth's most powerful nation, the quest never ceases. One incessant cry rings in the ears of everyone who has the ability to receive newscasts by the world's media. It is the call for *peace and security*.

Here are a few examples in just the last two presidential administrations:

George W. Bush, Address to the Nation, September 11, 2001: "America and our friends and allies join with all those who want peace and security in the world, and we stand together to win the war against terrorism."[82]

George W. Bush, Rose Garden Speech on April 4, 2002: "Israel has recognized the goal of a Palestinian state. The outlines of a just settlement are clear: two states, Israel and Palestine, living side by side, in peace and security."[83]

President Vladimir Putin, Joint Statement with President George W. Bush, May 24, 2002, taking this as their basis: "Russia and the USA intend to exert maximum efforts in order to realize this vision of a negotiated settlement of the conflict, which includes the existence of two states—Israel and Palestine—living in peace and security within recognized borders."

Meeting between Prime Minister Tony Blair and Prime Minister Benjamin Netanyahu. January 28, 2013: "It is up to us to work for peace and security, and no one is more fitting to work on this than you," he said (Netanyahu). Blair replied, "I look forward to working with you on matters of peace and security. We have many challenges, but I'm sure they can be overcome with good will and hard work."

Condoleezza Rice, American Jewish Committee's Ninety-sixth Annual Meeting, 2002: "On April 4, President Bush articulated a vision of two states, Israel and Palestine, living side by side in peace and security."[84]

Hillary Clinton, November 30, 2012 address in Washington: "America supports the goal of a Palestinian state, living side by side in peace and security with Israel."[85]

President Barack Obama, Jerusalem International Convention Center, Jerusalem. March 21, 2013: "I'd like to focus on how we—and when I say "we," in particular young people—can work together to make progress in three areas that will define our times—security, peace and prosperity.... First, peace is necessary. I believe that. I believe that peace is the only path to true security."[86]

The apostle Paul, as prophet, wrote the following:

> For when they shall say, peace and safety;
> then sudden destruction cometh upon them,
> as travail upon a woman with child; and they shall not escape.
>
> 1 Thessalonians 5:3

The Greek word for "safety" here is *asphaleia.* It is a feminine noun meaning "security from enemies and dangers; safety."

In the preceding verse, Paul had just foretold of the moment when the Tribulation would begin breaking on a world ripe for God's judgment:

> For yourselves know perfectly that the day of
> the Lord so cometh as a thief in the night.
>
> 1 Thessalonians 5:2

The rant we hear most prolifically today, with regard to the nation Israel, the city of Jerusalem, and the ongoing peace process in the Middle East is, "Peace and security." I could have added hundreds more such quotes.

Listen during the upcoming days for this cry from the diplomats of the world who will not have the God of heaven rule over them (read Psalms 2 again). It is a rant that pinpoints precisely just how near is the *thief-in-the-night* moment that Paul forewarned about: the Rapture.

MAY 2013

May 6, 2013
Tribulation Temple Talk

Just beneath the boiling surface of seething hostility there can be sensed a moving and shaking. Talk of the building of a Jewish temple atop the Temple Mount is beginning to escape into the back-channel atmospherics of the Mideast misery. How can such *not* be the case? Every direction the student of Bible prophecy looks, stage setting for the final act of this quickly decaying age is already on the scene.

God's land is being further divided (Joel 3:2), which portends God's bringing all nations into the Valley of Jehoshaphat—to Armageddon. The "Roadmap to Peace" is being dusted off and reintroduced as the blueprint for peace and safety for not only Israel and its blood-vowed enemies, but for the whole world, as insulation against the initiation of World War III.

The European Union is in turmoil. It is turmoil, however, that seems to have a smelting effect, preparing the iron of the legs, feet, and toes of Daniel's interpretation for Nebuchadnezzar—into their end of the age configuration. Technological wizardry of every description has made possible the bringing together of all peoples of planet earth into one world: the New World Order so desired by the globalist powers that be.

The economic upheaval experienced by most every nation cries out for a master manipulator that will institute an electronic funds transfer system in order to bring stability and order to the financial distress and perplexity that bedevils presidents, potentates, and dictators. Such a man can't be too far into the shadows of emerging world togetherness.

On the forefront of religious change is the call for a melding of every form of pathways to heaven. The pope and Islamist imams seem to be forging a synthesis of sorts in discovering many ways to God, a thing unheard of until very recently. Protestant America in large part seems not to oppose the feelers crawling toward their forms of Christianity. So-called Chrislam is appealing to them, and ecumenism beckons with allurement at many levels.

So, with all of this and much more going on, the talk of the building of a Jewish temple should surprise none of us. It is a key ingredient in the coming Tribulation mixture within God's cup of wrath. The talk of late on the possibility of a Jewish temple in the making revolves around the words of a Turkish TV producer, who is a Muslim. Sinem Tezyapar, as reported in the *Jewish Press* on March 14, said:

> There is a broad expanse of land around the Al-Aqsa Mosque and the Dome of the Rock. The land there is quite convenient in that respect, and the temple can be placed just a little way from Qubbat As-Sakhrah, and a little ahead of Masjid el-Aqsa.[87]

This train of thought, of course, conforms to the long-held opinions of some within the universe of those who observe matters involving plans to build a temple on Mt. Moriah. Bible prophecy foretells, through the vision given John, God's hand on the Tribulation temple:

> And there was given me a reed like unto a rod: and the angel stood, saying, Rise, and measure the temple of God, and the altar, and them that worship therein.
>
> But the court which is without the temple leave out, and measure it not; for it is given unto the Gentiles: and the holy city shall they tread under foot forty and two months.
>
> Revelation 11:1-2

The prophecy indicates, according to those with this view, that:

1. During the Tribulation era, there will definitely be a temple sitting where Solomon's Temple sat.

2. There is more than enough room surrounding where the temple must reside for the Muslim shrines to sit.

There is a ton of chatter going on about all of this within the Bible prophecy community. Many voices within this blogosphere hold that those Muslims who seem to be letting it slip (that Israel's Arab-Islamist enemies might be willing to talk about accommodation of a Jewish temple) must never be trusted. It is all being done for some surreptitious evil known only to the imams and to the master architect of their evil blueprint—Satan.

The very fact that there is talk coming from Israel's enemies about the heretofore unthinkable possibility of allowing a temple on Mt. Moriah is significant, I think. A phony—and deadly—peace is at the center of Satan's blueprint for usurping the throne of God on earth.

We can know this from Daniel's account of the covenant Antichrist will confirm, assuring peace for seven years (Daniel 9:26–27). Also, Isaiah the prophet says so (Isaiah 28:15, 18).

Satan intends to place his "messiah" right on the spot where the Holy of Holies sat, where the Ark of the Covenant resided within the temple of Solomon's day. So, I believe it is reasonable to look for the possibility of a rebuilt temple to become increasingly front and center in news and blog chatter as the age draws to a close.

May 13, 2013
Assessing the Syrian Situation

The Isaiah 17 prophecy looms heavily in cyberspace. Many continue to express concern that the present situation, in which Israel has as much as admitted attacking Syrian targets, will lead to Damascus' destruction as outlined by the prophet Isaiah.

To repeat that prophecy for the reader who might not be aware, it foretells:

> The burden of Damascus. Behold, Damascus is taken away from being a city, and it shall be a ruinous heap.
>
> Isaiah 17:1

Israel's involvement in the Syrian conflict makes the student of Bible prophecy come to attention—as it should. Actually, however, this is an indirect, not direct, involvement—at least according to the Israelis, themselves. Israeli authorities proposed that the raids were aimed at preventing Hezbollah and Iranian allies from acquiring weapons to use in striking Israeli territory. The air assaults were not connected to Syria's civil war. A report from CNN gives the salient points of the attack:

> A series of massive explosions illuminated the dark sky over Damascus early Sunday, igniting renewed claims that Israel has launched attacks into the war-torn country. Syria's government said the explosions were the second Israeli air strike in three days. The latest target, officials said, was a military research facility outside the Syrian capital. A top Syrian official told CNN in an exclusive interview that the attack was a "declaration of war" by Israel.[88]

It is amazing that such a stunning attack by the most-hated nation on earth drew so little vitriol from either the Islamist leaders or from Syria's chief big power protectors, Russia and China.

Russia did initially condemn the attacks that destroyed missiles, etc., destined for Hezbollah in Lebanon. The Russian mouthpieces called the actions a threat to regional stability. But, the hubbub seems to have quickly died down. Vladimir Putin's main concern seems to be that Bashar al-Assad's removal from power would erode Russian influence over Syria, and, once it was plain that Israel simply wanted to destroy missiles that would otherwise one day soon rain down on Tel Aviv, he backed off a bit in his rant against the Israeli action.

More perplexing is China's reaction. The Sino-Syrian linkage has been growing as Chinese leadership seeks greater influence in the region. The Chinese, always inscrutable, as we know, said only that restraint should be the order of the day. My own assessment is that the Chinese have possibly made even more productive linkages—for themselves—into the Islamist rebel leadership conclaves that drive the war against the Assad regime.

Sources for Israeli security let it be known to the above power players that the attacks on targets in southern Syria on Sunday were aimed at preventing the transfer of advanced Iranian-made missiles to the Shia Islamist movement, Hezbollah, in neighboring Lebanon—nothing more. They, it is reasonable to suspect, told Putin and the others that they intended no interference whatsoever with the civil war taking place.

The most logical analysis seems to reveal that:

1. Al-Assad's relative noncombative stance upon the Israeli attacks indicate that both Russia and China have told him that they won't back him to the hilt in an all-out attack by Syria on Israel.

2. Al-Assad's neighboring fellow Muslim powers have said—or demonstrated by their relative silence—the same. They are likely putting their shekels on Assad's ultimately being removed, and want to be on good terms with the Islamist brothers who are the victors.

The other element is the American administration's part in all of this: President Barack Obama has done or said little to try to influence Israeli Prime Minister Benjamin Netanyahu in trying to dissuade him from attacking and re-attacking the missile supplies headed for Hezbollah. Secretary of State John Kerry's hurried-up mission to talk to Putin indicates to me that there are back-room dealings afoot that we will perhaps learn of at some point in the Middle East future.

At any rate, none of the parties involved wants unleashed sarin and other chemical or biological agents that will upset power balances and/or wrest from them control of the Mideast situation. Tightening down on Assad's trying to widen the war with the exporting of missiles, etc., could seems to the powers that be a way to bring relative safety to the situation, while each re-evaluates and repositions for what is to come following the fall of the Syrian leader.

As for the Bashar al-Assad regime, the most it seems to be doing in retaliation is to say that Israel is effectively helping al-Qaeda Islamist "terrorists." The spokesman for the government threatens that the Israeli strikes "open the door to all possibilities." This most violent of the Islamist dictators seems out of character in his acquiescence.

What all of this means, I think, is that the Damascus destruction is likely on hold until new and more volatile dynamics develop as the world and the Middle-East march toward man's final act in this end-of-the age drama.

Any such action as total annihilation of the planet's oldest occupied city would make it a time unlike Jesus said would be prevalent when He next catastrophically intervenes into human history (again, read the business-as-usual description by the Lord in Luke 17:26–30 and Matthew 24:36–42).

I believe the Isaiah 17:1 destruction of Damascus is most likely a post-Rapture prophecy.

May 20, 2013
Demonic Divide

Dark, spiritual forces in high places are at work. There is no groundbreaking revelation in that statement regarding life in this nation and the world today. However, the true nature of the demonic delusion being foisted upon us is something even the most biblically mature among us will continue to miss if spiritual antennae aren't properly attuned.

Additionally, it is time like no other time before to put on the *whole armor* as outlined by the apostle Paul in Ephesians 6:12–18. I perceive a most troubling schism developing amongst the brethren. I refer to those who watch—like the Lord commanded (Mark 13: 37)—end-times developments in what many believe are the closing hours of the Church Age.

Reports come at us on an increasingly regular basis of behind-the-scenes activities that appear to be, to say the least, bizarre. I'm talking about things the equivalent of claims/reports of the U.S. government actually planning and carrying out the assassination of John F. Kennedy, and of George W. Bush's administration being behind the attack on the World Trade Center towers on September 11, 2011.

I'm certain that the reader of this essay has read the many articles of such mind-boggling reports—all written/presented as if they are unassailable truth. These accounts spring from unseen, fly-on-the-wall sources that give the impression they personally witness the making of plans to imprison believers or to implant us all with computer chips while we sleep, or...whatever the conspiratorial imagination can conjure.

I will already have angered those who send such email with that word portrait, no doubt. But before my thoughts on your side of the issue raise the blood pressure with words of anger, "I'll never send him another article," please hear me out. There is the other side of the developing schism. It, too, is deleterious to the task of being a watchman on the wall in these critical days leading up to our Lord's catastrophic intervention into the affairs of mankind.

I'm talking about the mindset that writes off as complete lunacy every report issued by the likes of Alex Jones crossing their computer screens. To fold up the antennae of discernment and simply lump all things that don't slip smoothly through one's anticonspiratorial filter, just might constitute a deadly delusion in the making.

The rift I sense developing between the watchmen during these fleeting days of the age is inflicted by the father of lies, himself. It is all part of the great, spiritual wrestling match Paul warns about in Ephesians 6:12. The devil likes to pit one side against the other, and it is easy for him to do, if the spiritual armor isn't the battle gear of choice.

One side of the divide most often sees only collusion of governmental diabolists at every level, thus is, understandably, accused by the secular world and fellow Christian watchmen alike of being conspiracy kooks. The watchmen on the other side of the divide too often, because of fear of guilt by association, run away from any talk of collusion of the human conspiratorial kind, sometimes failing to recognize the ways Satan directs his human minions to plot his end-times mischief.

Paul, mentioned at the beginning of this piece, must have, with his words of Ephesians 6:12–18, been given his inspired thought particularly to give to this generation so near the return of Jesus Christ. Each Christian should daily put on the *whole armor of God.* This obviously hasn't happened, and likely won't happen.

The vast numbers within the body of Christ are turned inward or in directions other than watching and yearning for the Lord's coming back to put an end to this evil world system. If we are honest, we must say that the body of Christ, as a whole today, isn't even pursuing the Great Commission left to us by Jesus to carry the gospel to the whole world and to do what He taught and instructed.

We must not seek out only the strange, secretive, evildoings in the dark underworld of governmental collusion so as to make the findings shocking or exciting. Neither should we think that such collusion doesn't exist at all and point to all reports as lunacy. Let's not wrestle violently and angrily against each other, but combine, with reasoned purpose, against our true foe. Here is how to dress for the battle that will surely grow more intensive by the hour as the Rapture of the church approaches.

> Finally, my brethren, be strong in the Lord,
> and in the power of his might.
>
> Put on the whole armour of God, that ye may be able
> to stand against the wiles of the devil.
>
> For we wrestle not against flesh and blood, but against
> principalities, against powers, against the rulers of the darkness of
> this world, against spiritual wickedness in high places.
>
> Wherefore take unto you the whole armour of God, that ye may be
> able to withstand in the evil day, and having done all, to stand.
>
> Stand therefore, having your loins girt about with truth,
> and having on the breastplate of righteousness;
>
> and your feet shod with the preparation of the gospel of peace;
>
> above all, taking the shield of faith, wherewith ye shall be able to
> quench all the fiery darts of the wicked.
>
> And take the helmet of salvation, and the sword
> of the Spirit, which is the word of God:

> Praying always with all prayer and supplication
> in the Spirit, and watching thereunto with all
> perseverance and supplication for all saints.
>
> Ephesians 6:10–18

May 27, 2013
In Antichrist's Shadow

I must admit up front that I have delved into now ancient archives of my own ponderings in writing this week's column. The things under consideration, however, are more relevant than ever. As a matter of fact, it becomes quite fascinating to look back at earlier times of analyses of issues and events. New perspectives and prospect-postulation can sometimes be derived from such retrospective.

A number of years ago, I put together (as general editor) a book with a number of prophecy scholars, broadcasters, and writers. That book was called *Foreshocks of Antichrist*. The compilation of chapters dealt with issues and events of the times, issues and events the other authors and I believed significant in considering prophecies that surrounded the coming of Antichrist to power, as foretold in chapters of the books of Daniel, Revelation, 1 John, and others.

That was about 1996, I think, and I believed at the time that conditions could not ripen much more so far as the world being ready to reap the bitter harvest concerning what the Antichrist will bring.

I was wrong, of course, which proves we must never be too quick to think that things can't get much worse. They can, and have gotten worse since my late colleagues such as Dr. John Walvoord, Dave Breese, Zola Levitt, and many others dissected the issues of our time with the omniscient scalpel of God's Word, in that Harvest House book more than a decade ago.

The shadow of the coming Antichrist looms more ominously than ever.

All one has to do is to consider the following report to see that dictatorship might be right around the proverbial corner. An Austrian newspaper reported the following result of a question posed to the citizenry of that nation: What about their opinion of Adolf Hitler and the Nazi annexation during World War II?

> Forty-two percent said life was not all bad under Hitler, while sixty-one percent said they would be interested in a strong-armed leader who did not have to deal with democratic challenges like political opponents and elections. The survey, published this weekend, is getting prominent play in the media in Israel, which is home to some 250,000 Holocaust survivors.[89]

Antichrist and the False Prophet of Revelation 13 will be the ultimate, final dictatorship. Their regime will be the drivers of the geopolitical and religious juggernaut that will crush anyone and anything that opposes it during the Tribulation era. The engine that will power Satan's cruel, soul-rending beast of Revelation 13:1–2 will be an all-controlling, enslaving economy. We see the beast described as follows:

And I stood upon the sand of the sea, and saw a beast
rise up out of the sea, having seven heads and ten horns,
and upon his horns ten crowns,
and upon his heads the name of blasphemy.

And the beast which I saw was like unto a leopard,
and his feet were as the feet of a bear, and his mouth
as the mouth of a lion: and the dragon gave
him his power, and his seat, and great authority.

Revelation 13:1–2

The control that beast will wield is described in this way:

> And he causeth all, both small and great, rich and poor, free and bond, to receive a mark in their right hand, or in their foreheads:

And that no man might buy or sell, save he that had the mark,
or the name of the beast, or the number of his name.
Revelation 13:16-17

The technologies for setting up just such a system of control over the people of planet earth have grown exponentially during the past several decades. Computer-satellite hookups between continents, linking most all of the world in a geometrically progressing network of electronic funds transfer capability, brings this generation ever closer to the type control prophesied in those familiar passages of Scripture.

The United States of America, the most materially blessed nation to ever sit atop earth's surface, has been concentric to the global networking. Most of the great contributions to the computer and satellite revolution have been spawned from this country. But other super-industrious peoples around the globe continue the "progress." Other nations are now taking the relevant technologies to new levels of "achievement." Now, it is America who seems to be dragging her feet in bringing in economic Utopia—or so it would seem...

As we looked as these matters of international finance a decade ago, it appeared that the U.S. was the holdup to bringing in a new world financial order. The refusal to relinquish paper and coinage as currency was viewed as a blocking agent to establishment of that changed monetary order.

With the unbelievable swiftness of movement involving all things fiscal since those earlier times, it becomes obvious that the powers that drive monetary movement determined to keep hard currencies in place with the U.S. dollar as the standard (until other dynamics of financial interlinkages brought sufficient chaos) to create critical need for a system other than paper and coinage to avert world economic disaster.

The United States' great wealth and power, represented in the mighty dollar, was thus held high as criterion for international trade until just the right political changes within America had been engineered. That political *change* has, with the Obama administration, now begun—and in a big way. The dollar's fate is sealed, as are paper currencies and coinage.

Is America, then, a stumbling block to—or a catalyst for—the emerging system that will almost certainly serve as the framework for the prophesied Antichrist's Revelation 13 hegemony over the earth?

Rationale prompts one to believe that something must happen to cause the U.S. citizenship to come around to acceptance of a total e-money solution to the confusing state of currency exchanges, etc. But, the process is agonizingly slow, and would likely have to take place with powerful opposition from the American congress and its constituencies and lobbyists.

Many observers of Bible prophecy, including yours truly, can't imagine a scenario that would allow, in America, a lengthy transition to the coming global order essential to the future Antichrist regime's system of control. This, because most all other prophesied signals for the Tribulation appear to now be in place, as far as stage setting for the Tribulation is concerned.

Again, the factor that fits perfectly into a scenario in which America instantly is brought to such a state of chaos that she acquiesces to the world's call for a cashless system of digital economics, is—you guessed it—the Rapture!

June 3, 2013
In High Places

International spy thrillers have always been among my weaknesses. I've spent far too much time over the years enmeshed cerebrally within one such story or another. Robert Ludlum was perhaps my favorite author within the genre, with such enthralling tales of espionage at the highest levels as *The Bourne Identity* and *The Matarese Circle*. I was also hooked at one point on fiction involving Blackford Oakes CIA intrigues authored by William F. Buckley, Jr.

It's difficult to find such books in electronic form (Word document) that my synthesized-voice computer program can read for me. I'm now blind due to a retinal disease, and the JAWS (Jobs Accessible Word System) program reads to me most all correspondence and other written materials over the Internet.

It's just as well that I can't easily access such books, because these, though entertaining, would be time-wasters for me, especially considering the compression of time I believe we are presently operating within as we move quickly toward the consummation of human history. There are far more important things to accomplish than being entertained by fictional stories of clandestine doings within top echelons of governments.

On second thought, we read in our headlines almost hourly of just such intrigues taking place in reality, that if not entertaining certainly are quite thrilling, in the frightening sense, at many levels. So, as a fellow watchman with many of you who are reading this column, I, like some of you, am really not missing anything but the love of fiction factor. And, things of factual import are developing at a pace and in fashion precisely the way the greatest of all authors, the Lord Himself, has foretold for all to read.

One such spy thriller comes to mind that helped bring out in me the interest in Bible prophecy that would in later years transform my thinking in a profound way. That 1960 novel's title is *In High Places*. Its author, Arthur Hailey, a British/Canadian writer who was among the first to produce such novels that later writers like Robert Ludlum and Tom Clancy would take to great book marketing heights.

In High Places is a story of a fictional Canadian prime minister and his political machinations while trying to maintain power during the time of the Cold War that was fraught with nuclear threat and Canada's troubled dealings with immigration. The author attempted and did a good job at showing the evil, wicked, and even perverse interactions of politicians at the very top of power politics and in governments at the highest levels.

Even as a very young man reading the novel, I noticed Hailey's use of biblical reference in selecting his title. The phrase "in high places." of course. is found in the apostle Paul's passages on spiritual warfare:

> For we wrestle not against flesh and blood,
> but against principalities, against powers,
> against the rulers of the darkness of this world,
> against spiritual wickedness in high places.
>
> Ephesians 6:12

I realized even as a young man of eighteen, upon reading the book and thinking on its title, that the Bible's use of the phrase was infinitely different in scope from Arthur Hailey's. Yet what I didn't understand at the time was that the malevolent forces in the fictional realm of Hailey's geopolitical thriller reflected and represented evil, other worldly forces at work in real life.

I'm not so sure that the author of the novel *In High Places* fully realized it, either. One thing for sure: No one in government in the highest of places today where true wickedness is happening, nor the journalists of our world who are supposed to be the watchdogs on behalf of the citizenry, indicates in the slightest way that they understand the true source from whence the wickedness this way comes.

If they do understand it, they must be in collusion with it, because they aren't letting us know. But, that's really a kook-conspiracy notion, is it not? (Human beings in power at the top levels in cahoots with the likes of Satan and his minions!)

Yet, I believe this is precisely what the apostle Paul was saying under inspiration as he penned the words to the Ephesian Christians, and to us who would follow.

The ultimate battle is being waged in the very highest places. The devil and his minions are using every device at their disposal that is allowed by the God of heaven, who is always in complete control. Those include human beings, who do the demonic entities' bidding, whether realizing it or not in many cases—probably most cases, in these end-of-the-age days.

Look for the demonic influences in high places to become ever more evident while evil men and seducers grow worse and worse, deceiving and being deceived (2 Timothy 3:13).

June 10, 2013
Rapture Reaffirmation

The TV teacher was finished with his first hour of "teaching" from the Bible. I know this not because I watched the first half hour of the one-hour daily, Monday-through-Friday program, but because I know the schedule. The program has aired for many years, and I have on occasion flipped through the channels and stopped just to hear what this man happens to be saying.

Some degree of what he "teaches" is in accordance with Bible truth, as best I can tell. However, much is almost anti-Semitic in its presentation in that he is of the view that Israel has been replaced in God's economy by the church. His view of Bible prophecy could hardly be more wrong. His almost total disregard for modern Israel having any place in God's prophetic plans brings his whole ministry into question, in my opinion.

The TV "teacher" says this generation is presently in the era of the sixth seal as given in the book of Revelation. He says that the prophetic trump of Revelation 11:15 is the same spoken of by Paul the apostle in 1 Corinthians 15:51–52. Here are the two passages:

> And the seventh angel sounded;
> and there were great voices in heaven, saying,
> The kingdoms of this world are become the kingdoms of our Lord
> and of his Christ; and he shall reign for ever and ever.
> Revelation 11:15

> Behold, I show you a mystery; we shall not all sleep,
> but we shall all be changed, in a moment,
> in the twinkling of an eye, at the last trump:

> for the trumpet shall sound, and the dead shall be raised incorruptible, and we shall be changed.
>
> 1 Corinthians 15:51-52

In other words, he teaches that believers will be changed into spiritual bodies at the end of the Tribulation period. When I heard this familiar television pontificator make this equally familiar proclamation this past Tuesday morning, rather than click to the next station as I would normally do, an inner tug at my spirit caused me to "stay tuned," as they say.

What happened next was quite revelatory to me. I determined that it was worthy of passing along. In fact, *it was such a strong impression* that I consider it yet another of the epiphanies I've received from the Good Friday April 22, 2011, widow-maker heart attack when my heart stopped beating on three separate occasions during a forty-five minute rush to the hospital and in the heart cath lab.[90]

Briefly, each time I heard an electronic-sounding blip, I stood instantaneously before a huge throng of magnificent young people—men and women who looked in the prime of life. They were beckoning me to come and join them.

Their hands were raised above their heads in a gesture of corporate victory, and the jubilation and warmth I viscerally felt at my very core made me never want to leave them. But I did leave them, only to return two more times to the same throng each time my heart stopped again. The third time I was in their midst, we were running, hands raised-high in the air, and it felt like a great victory lap.

Then I was hit with the defibrillation paddles for the third time, and I was again in the cath lab, the blockage to the major artery having been removed. Tuesday morning as I watched the TV preacher as he again proclaimed that the Rapture was a fraud—as he does every chance he gets—I saw in my mind's eye that group of cheering, jubilant young people, heavenly beings with their hands in the air in an unmistakable gesture of victory.

My irritation with the anti-Israel, anti-Rapture TV "teacher" instantly dissipated. Warmth not unlike the sensation that gave me peace beyond any I've felt before, or since that Good Friday made me know, gave reassurance that the pretrib Rapture is truth from God's Word.

Okay, I know that some will accuse my "epiphany" as being just an ecstatic rant from an emotional moment, thus not a valid proof of anything. I understand those who might accuse in that manner. If they truly knew me, they would know that I am among the least likely of individuals to embrace "experiential" Christianity in the ecstatic sense. But few personally know me, so I will add some other considerations to this account of my again being influenced by that *cloud of witnesses* (Hebrews 12:1–2).

Today, there are a considerable number of Bible prophecy anti-Rapturists like the gentleman I've just mentioned. Most include within their teaching, in addition to vitriol condemning all who teach and believe in a pretrib Rapture, that:

1) Israel, in the modern sense, has no relevance to Bible prophecy yet future. The church has now been given all of Israel's promises.

2) Many of these sorts teach that Britain and America are where the "lost tribes of Israel" settled. Thus Britain and America are now the Jews of God's promises.

3) They spiritualize and allegorize much of prophetic Scripture whenever it is most convenient, to fit within their false prophecy teaching/preaching schemes.

4) Many, like the TV preacher I mention above, include that we are already in the Tribulation era, usually proclaiming this generation is likely somewhere within the first six-seal judgment.

Israel alone is enough to show the foolishness of this teaching. The Jewish people are again a nation after nearly two thousand years of dispersion throughout the whole world, precisely as Bible prophecy foretells. They are at the center of hatred among all the nations of the world.

The U.N. body is almost totally against everything about Israel. Israel is seen as the occupier and aggressor, despite the absolutely undeniable fact that the tiny Jewish state has been attacked en masse by its neighbors in 1948, 1956, 1967 (Israel preempted Arab forces) and 1973. There have been many other, less major, attacks against this state.

Most spectacular of all as proof that the anti-Israel teachers are wrong is the fact that Israel has never been defeated in a major way. God has promised that Israel will be His nation forever. He still has His mighty hand on His chosen people!

For sake of brevity, I'll skip to the final category I mention that the anti-Rapturists most often claim. They believe we are in the Tribulation already, usually claiming that this generation is somewhere within the six seal judgments. Some proclaim that Barack Obama is to be the Antichrist, and even have given dates for when he will desecrate a future temple. Some, in fact, have claimed dates Antichrist would take power, dates that have already passed.

In total context, the pretrib Rapture view of unfolding Bible prophecy is proving daily to be the true biblical course of fulfillment. Every geopolitical, socioeconomic, religious, and technological indicator fortifies the sense that there is coming a catastrophic event that will bring all crashing down upon this world so ripe for judgment. I welcome, nonetheless, the reassurance that my throng of young, heavenly, friends continue to give in validating God's promises to call His people home before His wrath must fall.

June 17, 2013
Enslavement Evolving

Today's liberals, like progressives since the time of Woodrow Wilson, have most often viewed the U.S. Constitution contrary to the way it was held by America's Founding Fathers. "Truths" in the document that has made the nation the most envied ever to exist are not so "self-evident" to those who would take it apart and reconstruct it to fit their every ideological wind of doctrine.

The Constitution is, to them, not a solid pillar of security to which to tether the ship of state on the exceedingly dangerous waters of the times. It is a living, breathing organism—or, at least in their thinking, should be—that changes (or should) with the shifting morality and social mores of any given period in the country's history.

Shaped by entertainment media of our time and pushed along by the propagandist mainstream news media of the past half century, the assaults on our founding documents have been made in ways not unlike the assault these same entities have inflicted on our culture through the pseudo science they champion. I refer to, of course, their religion, *evolution.*

Their audience, the American people, is not without fault in the societal dissipation. We are all at fault for allowing the persistent undoing of the Judeo-Christian model within which Thomas Jefferson, Benjamin Franklin, James Madison, George Washington, and the rest framed this republic. Like Rev. Jeremiah Wright correctly stated (even though in a totally skewed context), "America's chickens have come home to roost."

We are now on the fast track to enslavement foretold in fiction by British writer George Orwell in his famous novel *1984*. Over the years, this column and many others have presented biblical prophetic truth about the eventual coming of Big Brother, the fictional dictator of Orwell's story.

We now see the evolution of that character as he comes to life on our front pages. As a matter of fact, "evolution" is the very term the most recent chief architect of the Orwell-Big Brother construct uses to shmooze us with his political rhetoric. He explained to us his changing coming of age in his thinking upon the issue of homosexual marriage, as but one example:

> As a presidential candidate, Mr. Obama's position hardened. In 2008, he visited the Saddleback Church in Orange County, Calif., where the pastor Rick Warren asked him to define marriage. "I believe that marriage is between a man and a woman," Mr. Obama said. "For me, as a Christian, it is also a sacred union."[91]

The president's "evolving" has brought him since that 2011 declaration, of course, to full support for "gay marriage"—which in God's economy must be considered an oxymoron, at the very least. It should now be increasingly obvious to even the most casual observer that this president and many of both major political parties have "evolved" in their understanding of the Constitution of the United States of America. There is simply so little pushback on the overt intrusions into the citizens' rights and privacy as to be the equivalent of a complete lack of resistance.

The exposure of the IRS' vile intimidation of the Tea Party and others who opposed the president's re-election would have, had it been a conservative core of IRS operatives working against a Democrat candidate, brought any Republican president down. The media propagandists would have been nonstop in the diatribes, as they were in the case of Richard Nixon and the Watergate break-in. Nixon's cover-up and involvement never came close to this grab for power and influence over America's political process.

Likewise, the Benghazi matter, with the subsequent lying and cover-up, far exceeded any political evil in Nixon's day. Nobody died in the Watergate scandal. At least four Americans serving our nation honorably died as a result of ineptitude, deliberate refusal to intervene, or both, in the Libyan massacre.

The Big Brother-like data collection apparatus and process used against U.S. citizens, recently exposed by National Security Agency (NSA) consultant Edward Snowden should have every U.S. senator and congressman up in arms. But, with few exceptions, our government is in lockstep with the obfuscation of the facts.

We are told by the administration and by the slavish national mainstream news media that all three branches—executive, legislative, and judicial—were well briefed on the fact that NSA gathered such data. Trouble is, none of *us* knew about it. It was done all in the name of the war on terrorism, we are told.

And, yes, George W. Bush and his administration's culpability in all of the liberty destruction involved with the Patriot Act deserve a proper part of the shame. Der Führer could have provided the manual for the march toward the installation of Antichrist that we see happening in America and the world at the present hour.

> The best way to take control over a people and control them utterly is to take a little of their freedom at a time, to erode rights by a thousand tiny and almost imperceptible reductions. In this way,

> the people will not see those rights and freedoms being removed until past the point at which these changes can be reversed.[92]

I'm in agreement with Hal Lindsey, that point of nonrecoverability has been reached and America's demise is likely irreversible. But, we who name the name of Christ have "hope" that is not a gamble, but a sure thing:

> Looking for that blessed hope, and the glorious appearing of the great God and our Savior Jesus Christ.
>
> Titus 2:13

June 24, 2013
Armageddon's Vortex

Recorded history's most powerfully destructive tornado tore through the Oklahoma City area May 31, 2013. The EF3, EF4, and sometimes EF5 twister was as large as two and a half miles wide during some points of its being on the ground for forty solid minutes. A number of people died in the vicious, multiple vortexes that raged within and around the central tornado, including three experienced storm chaser/researchers from Colorado.

The monster literally vacuumed even patches of earth and concrete roadways as it raged across the Oklahoma landscape toward the same places that were hit a week or two earlier by another massive tornado. Thirty square miles looked, one Oklahoma State governmental official said, like a gigantic lawn mower had cut its swath through the hundreds of homes that were completely sucked from their foundations.

While this commentary isn't about how the severity of storms and other natural disasters are causing records to fall in these closing days of mankind's rush toward the consummation of the age, these phenomena occurring are certainly an integral part of the matters I wish to present. Every signal on the scene today, whether considering geopolitics, socio-economics, religion, or natural upheaval, is caught up in an unstoppable, titanic, end-times storm. At the center of the vortex is the eye around which all other things swirl: the nation Israel.

The incessant call for peace—manifest in the "Roadmap to Peace" process—has been for a time obscured by the dark cloud of global distress and perplexities, but now is back on the radar of the world's diplomats, it seems. Israel, of course, is viewed by those diplomats as the hold-up to peace in the Middle East. It is the region of planet earth prophesied by the Word of God to be at the center of the great humanity-endangering storm at the very end of the age. Observers of these, goings on, especially those who watch for the unfolding of Bible prophecy, should take notice with an increased level of fascination. The Middle East is the region of the world that God says will produce the most destruction in human history.

That brewing storm is undeniably upon this generation, as the Bible prophecy student knows, and the tornadic winds that it is beginning to produce are vacuuming all of humanity into its massively expanding vortex. All is being drawn toward the valley of Megiddo and the land God promised will be Israel's forever. The last-days storm had fuel added to it its dynamic by a player on the world's diplomatic scene with whom we are familiar.

> "The only choice for Israel to remain a Jewish and democratic nation is to work toward a two-state solution," former U.S. President Bill Clinton said. Clinton was in Israel to attend celebrations marking the 90th birthday of Israeli President Shimon Peres.
>
> "You have to cobble together some kind of theory of a two-state solution, and the longer you let this go, just because of sheer demographics, the tougher it's going to get. I don't see any alternative to a Palestinian state," the former U.S. President said in a speech before the Peres Academic Center in Rehovot Monday night.[93]

Mr. Clinton, we remember, was at the helm of the U.S. ship of state during the Oslo Accords, in which Yasser Arafat was offered most anything he wanted if he would agree to simply acknowledge Israel's right to exist and vow to get along. Arafat refused, leaving it all on the table—

demonstrating to the sane thinkers of the world that the rage at the center of the Mideast storm has nothing to do with rationality or desire to live peaceably with God's chosen nation.

The storm is a supernatural one, and God, the only infallible forecaster, has told us what its course will be as we proceed deeper into history:

> For, behold, in those days, and in that time,
> when I shall bring again the captivity of Judah and Jerusalem,
> I will also gather all nations, and will bring them down into the
> valley of Jehoshaphat, and will plead with them there for
> my people and for my heritage Israel, whom they have
> scattered among the nations, and parted my land.
>
> Joel 3:1–2

JULY 2013

July 1, 2013
The Next Voice You Hear

The Next Voice You Hear is a black and white film released in June of 1950. It starred James Whitmore and Nancy Davis (who would become Mrs. Ronald Reagan some years later). It was sometime in the 1970s, probably, when I watched it as a late-night movie on television.

The movie portrayed Whitmore's and Nancy Davis' characters as a typical American couple residing in suburbia near Los Angeles, I believe. The husband worked in a factory—building aircraft, I think. He stormed out of his home early one workday headed for the factory. He was ticked off because he was late, thus in a rush. He was quite irritable as he backed in a rage from his driveway.

A motorcycle policeman pulled him over and gave him a ticket. Whitmore's character was even angrier, now. He stuffed the ticket between his teeth, put the car in gear, and took off as fast as the old sedan would move when the cop was finished with him. The policeman chased him down, as I remember, and gave him another ticket. The entirety of the stage setting of the film involved how angry people were with each other and how they treated each other in their hectic rush to do their own thing. Everyone was mad at each other, it seemed.

Suddenly, all radio broadcasts were interrupted. A voice spoke to the whole world at that moment through radios wherever they could be heard. Whitmore's character heard it and called his wife to hear the voice. Although we, the moviegoers, didn't hear the voice, we could see on the puzzled, shocked countenance of our hero that he had just heard something profound. He informed us that the voice said, "The next voice you hear will be God, and He will be with you for the next few days."

Over those days, the voice (we learn from the Whitmore character and his wife) was that of the Lord giving warning that people must change their ways and begin treating each other better. Judgment was coming, if this didn't happen. Rain began falling as it hadn't since the flood of Noah's time, but then it stopped. It was a warning.

How simple was that storyline! Compared to the world and its sins today, the Whitmore character and his family were living in Utopia!

When the film was released, America was a society and culture coming out of being on a war footing. The emphasis was on building families from a moral perspective based upon Judeo-Christian principles as conceived and perceived by the nation's Founding Fathers and the U.S. Constitution.

The Next Voice You Hear was produced from a book of the same name, a volume whose theme was that America should move forward as a good, moral people. French philosopher Alexis de Tocqueville put it this way:

> I sought for the greatness and genius of America in her commodious harbors and her ample rivers—and it was not there...in her fertile fields and boundless forests and it was not there...in her rich mines and her vast world commerce—and it was not

> there...in her democratic Congress and her matchless Constitution—and it was not there. Not until I went into the churches of America and heard her pulpits flame with righteousness did I understand the secret of her genius and power. America is great because she is good, and if America ever ceases to be good, she will cease to be great.

The rabid, voracious, anti-God, anti-America as founded detractor-revisionists are working every day to convince us that de Tocqueville never said or wrote this. When searching with Google, I found that this is the viewpoint that search engine seems to harbor. That everything "good" about America must be debunked seems to be at the heart of the revisionist efforts.

But, de Tocqueville did write it, and it is true: Anything "good" about America is because of what the Lord of heaven has done and continues to do. Good is found only in Jesus Christ, the Bible tells us. There should be little argument, in Christian circles at least, that in 1950, when *The Next Voice You Hear* was released, America was more morally in alignment then with its Constitution—which is based upon biblical principles—than it is now. As a matter of fact, there is little comparison, then to now. The morality deconstructionists (I'm being facetiously polite in calling them such, here) have done their work. America is no longer "good" under de Tocqueville's definition of the term.

Alexis de Tocqueville's extrapolation was correct. Each and every day, the headlines presenting all of the subterfuge, scandals, profligate mismanagement, and spending of this nation's wealth—every debauched, debased activity chronicled by entertainment and news media—prove that we are no longer a great nation. That a major Hollywood studio would in these times present such a morality tale under a biblical world view is unthinkable.

A prospective film's depiction of the God of heaven giving warning through reminder of a biblical flood that once "corrected things" would likely never enter the minds of Hollywood producers these days. Or, if the thought of God giving such warnings ever did percolate in the minds of the entertainment industry geniuses, it would never include thoughts of the true Creator of all that is.

Especially troubling in all of this is that most within the church today likely wouldn't think to consider that such a message as God warning this generation was even relevant to them, should such a movie be made. The church has been so desensitized to what is going on around them, and so caught up in living snuggly within their own comfort zones as to prefer to not think about the dangers of being caught up in the pleasures of worldly pursuit.

The messages these get from the pulpits are sugar coated. They learn how to go through life ignoring the Holy Spirit-engendered conviction of living like the world during these final days of the age. They are all too comfortable in their blissful ignorance of Christ's call for repentance. Bible prophecy never enters their thinking; they never hear about it for the most part, and that, it seems, is fine with them. Strive to be among those of Christ's bride who are longing for His coming for them. The next voice you hear just might be the one that shouts: "Come up hither!" (Revelation 4:1)

July 8, 2013
"Perilous Times" Headlines

No prophetic indicator more precisely relevant to our time can be determined than what we have seen develop within recent weeks and days.

Specifically, I would like us to examine in this brief commentary things in our headlines of late that I believe parallel Paul's "perilous times" forewarning found in the following portion of 2 Timothy 3:

> This know also, that in the last days perilous times shall come.
> For men shall be...traitors, heady, highminded...
>
> 2 Timothy 3:1a, 2a; 4a

First, we should get these words down in terms of the definitions given in the Greek language, in which the New Testament was written. I invite you to check out the Greek in the *Strong's Greek Lexicon* or another source to get the exact Greek word. I deal here only with the definition of each of these words that I believe so fit our day in regard to being end times:

Traitors: A betrayer—in the sense of giving forward into another's (the enemy's) hands.

Heady: 1) To fall forward, headlong, sloping, precipitously; 2) precipitate, rash, reckless (example: Acts 19:36; Paul advises to never act rashly).

Highminded: 1) To make proud, puff up with pride, render insolent, to be puffed up with haughtiness or pride; 2) To blind with pride or conceit, to render foolish or stupid.

These characteristics have in recent days been on display in glaring, unmistakable fashion for anyone who is willing to honestly acknowledge America's slide into reprobate thinking, as Paul forewarned:

> And even as they did not like to retain God in their knowledge,
> God gave them over to a reprobate mind,
> to do those things which are not convenient.
> Romans 1:28

One particular young man is at the center of this end-of-the-age display of God's prophetic truth, manifesting before our eyes on an hourly basis. Edward Snowden, as of this writing, is stuck in a Moscow airport, awaiting word on possibly being given sanctuary in Ecuador. Of course, we all know his story by now. He divulged massive amounts of National Security Agency (NSA) information regarding the snooping agency's intelligence gathering.

Most troubling, apparently, to the powers that be in Washington is the revealing of the methodologies the NSA uses to collect the data and use it—even against American citizens. The thirty-year-old contractor, who reportedly doesn't have a college degree, was in a position to collect information on the capabilities of, arguably, America's most secretive clandestine service.

Everyone in power, from the Obama administration to senators and representatives and mainstream media pundit-types, is calling him a traitor and demanding that he be immediately extradited to the U.S. Snowden claims he divulged the information and will divulge a lot more because the NSA and other clandestine services are spying on individual American citizens and collecting dossiers in a way that violates the Constitution—for example, the Fourth Amendment.

Snowden went to China and to Russia (America's traditionally most powerful, antagonistic opponents) with the information, so "traitor" is a term that is appropriate, it can be argued—thus, although the betrayal might be viewed as well as being carried out against a corrupt, intrusive government, not as against the American people.

Regardless of his motive, he has opened up himself to appear to have selfishly performed a traitorous act by placing himself in a position to be debriefed on these sensitive documents by America's most dangerous foes, in terms of geopolitical intrigue.

Now, I would like to look at an even more worrisome matter in all of this—the betrayal or traitorous activities by those in the high places of government who are so heady and highminded, to use Paul's Holy Spirit-inspired words. Those in the NSA, the Internal Revenue Service, and other such agencies who have wantonly and recklessly disregarded the Constitution the Founding Fathers gave this nation have violated the very spirit of what has made this unprecedented experiment in human liberty unique in all the ages of human history. That they do their dastardly, enslaving activity under the guise of "national security" makes the crime worse.

They continue to betray the trust a people must have in its leaders in order to carry on with civil and productive society and culture. Make no mistake: There are those principalities and powers in the high places, both human and supernatural, who want you to be the servants of the ruling class, rather than those whom are served, as the Founding Fathers wrote into that most noble document. Here is what Benjamin Franklin had to say about a national, salaried bureaucracy:

> Sir, there are two passions which have a powerful influence in the affairs of men...ambition and avarice-the love of power and the

> love of money.... What kind are the men that will strive for this profitable preeminence, through all the bustle of cabal, the heat of contention, the infinite mutual abuse of parties, tearing to pieces the best of characters? It will not be the wise and moderate, the lovers of peace and good order, the men fittest for the trust. It will be the bold and the violent, the men of strong passions and indefatigable activity in their selfish pursuits. These will thrust themselves into your government and be your rulers.[94]

Franklin said further:

> There will always be a party for giving more to the rulers, that the rulers may be able, in return, to give more to them.... The more the people are discontented with the oppression of taxes, the greater need the prince has of money to distribute among his partisans, and pay the troops that are to suppress all resistance, and enable him to plunder at pleasure. There is scarce a king in a hundred who would not, if he could, follow the example of Pharaoh—get first all the people's money, then all their lands, and then make them and their children servants for ever.... I am apprehensive, therefore—perhaps too apprehensive—that the government of the States may, in future times end in a monarchy...and a king wills the sooner be set over us.[95]

The traitorous, heady, and highminded are among us. These times in which we live look to be the perilous times that Paul said will be prevalent at the moment Christ calls His church to be with Him forever.

July 15, 2013
Egypt in Prophetic Perspective

Events in the Middle East are moving rapidly, stirring many prophecy students to speculation—as always happens when things flare in the region. The current focus for rumination is on Egypt and the chaos that doesn't yet rival that of what has been happening in Syria, but which is obviously building toward a similar level of trouble.

The speculation I've been receiving centers mostly around the question of whether the Egyptian military vs. the Muslim Brotherhood is the beginning of prophecy yet future laid out in Isaiah 19. Superimposed over both the Syrian and the Egyptian turmoil, along with all other physical and polemical dynamics surrounding Israel today, is the question: Is this all leading to the fulfillment of the Psalm 83 matter involving Israel's surrounding, Arabic, Islamic enemies?

Egypt is the most recent recipient of the destructiveness of the Arab Spring's "democracy movement."

Despite warnings by many geopolitical thinkers who genuinely employ cognitive reason, not to mention those who have spiritual discernment at the helm of their thinking, the Obama administration threw the diplomatic blessings of the U.S. behind the deposing of Hosni Mubarak and the subsequent installation of that great champion of democracy, Mohammed Morsi. Doing so was a fool's errand.

No sooner was the election done and Morsi installed than the Islamist enslavement began. Only, the people of Egypt, more than seventeen million strong in their response, would have none of it. As of this writing, it has yet to be determined where it will all lead.

The questions we are considering here are:

- Does the current Egyptian maelstrom indicate that fulfillment of Isaiah, chapter 19 has begun?
- Does this mean that Psalm 83 is on the verge of fulfillment?

Space for this column doesn't permit the full examination of what these portions from the great prophet, Isaiah, and the psalm entail. In brief, however, Isaiah 19, according to some prophecy students, is thought to indicate that Egypt might, with the current crisis, become—like the prophecy details—under great internal strife, and will be judged by God for its idolatry and for its treatment of Israel. God will send great trouble; most specifically, the Nile will dry up and there will be great destruction of Egypt's economy and environment, including devastation of much of its land.

The following is a part of the prophecy about Egypt's fate in question. I suggest you read chapter 19 from the beginning.

> The Lord hath mingled a perverse spirit in the midst thereof:
> and they have caused Egypt to err in every work thereof,
> as a drunken man staggereth in his vomit.
>
> Neither shall there be any work for Egypt,
> which the head or tail, branch or rush, may do.
>
> In that day shall Egypt be like unto women: and it shall be
> afraid and fear because of the shaking of the hand of the
> Lord of hosts, which he shaketh over it.
>
> And the land of Judah shall be a terror unto Egypt,
> every one that maketh mention thereof shall be afraid in himself,
> because of the counsel of the Lord of hosts,
> which he hath determined against it.
>
> Isaiah 19:14–17

The Psalm 83 Scripture, a seemingly growing number of prophecy students believe, foretells a soon-coming war between Israel and its immediately surrounding Arab Islamist neighbors (the inner ring, as it is termed). Israel's military, the Israeli Defense Force (IDF), is, many who hold this view believe, part of the revived army mentioned in the following prophecy by Ezekiel:

> So I prophesied as he commanded me,
> and the breath came into them, and they lived,
> and stood up upon their feet, an exceeding great army.
>
> Ezekiel 37:10

This army, those who believe the Psalm 83 passage to be a coming war assert, will completely defeat the inner ring of Israel's enemy nations and will win back for Israel portions of the land God promised them. Those who hold to this relatively new view of this part of the psalm, in fairness, believe it will be the Lord, using the IDF to bring about this result. They see this as a prophecy that could take place at any time, as things stand now in the Middle East.

The conflagration continues to rage in Syria, with the Damascus matter in view (the Isaiah 17:1 prophecy). That real and present danger to world peace, combined with all that has taken place as the Arab Spring inflamed the whole region, now has been doused with the accelerant of Egyptian pyrotechnics, fed and fanned, it seems, by an American presidential administration that hasn't a clue of what all of it portends.

While I continue to believe that the Psalms 83 passages refer to an imprecatory prayer of God's chosen people to vanquish all of their traditional enemies, I do believe that prayer will be answered with exactly that vanquishing. This will happen, I believe, during the Gog-Magog assault of Ezekiel chapters 38 and 39.

The Damascus destruction, likewise, will occur when the Middle East ignites and the world implodes economically and most every other way.

I am firmly convinced that immediately upon Christ calling the church to Himself in the Rapture, Egypt will undergo the prophesied judgments of Isaiah 19, while Israel, following the confirming of the covenant of Daniel 9:26–27, is undergoing Jacob's trouble as given in Jeremiah 30:7 and outlined within other prophetic areas of God's omniscient foretelling.

Primary in my thinking on all of this is the fact that Jesus tells us plainly that His next catastrophic intervention into the affairs of mankind will be at a time when things are still going on relatively as usual. Wars and rumors of wars have always been "business as usual" with mankind since the Fall in Eden.

Jesus tells us that the day Noah went into the ark and the door was shut, and when Lot went out of Sodom—the very day each was removed by the hand of God, judgment fell. Jesus said that it would be exactly like that when He next catastrophically intervenes. It will be business pretty much as usual right up until that stunning moment. This cannot be referring to the end of Armageddon, when perhaps three-fourths of mankind will have perished during the most horrendous time of human history. This has to be the Rapture of the church! (Read Luke 17:26-30 and Matthew 24: 36–42.)

Keep in mind that when the Middle East explodes in such a massive way as Bible prophecy indicates, "business as usual" will go out the window. Jesus' description of how the conduct of human activity will be at the time He next catastrophically intervenes would be off the proverbial table of end-times arrangement, if these devastating things were happening prior to the Rapture.

My own perspective is that all of this is stage setting for the sudden destruction that God has prophetically scheduled. Here is a key to when these things will likely come to fulfillment:

> But of the times and the seasons, brethren,
> ye have no need that I write unto you.
>
> For yourselves know perfectly that the day of the
> Lord so cometh as a thief in the night.
>
> For when they shall say, Peace and safety;
> then sudden destruction cometh upon them,
> as travail upon a woman with child; and they shall not escape.
>
> 1 Thessalonians 5:1–3

July 22, 2013
Sunset of Empires

Some will remember the boast, "The sun never sets on the British Empire." It was true for a considerable period of time. Between the sixteenth and eighteenth centuries, the British Empire was the most expansive in history, basically touching, in terms of modern time calculation, all time zones with its overseas possessions and trading posts. Thus, the sun was just arising on one part of the empire while it was in process of setting on another.

Even the Roman Empire, which many of us who study Bible prophecy believe is referenced in the book of Daniel and other scriptural places, came nowhere near matching the British Empire in scope and influence. Some Bible prophecy scholars and students believe that Britain and its influence is, in fact, mentioned in prophecy yet future, although obliquely. These references, it is conjectured, are found in Daniel:

> Daniel spake and said, I saw in my vision by night, and, behold,
> the four winds of the heaven strove upon the great sea.
>
> And four great beasts came up from the sea,
> diverse one from another.
>
> The first was like a lion, and had eagle's wings:
> I beheld till the wings thereof were plucked,
> and it was lifted up from the earth,
> and made stand upon the feet as a man,
> and a man's heart was given to it.
>
> Daniel 7:2-4

The lion in this prophecy might be Britain, those prophecy watchers believe. Certainly, England has been symbolized by the lion in legend, lore, and the annals of war.

Another place in Scripture that many—including me—believe Britain is likely mentioned is in Ezekiel's prophecy about the Gog-Magog attack on Israel:

> Sheba, and Dedan, and the merchants of Tarshish,
> with all the young lions thereof, shall say unto thee,
> Art thou come to take a spoil?
> hast thou gathered thy company to take a prey?

> to carry away silver and gold, to take away
> cattle and goods, to take a great spoil?
> Ezekiel 38:13

Here, those who hold that Britain is referenced believe the term "merchants of Tarshish, with all the young lions thereof" is significant proof of their position. The area of Tarshish ("land of tin") is thought to be where the isle of today's England sat in ancient days. They believe "the young lions" of this Scripture likely refers to the United States and other of Great Britain's offspring.

Upon hearing the news pundits going a bit gaga over the approaching birth of a royal British baby, my thoughts ran with cogitations of contrast to another news item in today's headlines. All of the talking heads have been conflabbing about the upcoming birth of the baby who will become fourth in line to succeed the present queen, I believe. There seemed some confusion among the pundits about exactly what number in line the child will be.

I searched ABCnews.com to find out just who were the royal parents and other details. No problem: The first link said: "Royal baby due date has world on pins and needles."

The headline was far elevated above the other matter—the matter starkly in contrast:

> Gay marriage is set to become law after clearing the House of Lords. The Queen is expected to be asked to give her approval to the Bill—one of the most radical pieces of social legislation of her reign—by the end of this week.
>
> It opens the way for the first legally recognized same-sex weddings to take place in England and Wales by next summer and brings the centuries-old understanding of marriage as being solely between a man and a woman to an end. Peers gave their assent to the third reading of the Government's same-sex marriage bill without a formal vote after a short debate in the Lords,

> also backing plans for a review of pension arrangements for gay couples....
>
> Baroness Stowell, the Government spokesman who steered the bill through the Lords, told a chamber packed with peers wearing pink carnations, that it was an "historic" achievement.[96]

My first thought was to whisper to myself the (I guess mean-spirited) statement, "Well, there will be no royal babies produced from those unions."

On second and third thoughts, however, with all of the gene splicing and other corrupting of genetics being carried on today, who knows?

The Creator—the Lord Jesus Christ—laid down the rule and provided the physiological means to produce offspring: one man and one woman, in marriage, for life. The sun has definitely set on that law, so far as the humanist God-rejecters are concerned.

It is appropriate to consider, in thinking on the upper house of Parliament's decision, that the sun set long ago on the British Empire. It is in process of setting on the greatest of all empires in history to date—the American empire of influence. America is following directly in the footsteps of Mother England, it is apparent. The final throes of decline and fall of world empires are easily determined by study of the greatest of them.

Greece, Rome, Britain—each saw a marked influence of homosexuality as their demise approached.

Enough said.

The words of the Lord Jesus apply to empires as well as to individuals, and none of Christ's words are more apropos in regard to all of the above than the following:

> And every one that heareth these sayings of mine,
> and doeth them not, shall be likened unto a foolish man,
> which built his house upon the sand: And the rain descended,
> and the floods came, and the winds blew, and beat upon that
> house; and it fell: and great was the fall of it.
>
> Matthew 7:26-27

July 29, 2013
Peace: The Number-One Sign

Bible prophecy's number-one sign that God's next intervention into the affairs of mankind is near at hand is again front and center in our headlines. U.S. Secretary of State John Kerry just completed a mission for the Obama administration, consulting (to some extent) with Israeli Prime Minister Benjamin Netanyahu about getting the "Roadmap to Peace" process back on track. The process has been on hold for an extended period, but with apparent loosening of stipulations involving the 1967 borders by both sides, the Israel and the Palestinian Authority, the deadly peace process is seeming to once again get traction.

I use the word "deadly" without reservation, because that's exactly the way the Lord portrays any man-made peace process involving Israel and its enemy neighbors that excludes Him. His Words through the prophet Isaiah spell out God's anger against subterfuge in the matter of human attempts to impose godless peace on His chosen nation. He minces no words in admonishing those of His nation who would be part of this subterfuge.

> Because ye have said, We have made a covenant with death, and with hell are we at agreement; when the overflowing scourge shall pass through, it shall not come unto us: for we have made lies our refuge, and under falsehood have we hid ourselves....
>
> And your covenant with death shall be disannulled, and your agreement with hell shall not stand; when the overflowing scourge shall pass through, then ye shall be trodden down by it.
>
> Isaiah 28:15, 18

The land in the long-disputed territory involved is God's, and He gave it to Israel forever. He is jealous of any attempt to change things in that regard. He is so adamant about this, as a matter of fact, that His Word, through His prophet, Joel, foretells that God will bring every nation to

Armageddon precisely because they attempt to change His directive in this matter.

> I will also gather all nations, and will bring them down
> into the valley of Jehoshaphat, and will plead with them
> there for my people and for my heritage Israel, whom they have
> scattered among the nations, and parted my land.
>
> Joel 3: 2

America is at the forefront of again trying to impose such peace as is forbidden by the One who made the covenant with Abraham, Isaac, and Jacob. And it doesn't take much to read between the lines as to whose side this administration and its State Department wants most to listen to in the process. One report summarizes:

> On his visit, Kerry had marathon talks with Palestinian leader Mahmoud Abbas—including a stop Friday in Ramallah. Kerry also met Palestinian negotiator Saeb Erekat in Amman and had been consulting Israeli officials by telephone, a U.S. official said. The Palestinian leadership on Thursday did not accept Kerry's latest plan, but signaled that it was leaving the door open for him to continue pushing for talks.[97]

This is the way President Obama has seen fit to deal with Israeli leadership in almost every situation. We remember when, immediately following his first election, the president summoned Israeli Prime Minister Benjamin Netanyahu to the White House. He then talked *to,* not *with,* him for a few minutes before saying that he had to go have dinner with his family, leaving a condescended-to Netanyahu sitting alone and perplexed.

During the course of their relationship over the next five years, it's reported that the president calls Netanyahu and tells him what's what, but rarely listens, even refusing to take calls from the Israeli leader at times.

But, this is pretty much the way Mr. Obama handles all of his meetings. Notice how abbreviated is his response to serious questions he doesn't want to address, like those about Benghazi, the Internal Revenue Service scandal, the National Security Administration scandal...well, you name it.

And, the press conferences are so few and far between with the president before the microphones that the press must wonder why they even attend them, just to hear Jay Carney play ring around the rosy with them. But, members of the mainstream news media are so devoted to keeping this president from any political fallout that we have our answer as to why they keep coming to hear the president's propaganda minister instead of the man himself.

So, the Israeli prime minister is just like the rest of us. He, like American citizens, must wait, and then endure the phone call or press conference in which Mr. Obama, like when he depends upon the teleprompters, gives a one-way lecture.

> U.S. President Barack Obama on Thursday urged Prime Minister Binyamin Netanyahu to resume negotiations with the Palestinian Authority "as soon as possible," the White House said in a statement quoted by AFP. The two leaders spoke by telephone as Secretary of State John Kerry made his latest trip to the region as part of marathon efforts to re-launch the stalled peace talks.[98]

The thing to consider is that the "Roadmap to Peace" seems to be on again. It has been conspicuously absent from the mix of end-times issues and events until this past week. The president is looking for accomplishments to divert attention from some miserable failures in the economy and from the political shenanigans in which his administration has been caught. John Kerry, no doubt, would like nothing more than to hang a peace covenant on his political belt, regardless of its damage to Israel and to this nation.

Just my opinion...

But it is fact, not just my own view, that the issue of peace involving Israel is the number-one issue and signal that shows the nearness to Christ's call to His church in the Rapture.

AUGUST 2013

August 5, 2013
Dining with Danger

Which of us who, upon learning that Islamist terrorists were responsible for the most horrific attack ever against America on this continent, would have believed it? Who would have believed that an American president of the United States with the middle name "Hussein" would a little over a decade later be hosting a dinner in the White House in celebration of the very religion that spawned the attacks by murderous fanatics who reportedly shouted: "Allah Akhbar" (from Arabic, literally, "God is most great"), just before slamming three airplanes loaded with humanity and jet fuel into the World Trade Center towers and the Pentagon?

This is not to equate all who believe in the religion of Islam to being people who want to murder all others who don't agree with them. But this is indeed meant to equate the religion itself to one whose so-called holy book—the Koran—advocates the murder of all who will not yield to the supposed edicts of their supposed god, Allah. The same president who let us know that America is no longer a Christian nation has since his election in 2008 shown himself to be, if not a closet Muslim, certainly one sympathetic to Islam. His family history is steeped in the Islamist faith, even though he has told us he is a Christian.

I must and will leave that determination to Christ and those who claim to be His followers. However as a fruit inspector, as I believe we who name the name of Christ are instructed to be (Matthew 7:16, 20), it is my observation that the president's is far from a belief system that holds to major precepts of the Christian faith. He openly supports abortion—the murder of children in their mother's wombs, and even outside the mother's wombs under certain conditions. He supports the homosexual agenda at a number of levels, including gay marriage initiatives. He advocates change in areas where God's prescription throughout the Bible hasn't changed—or God does not change.

It is an interesting exercise to wonder how America's Founding Fathers might react, should they suddenly return to this earthly sphere and be confronted by the way the country has drifted from the Judeo-Christian principles upon which they founded the nation. Even the most secular of them like Thomas Jefferson and Benjamin Franklin, would be absolutely amazed and chagrined.

They would, I think, be completely perplexed, even angered, to see a president honoring the Muslim religious holidays with a White House celebration, while consistently casting aspersions on the Christian religion and favoring the elimination of its influence throughout America at every opportunity.

The president celebrated Ramadan this week by hosting a traditional late dinner in the state dining room of the White House. He remarked that throughout America's history, "Islam has contributed to the character of our country." In his remarks before the Iftar dinner eaten by Muslims after sunset to end the day of fasting, the president quoted from the Koran: "As the Koran teaches, whoever does an atom's weight of good will see its results." Mr. Obama said further, "Muslim-Americans and their good works have helped to build our nation, and we've seen the results."

Within the Koran's system of righteousness, "good," is, it seems, a relative term. The only "good" that there is apparently resides within works done for the putting forward of Allah's will—as given in the shouts the murderous terrorists screamed just before guiding the fuel-laden passenger planes into the Trade Center towers: "Allah Akhbar!" If I may, Mr. President, I hereby alert you to the dangers presented by inviting the Koran's duplicitous influence upon this nation you claim to love, in honoring its religion with an official state dinner.

The following synopsis encapsulates those dangers inherent within the Koran. This excerpt was written by Frosty Wooldridge, a journalist who for many years worked and lived around Detroit and watched Islamist influence help bring that once great city to destitution.

> You have already seen it in Madrid, Spain, London, England, and Paris, France with train bombings, subway bombings and riots. As their numbers grow, so will their power to enact their barbaric Sharia Law that negates republican forms of government, first amendment rights, and subjugates women to the lowest rungs on the human ladder. We will see more honor killings by upset husbands, fathers and brothers that demand subjugation by their daughters, sisters and wives. Muslims prefer beheadings of women to scare the hell out of any other members of their sect from straying. Multiculturalism: what a perfect method to kill our language, culture, country and way of life. The God of Israel gives the penalty for following any false religious system.

> But if thine heart turn away, so that thou wilt not hear, but shalt be drawn away, and worship other gods, and serve them;
>
> I denounce unto you this day, that ye shall surely perish, and that ye shall not prolong your days upon the land, whither thou passest over Jordan to go to possess it.
>
> Deuteronomy 20:17–18

August 12, 2013
Third Temple Temperature

Third Temple fever is rising surrounding the Temple Mount. It is, I believe, the most burning issue of our time, although simmering just beneath the surface of Middle East madness, just out of sight and mind most of the time.

Upon researching and writing for *Cauldron: Supernatural Implications of the Current Middle East*, the Temple again shouldered its way to the top of my thinking.

This is for good reason. The Temple Mount, Mt. Moriah, is the center of the earthly battle in the war Satan has waged against God since being ejected from heaven with the one-third of the rebel angels that followed him.

Moriah is the spot on the planet where some believe the Garden of Eden was centered. Some hold that the stone under which the Dome of the Rock sits was the place where Adam, then Eve, was created. I don't necessarily hold to this, but there are serious scholars within Christendom who do. The surface of Mt. Moriah is the place where Isaac was to be offered as sacrifice by his father, Abraham, when God intervened and provided the ram caught in the thicket by his horns. Moriah is the place where the Holy of Holies sat with in the two previous temples. It is the place where the Ark of the Covenant resided within the Holy of Holies. It is the place where the veil was torn from top to bottom the moment Jesus Christ said, "It is finished," and gave up His life to death and the grave, to be raised on the third day.

As we have written many times in these commentaries, the signals of this Age of Grace dispensation coming to an end soon are everywhere. It is absolutely mandatory, if that is true, that the most important signal of all be in view at this time. I believe with all that is within me that matters involving the rebuilding of the temple atop that most centrally important piece of rock must be clearly in view in proving that this generation is near the end of the Church Age.

Some excellent scholars believe and teach that the Tribulation Temple (Third Temple) doesn't have to be located atop Mt. Moriah. Rather, they believe it will possibly be a synagogue-type structure somewhat north of Jerusalem—Shiloh, to be exact—where the tabernacle stood for four hundred years. I respectfully disagree. Satan wants to usurp the throne of God. He cannot do so by taking over the throne of God in heaven. He has already been banished from that kingdom, except for having the privilege of accusing the brethren.

The devil does want to usurp the earthly throne of God, however, and, in his totally depraved thinking still believes he can do so. That "throne," which I call God's touchstone to humanity, is where the Holy of Holies sat, where the Ark of the Covenant resided within Solomon's Temple. Lucifer the fallen isn't interested in a second choice for a place to place his "man of sin." Antichrist must sit right where the vessel containing God's Law, the tablets (Ten Commandments), rested.

Antichrist will, of course sit in that spot, declaring himself to be God, according to 2 Thessalonians:

> Who opposeth and exalteth himself above all that is called God, or that is worshipped; so that he as God sitteth in the temple of God, shewing himself that he is God.
>
> 2 Thessalonians 2:4

Satan will apparently indwell this "prince that shall come," thus achieving, in his own demented mind, at least, the usurpation of God's earthly throne. This, after all, is the place within the Temple Jesus will one day sit as King of Kings during the millennial kingdom.

Now, I know the mountain of Moriah will be split in the middle and the Tribulation Temple will likely be completely destroyed. After all, it is the Third Temple built, I believe, by unbelieving Jews; thus, it doesn't meet with God's approval. Mt. Zion, as it will be known, will be supernaturally elevated in the tremendous topographical changes that will take place when Christ's foot touches the Mt. of Olives when He returns. Christ will, Himself, build the Millennial Temple upon Mt. Zion, where He will reign and rule with a rod of iron for one thousand years.

The thing we are considering here is: Do we see signs of the call to rebuild the Temple? The answer is, of course, "Yes!"

Great tensions are currently building around the Temple Mount. Both the Jewish community, which wants to worship on top of Moriah, and the Arab Islamists, who are determined the Jews will never do so, are revving up their emotional engines. The temperature is rising, and the diplomats of the world realize that it is potentially the one place on earth that is the greatest trigger point to start nuclear Armageddon.

The following two news excerpts lay out the building fever surrounding the Temple Mount.

Israelis who believe the Temple Mount should remain in Israeli hands must take urgent action, Likud MK Moshe Feiglin warned Thursday. Feiglin, who heads the Jewish Leadership faction of the Likud party, visited the Temple Mount on Thursday despite knowing he would find it locked to Jews, as a display of protest.

In an "unprecedented" move, police on Wednesday informed Jewish groups that the Temple Mount will be closed to all non-Muslims until at least the end of Ramadan, on 11th August. The announcement has provoked renewed anger over anti-Jewish discrimination on the Temple Mount, and sparked calls by activists for a mass-protest on 7th August, at the start of the Hebrew month of Elul.[99]

A Jewish website that aims to teach Israelis about the Temple has been met with an angry backlash from the Arab Muslim community. The Har Hakodesh (lit. "The Holy Mountain") website includes educational material about the history of the Temple Mount, which was the site of the First Temple and Second Temple. The Temples were the focus of divine service for the Jewish nation. The site also includes stunning photographs of the Temple Mount, including pictures taken by a non-Jewish photographer from parts of the Mount which Jews may not enter.

What has caused upset in the Muslim world is a representation of the Temple Mount as it would appear with a rebuilt Jewish Temple atop it rather than Al-Aqsa Mosque that currently stands there.

The site has been repeatedly targeted by hackers, and has been the focus of criticism in the Arab media. Sheikh Raed Salah, who heads the hardline northern branch of the Islamic Movement in Israel, has called for an "Islamic awakening" in response to the website....

The desire to see a rebuilt Temple is central to traditional Judaism, and the Amidah prayer, which religious Jews recite three times daily, calls for the Temple to be rebuilt.[100]

Because we are so near the end of the Church Age (Age of Grace), look for the temperatures of both the Jews and the Islamists to continue to rise as end-times events continue to unfold.

August 19, 2013
Race-Baiting Fitting the Prophetic Pattern

Mankind continues to rage toward Armageddon. The hatred flows from an anger that seems ready to blow uncontrollably, like a massive volcano seething just beneath the not-so-tranquil surface. Man's hatred for his fellow man is more and more bursting forth from the angry substrata of even the most civilized places, to shock the rest of us who just want to live peacefully among each other.

While the brutal attacks are becoming obvious to the point of alarming the general populace of America, the racial-based assaults of a certain sort are almost never reported by U.S. mainstream news media. People can see the attacks for themselves, and, thankfully, the alternative media is more and more getting out the facts about the brutality.

Mainstream reporters are quick—and rightfully so—to point to any reprehensible act of white assault on black, Hispanic, or other racial minority. We have only to consider the case of George Zimmerman and Trayvon Martin to see this. The case was treated as cataclysmic for race relations. However, the recent case of a mob of black youths beating a lone white young man has hardly been touched by the major news sources.

While the absolute insanity of this imbalance of treatment is overtly apparent, the bigotry of sycophantic mainstream news journalism isn't my primary point of concern for this commentary.

I say "sycophantic, mainstream news journalism" because the journalists of this stripe are overwhelmingly and demonstrably on the take, as is said, for this president. They want to ignore the reporting of any news that they perceive would in any way reflect negatively on America's first African-American—and, may I add, thoroughly liberal—president.

This has been true in most every issue, whether talking about the way this administration has, in my estimation, run the economy of this nation into the ground; the way it has helped degrade the military with various cuts and with opening the armed services to homosexual influences; how it has, through this Department of Justice, divided the nation racially as it has not been since the pre-1957 era; and in numerous other ways.

It is this last point that enlightens further on where this generation stands on God's prophetic timeline.

America's racial divide is illustrating the Lord Jesus Christ's Olivet Discourse prophecy as surely as have the horrific ethnic cleansings of nations like those found in Africa, Asia, and other places of the world. The atrocities might not have yet reached the levels of those that have occurred in places like Cambodia, Somalia, Ethiopia, and others, but the visceral hatred is there just as strongly as in those places where the results have been genocide.

The following story has made it into the public light, thankfully, because of the alternative media, as stated above.

> A St. Paul, Minn., man is in a coma today, fighting for his life after a black mob beat him, stripped his clothes off and left him for dead. Even if he recovers, he will have permanent brain damage.
>
> Ray Widstrand thought he had nothing to fear from moving into a black neighborhood on the East Side of St. Paul. This young white guy and aspiring filmmaker thought he had nothing to fear when he decided to take a Sunday night stroll through his adopted part of town. Nothing to fear from a crowd of 50 black people fighting outside a nearby party. So he stopped to check it out. Soon, however, the mob's attention turned on him....
>
> When police arrived, the black mob scattered, leaving only Ray behind.
>
> "He had blood coming from his nose and mouth and was unresponsive," said the police report. "As of August 8th, the prognosis for recovery is slight, and should he live, he will suffer permanent and protracted loss of brain function."[101]

Again, this is a story you will likely not see in a mainstream news article. Or, if you do, the word "black" will not be found. The opposite will invariably be the case in a case where a black, Hispanic, or other minority of so-called color has been the victim of an attack by a Caucasian.

The tragedy here is that we are all just people just beneath the epidermis, and the racism has and is being stirred by forces that wish to attain political capital or other advantages from the race-baiting in which they engage.

Again, this was on display in the case of Zimmerman and Martin. The mainstream journalists made it their groundbreaking purpose to refer to Mr. Zimmerman, a darker-skinned man, of being a "white Hispanic." The community organizer types, from Eric Holder, the U.S. Attorney General, to Revs. Al Sharpton and Jesse Jackson and others, immediately did all they could to rev up the race-baiting, even bussing in hundreds to demand the firing of the sheriff involved in the initial investigation of the case.

And there we have, in microcosm, the nucleus of Jesus' prophecy about the ethnic strife that will be prevalent at the time of His return to planet earth. The Lord said that these uprisings would be unusual, in that they would be based in *ethnos,* the Greek word, here, for "nation." They would be ethnic in origin. They would pit ethnic or racial group against racial group.

It is equally true that ethnic factors have been the cause of many wars throughout the centuries. The Arabs and Jews—as a matter of fact, many ethnic peoples against the Jews—marked the conflicts of Old Testament times. Almost without exception, those early wars were "ethnic" in origin.

Things have not changed. Arabs and Jews still have the ethnos factor at the heart of their differences. And, never in history has the conflict been more virulent, in rhetoric, if not in fact. The Islamic nations, mostly Arab, are blood-vowed to push the Jews into the Mediterranean Sea and to wipe the Jewish race from the planet. Some Arab leaders of the past and other leaders—e.g., the Iranians—continue to want all Jews expunged from the region, and even off the globe. They have made it their national policy through their oratorical invectives. There have been conflicts in the century just passed involving peoples of the Caucasus, the Balkans, etc., and horrific slaughters in Africa, and other places—all based upon ethnic differences.

The words of Jesus Christ reverberate throughout these strange days when God's wrath is building. His words and what we see at the basic levels of American societal upheaval show this generation is nearing midnight and the Rapture of the church.

> And ye shall hear of wars and rumors of wars: see that ye be not
> troubled: for all these things must come to pass,
> but the end is not yet. For nation shall rise against nation.
>
> Matthew 24:6–7

August 26, 2013
Caught Up

We just upgraded to a system that has added an extra five hundred channels or so to our television programming. All of it comes automatically with what I really wanted to acquire, Internet service that increases my download capacity and speed by a factor of three or four.

I realize there are many who read these columns who believe strongly that there should be no television in the home whatsoever, so I'm almost apologetic—but not quite. I was sick and tired of waiting sometimes hours to download materials I needed to do my work for Rapture Ready and for other work.

Clicking through the myriad TV channels I now have, I am amazed at all of the things of life that bombard us. I can no longer "see" the programs and their content because of retinas that no longer work (which I suppose makes the upgrade sound ludicrous). I do hear, however, with at least a modicum of ability in my closing ears and years, so I get the gist of the programming. The many aspects of everyday living in America today are astonishing—not in scope, but in the absence of the profound.

By this, I mean that in America all that is presented on the programming revolves around nurturing self-centeredness that directly affects the average U.S. citizen in one way or another—love, sex, finance, lifestyle, and health.

Religion is covered by TV entertainment and news to a much lesser degree, and increasingly in a way that moves ever farther from the biblical fundamentals of the faith once delivered to the saints. The only things that matter for life more abundantly, according to Jesus Christ, are conspicuously absent from this massive programming regime. Things of truly eternal value are sequestered in the corners of the religious channels, and few of those Christ-centered programs exist. The majority of so-called Christian programming involves prosperity-a-thons that are almost as ubiquitous as the secular infomercials that incessantly barrage the late-late-night/early-morning viewers. Most in America in these closing days of this Church Age comprise a generation caught up in a world system that long ago pushed God out of the equation for living on the planet He designed for mankind.

Jesus forewarned of a future generation of believers that would be caught up in such a world system at the time when His return neared. He had just gone through the many signs of His coming again, and had given His disciples the answer to their questions: "Master, but when shall these things be? and what sign will there be when these things shall come to pass?"

Jesus said in forewarning that future end-times generation:

> And take heed to yourselves, lest at any time your hearts be
> overcharged with surfeiting, and drunkenness,
> and cares of this life, and so that day come upon you unawares.
>
> For as a snare shall it come on all them that
> dwell on the face of the whole earth.
>
> Watch ye therefore, and pray always, that ye may be accounted
> worthy to escape all these things that shall come to pass,
> and to stand before the Son of man.
>
> Luke 21:34-36

Sadly, Christians in mass numbers seem to fit the description of that final generation of the Age of Grace. If we are honest, we have to consider that it appears that the everyday cares of life hold most captive like the Lord's description of those who will be alive at the time of the "snare" that will come upon the whole earth. That "snare" will be none other than the Rapture of the church.

It will be a startling thing for those so married to this world to suddenly be in the presence of their Lord. Having been caught up in the world and all of its quicksand of immorality, they will suddenly find themselves caught up into the holy presence of the One who died for them.

While every true believer will meet the Lord in the air when He calls, "Come up here," the above Scripture leaves little doubt that there is a most serious issue involved in the words the Lord used:

> Watch ye therefore, and pray always,
> that ye may be accounted worthy to escape all
> these things that shall come to pass,
> and to stand before the Son of man.
>
> Luke 21:36

Christians are not to be caught off guard like the lost of the world, for whom the Rapture will be a thief-in-the-night experience. To be caught off guard in the sense that we are living like the world, with little thought of Jesus' coming back for us, will demonstrate unworthiness to stand before Him at that monumental moment. Our worthiness will determine whether we hear Him say to us, "Well done, good and faithful servant," when we then move to heaven and the Judgment Seat of Christ for rewards earned in this life.

SEPTEMBER 2013

September 2, 2013
Tribulation Actors on Scene

It is an amazing thing to watch and hear. Tribulation-era nations are gathering and making their presence known with headlines-grabbing statements while surrounding one of Bible prophecy's key, judgment-bound cities.

Strangely, however, the most powerful of the nations gathering about Damascus is the one out of all of them that has no apparent prophetic mention. More about that later.

Let's consider some statements coming from the leaders of these nations of end-times Bible prophecy.

> Israeli Prime Minister Benjamin Netanyahu said Israel and France share an interest in having the "tragic" events in Syria come to an end. "I think what is going on there is a crime committed by the Syrian regime against its own people. It's truly shocking," Netanyahu said. He added that the Assad regime was being actively aided and abetted by Iran and Hezbollah. "In fact, Assad's regime has become a full Iranian client and Syria has become Iran's testing ground," Netanyahu said. "Now the whole world is watching. Iran is watching and it wants to see what would be the reaction on the use of chemical weapons." Earlier in the day at the weekly cabinet meeting, Netanyahu said that Israel's "finger is on the pulse" following the situation in Syria, and—if needed—its finger will also be on the trigger. These were his [words] in his first public comments on the reports that hundreds of Syrians were killed last week by chemical weapons....

> Netanyahu said that Israel drew three conclusions from this incident. "One, this situation must not be allowed to continue. Two, the most dangerous regimes in the world must not be allowed to possess the most dangerous weapons in the world. And three, we expect that this will stop, of course, but we must always remember our sages' ancient principle: 'If we are not for ourselves, who will be for us?'"[102]

Russian President Vladimir Putin has been blustering during the lead-up to Western powers entering into the Mediterranean near Syria. The quasi-official statement by Russian foreign ministry spokesman Alexander Lukashevich seemed to have a more subdued tone than the macho Putin's demeanor earlier on. He said in a statement:

> Attempts to bypass the Security Council, once again to create artificial groundless excuses for a military intervention in the region are fraught with new suffering in Syria and catastrophic consequences for other countries of the Middle East and North Africa.

The Chinese weighed in on the developing Syrian situation. They accused through the official news agency, Xinhua, stating that Western powers were rushing to conclusions about who may have used chemical weapons in Syria before U.N. inspectors had completed their investigation.

Both Russia and China have warned the U.S. with subtle threat that they will join forces to oppose any military action.

Syrian Foreign Minister Wallid Moallem, in a press conference last Tuesday, let it be known that Syria sees its options as being one of two. The Al-Assad government can either surrender or defend against aggressors. It chooses the latter, he said. Moallem said that a U.S. strike on Syria would serve the interests of al-Qaeda-linked groups. "Syria will press on with military campaign," he added, "despite any possible foreign strikes."

Iran, a key prophetic entity (Persia), has been eyeing the Syrian situation warily.

Some experts in dealing with Iran believe they will study the present U.S. course of action against Syria, thus to use any weaknesses they perceive to move on the diplomatic/military chessboard against their hated enemy, Israel.

Iranian Foreign Minister Mohammad Javad Zarif warned U.N. political affairs chief Jeffrey Feltman, who was in Tehran for talks that included Syria, of grave consequences for any attack on Syria.

Foreign ministry spokesman Abbas Araqchi, in relaying what was said during the meeting said, "The use of military means (against Syria) will have serious consequences not only for Syria but for the entire region."

The lone superpower of all the nations gathering to force Syria into compliance with what the Western powers consider to be civilized behavior is the one nation that, so far as even oblique mention, isn't in the biblically prophetic picture. That is, with the possible exception of being mentioned as one of the "young lions" referenced in Ezekiel 38:13.

The United States of America is nonetheless the primary mover in bringing this military pressure in order to force Bashar al-Assad into compliance with the "red line" restriction on use of chemical weapons he is alleged to have crossed. I say "alleged," because it seems to make no sense that at this crucial time of his dictatorial rule over his nation he would use such weapons, knowing he is inviting the wrath of the international community to fall upon his regime. But, then, we remember all of Saddam Hussein's machinations to try to hold to power…

U.S. Secretary of State John Kerry said the use of chemical weapons is a "moral obscenity." He said the delay in allowing U.N. inspectors to the sites was a sign the Syrian government had something to hide.

"What we saw in Syria last week should shock the conscience of the world. It defies any code of morality," Kerry said on Monday in a news conference. "Make no mistake, President Obama believes there must be accountability for those who would use the world's most heinous weapons against the world's most vulnerable people."

It is fascinating that at this late moment of this dispensation, America—mentioned nowhere in Bible prophecy—is directing traffic for the nations that God's Word proclaims will be actors during that coming time of Tribulation.

Bashar al-Assad, I sense, is one who understands how the so-called international community works in deposing his kind. He watched under his father's tutelage while the presidents Bush removed Saddam from his firmly ensconced dictatorship. He observed from the top perch in Damascus while the Obama era influenced the violence-wracked people of Libya to brutally remove Moammar Gadhafi.

The question keeps running through my thoughts, considering Bible prophecy and the Middle East madness: Might the Syrian tyrant decide it would be a far better ending—a glorious going to his version of Allah—to light up Damascus in a nuclear fireball, rather than to suffer Hussein and Gadhafi's fates?

We will definitely stay tuned…

September 9, 2013
The Ezekiel Wimp Factor

The Syrian situation continues to be up in the air as of this writing. While the matter of the chemical weapons of mass destruction—much of which were sent by Saddam Hussein to Syria when it looked like Saddam's jig was up—is important, and cries out for a response from the civilized peoples of the world, there is, for the purposes of this commentary, another facet of this subject I wish to broach.

This presidential administration is at the center of all kinds of controversial speculation, some coming from within Mr. Obama's own ranks. Some of his Democrat partisans accuse the president of being just like the Bushes in beating the drums of war. They prefer to avoid all armed conflict. Others accuse him of getting the U.S. aligned with the likes of Al-Qaeda and other terrorist types, giving them weapons that they will one day turn on America, Israel, and Western Europe. The speculation has grown from Obama being considered a bumbling Jimmy Carter look-alike (in Carter's inept handling of the Iranian revolution) to the current president being so conniving in his desire to win votes for his own power's sake in the 2014 midterm election that he helped plan the Syrian rebels' framing of Bashar al-Assad in their use of chemical weapons against their own.

We watched and heard President Obama come out strongly to assist the rebels in every way possible except to put "boots on the ground." We watched and heard Secretary of State John Kerry give a rousing speech that America was morally obligated to lead the way in taking out al-Assad's capability to wage chemical war. We watched and heard the mainstream news media remain silent as to the sort of opposition with which they once lambasted George W. Bush for the same kind of preparatory war rhetoric.

The president said flatly that he didn't need any approval from Congress; he needed no coalition to go in and do what had to be done. He said all of this, having accused George W. of being a "cowboy" for doing the same.

Then the prime minister of Britain consulted Parliament and they said "no" to the U.K. entering the fray in a military way—that is, joining in the inevitable sending of cruise missiles, etc. France and other "allies" decided they wouldn't be a part of overt military action, but would back the international community principles in the matters involved.

President Obama then had a forty-minute walk on the White House grounds with one of his closest advisers. When the walk was done, Obama had changed his mind and would now wait until after September 9 when Congress returned to Washington in order to get their vote (although he continues to assert that he has the right as commander in chief to go to war against the al-Assad regime, or at least conduct limited strikes...).

All of this brings us up to date, as of this writing. That's where the president—the U.S. and we the people—stands.

Is that what we are doing? Standing?

For what? Against what?

What I'm leading up to in all of this is the thought implicit within the title of this commentary, "The Ezekiel Wimp Factor."

America's liberal, woolly-minded detractors within our own nation have long thought of the United States as a bully on the world scene. We wish to always impose our values, our will, upon the weak, helpless of the world. This has been the mantra of the left and their mouthpieces, the mainstream news conglomerate, for many decades. Until, that is, the likes of Jimmy Carter, Bill Clinton, or, especially, Barack Obama control things. When that is the case, a strange silence develops, such as now, while this president is maneuvering to launch a cruise missile or a half dozen into his own version of Clinton's aspirin factory attack.

Even Obama's own chairman of the joint chiefs, Gen. Martin Dempsey, has expressed grave concerns about interfering in the civil war going on in Damascus and surrounding area. Many who watch Middle East madness say that numerous incalculable dangers are involved in interjecting U.S. power into such a volatile powder keg as the Middle East presents today. It is especially foolhardy to do so when we can't even offer absolute proof of who used the chemical weapons. The vacillation shown by the U.S. in this Mideast violence is perhaps the most dangerous aspect of what's going on.

We who watch Bible prophecy often review Ezekiel the prophet's foretelling of the Gog-Magog assault against Israel. We wonder just what is meant by the words of Ezekiel 38:13:

> Sheba, and Dedan, and the merchants of Tarshish, with all the young lions thereof, shall say unto thee, Art thou come to take a spoil? hast thou gathered thy company to take a prey? to carry away silver and gold, to take away cattle and goods, to take a great spoil?

This weak, diplomatic note of protest will be the only apparent response to the assault by Russia, Persia (Iran), and the rest as they rush toward Israel. With the on-again/off-again decision-making of this president, it isn't hard to understand that the Ezekiel wimp factor is alive and well and will likely soon play out in that Middle East conflict that will be far more devastating than even the destruction of Damascus that is prophesied by Ezekiel's colleague, Isaiah.

September 16, 2013
EMP and Gog

It's a frightening thing to consider. For the most technologically endowed nation to ever exist on planet earth, it would be a nightmare of almost unimaginable proportion. I'm referring to an attack on the U.S. by EMP (electromagnetic pulse), about which there continues to be much chatter in the cybersphere. Most feared is a nuclear blast that could interact with the ionosphere, the shell of electrons and electrically charged particles surrounding earth, to create a series of electromagnetic pulses that could reach across the North American continent, according to the scientists who study such matters.

In such an apocalyptic scenario, an American enemy would explode a nuclear weapon a certain number of miles above a central point above the continent. This would cause everything that is controlled by electronic circuitry to fail, bringing society and culture as we have known them to an instantaneous conclusion. All modern transportation would be stopped, with planes falling from the air. Car engines and circuitry would cease to function. From the sophisticated technologies of the hospitals, banks, and electric power-generating plants to the electronically powered, smallest conveniences such as coffeemakers, all would be instantly fried, and we would be sent back to the 1850s in a millisecond, according to the experts.

There would be no more TV watching, electronic devices to play music, no cell phone talk, or texting! Now, I know that last bit got your attention. The only positive might be that car accidents caused by texting would cease to occur. For sure, the insurance industry would be out of business. Their electronic files on the texting-caused accidents would be no more…

The stores would be out of food within a day because the vehicles to resupply would no longer be operating. Whoever could get to the shelves first on foot or bicycle would get the quickly disappearing grocery items. Water and sewer systems would begin to undergo contamination and disease would begin to spread.

Those who warn of such things worry that America's military capabilities would be degraded to the point that the U.S. would have no course of action that would protect the nation from invasion. The military machinery and personnel would be as adversely affected as would we civilians.

It is indeed a nightmare to consider.

This is all predicated upon the postulation that it would be an enemy nation or possibly terrorist group that would attack with EMP. However, America has nuclear submarines and many other assets that—like in the case of the cold war and MAD (Mutually Assured Destruction)—would devastate any enemy who dared to knock out the American power grid. Even if the enemy could not be determined, such as if Al-Qaeda launched an EMP off a freighter on the Atlantic coast, there are automatic responses programmed that make any enemy think twice before attempting such an untried assault on the most awesome war-making entity ever to exist.

Well, maybe that doesn't exactly apply any longer. Remember Tuesday, September 11, 2001. Those nineteen terrorists did not seem to regard the awesomeness of America's military. It's true they have paid the price for the attack. But the price we've paid since is far greater, not just in the trillions of dollars spent and still being spent, but in lives lost and continuing to be lost.

Disregarding such an enemy for the moment, the experts tell us we face the possibility of an EMP attack from the cosmos. Now, there's something to truly be concerned about!

Solar flares are the real danger, according to the scientists involved in study of this sort of EMP assault. These coronal mass ejections are enormous sun eruptions of super-hot plasma that spews charged particles across the solar system. They do the same sort of damage that the nuclear weapon EMPs might do, as I understand it.

The earth is in a period of high likelihood for these types of coronal mass ejections for the rest of 2013 and all of 2014, according to the authorities on such things. Although Congress has been given ways to help prepare for damage such EMP events can do, there has apparently been little interest from that quarter in making preemptive preparation. We remember the same sorts of fears and warnings about the year 2000

(Y2K) event. In that instance, billions of dollars were thrown into fixing the feared problems.

This time around, unlike in the case of the Y2K scare, the mainstream media seems to have all but ignored the EMP concerns. Even peripheral media cable networks and other such media have remained silence. Only the blogosphere is alive with details of the possibility of impending doom.

My own thought is that the Lord has always been in complete control of the fate of individuals, nations, and the entire earth, which He created. That's why there hasn't been all-out warfare—nuclear war. That's why there hasn't been an EMP event that sets us back to the 1850s or so…

However, there is a prophetic thought that has nagged for a long time. That's all it is, a thought.

Salem Kirban wrote the novel *666* in the 1960s. He portrayed the Ezekiel 38–39 Gog-Magog attack as being waged totally like the Scripture depicts. There were only horses, bucklers, shields, etc., as they stormed like a cloud to cover the land as the Gog forces raged toward Jerusalem. All modern weaponry had been rendered useless—I can't remember why or how.

An EMP event from earth's sun could apparently make Mr. Kirban's novel truly prophetic, if all we've been told about EMP is correct. The way things are shaping in that region of the world should alert us that maybe we don't have too long to wait to find out about how Bible prophecy plays out.

September 23, 2013
Brave New World's Big Brother

Aldous Huxley had published in 1932 his futuristic novel *Brave New World,* in which every facet of humanity came under central control of the ultimate, despotic government. The author described some pretty amazing technological tools for the times for use in enslaving all peoples.

Evidence mounts that our own generation is moving swiftly into a new, troubling world, and the tools Huxley's fictional world utilized seem like child's toys by comparison with what is in view now. The technologies that have developed truly constitute what could be termed the "big brother" of those technological instrumentalities described in the long-ago novel. More about that in due course. For now, let's look at the intrusions into everyday life that increase with each passing day.

Less than a year ago, I received a troubling news report about a small town near where I once lived in northern Arkansas. The town is about an hour away from Memphis, which lies to the east. The chief of police was acting like a Nazi thug, as best I could determine from the report. The headline of the story was "Police State Comes to Arkansas." The police chief reportedly said, "[Police are] going to be in SWAT gear and have AR-15s around their necks." He said further: "If you're out walking, we're going to stop you, ask why you're out walking, check for your ID."

The head policeman said that while some might be offended, they shouldn't be. "We're going to do it to everybody," he said. "Criminals don't like being talked to."

One of the town officials backed the chief of police. He said: "[The citizens] may not be doing anything but walking their dog," he said. "But they're going to have to prove it.... This fear is what's given us the reason to do this. Once I have stats and people saying they're scared, we can do this," he said. "It allows us to do what we're fixing to do."

The chief of police added, "To ask you for your ID, I have to have a reason," he said. "Well, I've got statistical reasons that say I've got a lot of crime right now, which gives me probable cause to ask what you're doing out. Then when I add that people are scared...then that gives us even more [reason] to ask why are you here and what are you doing in this area."

Individuals who do not produce identification when asked could be charged with obstructing a governmental operation, the policeman said. He added that he realized what he was proposing was much like martial law, but that he really didn't care.

The report gave statistics on the fact that increasing percentages of towns, especially some of the larger cities, are using SWAT teams to do routine patrols, following the models in other parts of the world.

In one area of the beleaguered city of Detroit, the Nazi-like tactics—or perhaps Soviet-style tactics—were recently employed against citizens.

Government officials decided to cut off a large portion of the power grid because there wasn't enough cooperation from the citizenry. When the levels of cutting off air-conditioning weren't satisfactorily complied with, the authorities cut off all power to the grid. This was done to "send a strong message" that the orders must be obeyed, one of the officials said without apology.

Now to the latest technology that surpasses the imaginations of even Huxley and George Orwell. But, this is real, not fictional, technology that has already been proven in places like the battlefields of Afghanistan in 2011. The technology mentioned here is one of the least draconian of the many that are in development and even in use in some areas of the world.

> A new gadget built by Diehl Defense, much like a portable Electro-Magnetic Pulse ray gun, can disable a vehicles electronic circuitry rendering it useless in battlefield or pursuit conditions....
>
> Police departments and militaries around the world will likely grovel over the device. The official website for Diehl Defense explains the use for the device in a convoy protection scenario reading, "The new HPEM (High-Power-Electro-Magnetics) technology protects convoys against improvised explosive devices (IEDs), can stop get-away vehicles and prevent unauthorized access to limited access areas....
>
> HPEM sources can be used for personal and convoy protection, for instance, to overload and permanently destroy radio-based fuzing systems. In contrast to conventional jammers, the HPEM convoy protection system is also effective against new types of sensor-based IEDs. Enemy vehicles with electronic motor management can be stopped inconspicuously by mobile and stationary HPEM systems (car stopping).[103]

Move over, Captain James T. Kirk. The phaser is here, now. And it's apparently set to stun America's own citizenry at some point as policing technologies incrementally take over our lives!

> And he causeth all, both small and great, rich and poor, free and bond, to receive a mark in their right hand, or in their foreheads.
>
> Revelation 13:16

The beast system that will make Huxley's fictional dictatorship seem child's play by comparison is approaching rapidly. You don't have to be a part of that new, deadly world. Accept Christ today and not Antichrist.

> That if thou shalt confess with thy mouth the Lord Jesus,
> and shalt believe in thine heart that God hath raised
> him from the dead, thou shalt be saved.
>
> For with the heart man believeth unto righteousness;
> and with the mouth confession is made unto salvation.
>
> Romans 10:9-10

September 30, 2013
Temple Mount Still the Fuse

While the nations of the world gathered in New York City at the United Nations building for what is called by some "Dictators Week," the single-most reason for the gathering continues to boil in turmoil. Mount Moriah, the Temple Mount, continues to be the fuse that will trigger mankind's final war prior to Christ's Second Advent.

The primary talk at the beginning of the big New York gathering was of the potential meeting between President Barack Obama and the new Iranian second in command, President Hassan Rouhani. All the news media was in a twitter over whether the two would shake hands, thus healing the breach that has split America and Iran since the Jimmy Carter administration in 1979 saw the Ayatollah Khomeini return to Tehran with the Iranian Revolution. Their hopes were dashed as the Iranian would have no part of the handshake. Despite the Obama administration going so far as to have the president say in his speech before the U.N. assembly that he was opening new talks over the Iranian nuclear program, administration officials soon backtracked to say that such "sidelines" talks with Rouhani were never on the table.

The point I would like to make is that despite all of the high-powered world leadership in attendance in the U.N. summit, world peace really boils down—whether thinking in terms of secular perspective or in Bible prophecy perspective—to the matter of Jerusalem, Israel, and, most particularly, the Temple Mount. Iran's nuclear development program, almost certainly for the primary purpose of producing nuclear weaponry, directly relates to Jerusalem, Israel, and the Temple Mount.

The Iranian Islamist leaders want Israel off the Holy Land, out of the Middle East—removed from planet earth. Ditto for a large majority of all leadership gathered at the U.N. summit. The leaders of the Muslim states surrounding Israel and those other Islamist dictatorships all want Israel bulldozed into the Mediterranean so they can then begin concentrating on killing each other.

All Muslim vitriol can be characterized as directed at that one spot on the planet that Satan most wants to claim as his own, Mt. Moriah. He will indeed do so, the Bible tells us, when his chosen vessel, Antichrist, sits in the Tribulation Temple and declares himself to be God (2 Thessalonians 2).

Signals that Satan is stirring his minions, both demonic and human, toward causing troubles on this spot where the two previous Jewish Temples sat—where Abraham brought Isaac to be a sacrifice, where the Ark of the Covenant sat, and near where Jesus Christ was crucified for the sins of man—are in evidence, as always. The violence exploded again during the Jewish Sukkot holidays just past, as the following excerpt reports. The Al-Aqsa mosque on the Temple Mount was the scene of clashes between Palestinian youths and Israeli police Wednesday morning, the latest in a series of skirmishes as Jewish pilgrims have flocked to the site over the holiday.

> After Palestinians in the courtyard began stone-throwing and rioting, police officers stormed the compound. Ma'an News Agency reported that police fired stun grenades at the rioters. Seven Palestinians were injured, according to Ma'an....

> Just before the Jewish New Year, on September 4, 15 Palestinians were arrested after fighting with police, and hundreds of Muslims were denied access.
>
> Security forces have been on high alert during the entire holiday period.[104]

It seems something akin to insanity, the fact that Israel has been attacked in major assaults on three occasions by Muslim coalitions—in 1956, 1967, and 1973. Each time, Israel defeated the vastly superior in numbers forces and won territory from its attackers. Then, each time, Israel, under U.N. pressures, gave back much of what was won in war. Particularly flabbergasting is the fact that Israel gave controlling authority over the Temple Mount to the Muslims following the 1967 Six Day War. No one has been able to fully fathom to this day why the hardened Israeli general, Moshe Dayan, did so.

All of that, then to consider that Muslims are given free rein to worship and visit its shrines atop Mt. Moriah while Jews are strictly forbidden from worshipping there and from visiting except under the most stringent of regulations, is just mind-bending.

There is building a desire by the Jewish people to push back against this intolerable restriction against interacting with this most holy place in its history. The Muslim Arabs and others are becoming just as exercised while the Jews are ratcheting up demands that they be given access to the Temple Mount.

Bible prophecy tells us that there will be a Third Temple atop Moriah, the Tribulation Temple. Also, it is foretold that Israel's land will be divided in an act that will cause God to bring all of Israel's antagonists into the Valley of Jehoshaphat for punishment—to Armageddon (Joel 3: 2). The U.N. dictators see a "two-state solution"—an Israeli state and a Palestinian state—as the formula for Middle East and world peace. In actuality, they want Israel gone, and believe when there is a Palestinian nation, Israel will be so surrounded as to set it up for complete destruction.

The God of heaven, of course, has other ideas. Israel, although its people don't know it, is the one nation on earth that never has to worry about being destroyed by its enemies.

> Also I will restore the captivity of My people Israel,
> and they will rebuild the ruined cities and live in them.
> They will also plant vineyards and drink their wine,
> and make gardens and eat their fruit.
>
> I will also plant them on their land, and they will not
> again be rooted out from their land which I have
> given them, says the Lord your God.
>
> Amos 9:14-15

OCTOBER 2013

October 7, 2013
Persian Prince and Pawns

Persia is credited with inventing perhaps the world's most recognized intellectual game: chess, having appropriated its primitive form from India, by way of ancient Afghanistan. The Persian ability to anticipate and formulate strategic moves seems to have successfully spanned the centuries to inhabit the brain trust of Iran's Israel haters. In the battle of mind games on the diplomatic front, their negotiators certainly appear to be using the U.S. presidential administration like pawns to try to—pardon the pun—rook Israeli Prime Minister Benjamin Netanyahu in the deadly game of Islam against Israel.

John Bolton, former U.N. ambassador and current senior fellow at the American Enterprise Institute, said recently that Iran's new president,

Hassan Rouhani, is telling President Obama things he wants to hear, all the while buying time to move Iran's nuclear program toward Iran's objective, development of nuclear weaponry. The biblical prince of Persia, it seems, is alive and well and working his mischief just as when he hindered the angel in delivering God's message to the prophet Daniel—still making his own devilish brand of chess moves in Satan's incessant battle for the souls of mankind.

Bolton wrote in a Sunday *Wall Street Journal* op-ed:

> Just as Vladimir Putin had played him for a fool over Syria, Mr. Obama was initially snubbed by Iranian President Hasan Rouhani despite frantic White House efforts to produce a handshake.

Bolton said in the piece that this isn't the first time Rouhani has played the West like a master chess player. Bolton wrote in effect that the Iranian worked his same sleight-of-hand wizardry when he was Iran's chief nuclear negotiator from 2003 to 2005, when he successfully followed the same playbook.

The former ambassador listed what he considers the president's failures on the diplomatic front that he thinks leads the Iranians to believe he can be had, in the sense of one's being conned.

> Mr. Obama failed in his stated objective to oust Syria's Assad regime from power; failed to impress Assad that his "red line" against using chemical weapons was serious; failed to exact retribution when that red line was crossed; failed to rally anything but small minorities in either house of Congress to support his position; and failed to grasp that agreements with the likes of Syria and Russia prolong, rather than solve, the chemical-weapons problem.

Bolton said further that the Iranian ayatollahs know that the "all-options-on-the-table" threat have no teeth. They are without weight. As for the other player on this most crucial chessboard of end-times matters,

Netanyahu is observing the board's configuration and the lessening of distance between the American president and the Iranian regime.

Netanyahu doesn't seem to mind standing alone and speaking up in terms of resisting the cozying up to the Iranian diabolists. What worries the international community's diplomatic complex, and thus, the State Department in particular, is the Israeli prime minister's potential for acting alone in opposing Iran's getting an atomic bomb. This, he has declared on numerous occasions, will not be allowed during his time as head of the Jewish state.

Addressing the subject of the Iranian Charm offensive designed to rook Obama, Netanyahu recently told a group of reporters while flying on the Boeing 767 aircraft bringing him to the United States, "I will tell the truth in the face of the sweet talk and the onslaught of smiles. One must talk facts and one must tell the truth."

He has laid out four areas he insists his Persian chess opponent-antagonists must agree to in order to begin truly moving toward resolving the ever-increasing buildup toward likely Mideast war:

- Halt uranium enrichment.
- Remove already enriched material.
- Close the Fordo nuclear facility.
- Discontinue the plutonium track in Arak.

As for the Persian mindset in this most dangerous game, Iranian Foreign Minister Mohammed Javad Zarif accused the Israeli prime minister of "lies and actions to deceive." The Iranian said further:

> International public opinion will not let these lies go unanswered....
>
> For 22 years, the Zionist regime has been lying by repeating endlessly that Iran will have the atomic bomb in six months. After all these years, the world must understand the reality of these lies and not allow them to be repeated.

With the prince of Persia whispering in the ear of the Iranians, who are in turn whispering in the ear of Mr. Obama, trying to convince him and the West that their intentions are to simply develop nuclear power for peaceful purposes, Mr. Netanyahu's response was to offer his own assessment to the president, according to the following account:

> In his Oval Office meeting with Obama on Monday, Netanyahu urged the US president to tighten sanctions on Iran and said that Israel reserves the right to wage a unilateral military campaign against Iran's nuclear facilities should the words of Iranian President Hassan Rouhani not quickly be followed by constructive action.[105]

There's another prince who will stand with Israel, when all others abandon God's chosen nation:

> And at that time shall Michael stand up, the great prince which standeth for the children of thy people: and there shall be a time of trouble, such as never was since there was a nation even to that same time: and at that time thy people shall be delivered, every one that shall be found written in the book.
>
> Daniel 12:1

October 14, 2013
Satan's Number-One Priority

There are today so many obvious assaults against God-given principles through which we are meant to comport ourselves, that choosing any as the number-one assault should be a difficult thing to do. But, it isn't, as I believe we will understand upon reaching the end of this essay.

We can with certainty state that in America at this moment, Satan is leading assaults on God's prescription for marriage. It is working. Not too many years ago, more than 70 percent of people involved in romantic relationships in the United States got married, in the legal sense. These were man-woman marriages. Today, fewer than 50 percent are getting married, choosing to engage in live-in arrangements. But, the number of marriages of men to men and women to women, although still low, is growing. It is more than obvious that this is a satanically inspired trend that is prophetically scheduled to increase. (Jesus said it will be like it was in the days of Lot when He next intervenes, catastrophically, into the history of man. Homosexuality was at the heart of Sodom's society and culture.)

This isn't, however, the top assault Satan and his minions are making on this generation.

An even more horrific attack on humanity is the murder of babies in their mothers' wombs. The evil one has convinced a large section of those who claim to be the most compassionate, caring, intelligent among us—the "progressives"—that burning little ones to death in the womb, ripping them apart, or—if still breathing upon making it to birth—killing them by severing the spine is nothing more than birth control after the fact. At this infanticide—getting rid of human beings like refuse—the devil has been most successful.

This isn't, though, his number-one priority.

The great deceiver incessantly attacks the human, fallen mind, inciting the greed within, fanning the flames of avarice. The result is movement toward one-world, economic enslavement, in which the few intend to control the rest of us by severely governing our ability to buy and sell. The devil is working, seemingly to perfection, his plan to one day install the 666 beast system of Revelation 13:16–18. Even this love-of-money incitement, though, is not the number-one assault being made by Lucifer, the fallen one.

His absolute hatred for the creation called man is eclipsed only by his insane detestation of the God of heaven. He drives the hatreds man has for his fellow man, instigating conflicts and wars at every opportunity. In this he has been highly successful, with well over fifteen thousand wars being waged and countless millions of lives being destroyed over the centuries.

This carnage is increasing, with the twentieth century seeing the most prolific loss of life in war ever, due to the horrendous capability of modern weaponry. With the fantastic weaponry available now—and that's on the drawing boards of the military-industrial complex that studies war-making—there will come warfare that will make even World Wars I and II pale by comparison. We know that Armageddon looms.

But, again, this is not Satan's number-one assault on this generation.

Then, his number-one assault must be to bring all the world into a hatred for God's chosen people, Israel, I can hear some surmising. Certainly the words of the prophet Zechariah can be seen materializing into reality before our amazed eyes:

> The burden of the word of the Lord for Israel, saith the Lord, which stretcheth forth the heavens, and layeth the foundation of the earth, and formeth the spirit of man within him.
>
> Behold, I will make Jerusalem a cup of trembling unto all the people round about, when they shall be in the siege both against Judah and against Jerusalem.
>
> And in that day will I make Jerusalem a burdensome stone for all people: all that burden themselves with it shall be cut in pieces, though all the people of the earth are gathered together against it.
>
> Zechariah 12:1–3

We have gone over many times how this is an all-important plan of Satan—to destroy that people. God's ultimate salvation plan would be thwarted, were this to happen, because the Lord's promises would have been proven false. The fallen one has made great strides in bringing all against Israel, and this assault certainly continues—sometimes seemingly unabated.

Yet, as integral to Satan's war on God and man is to his fiendish intentions, the destruction of Israel is not his number-one objective in assaulting this generation. Time after time it has been seen that the most powerful plans are often the simplest. So it is with Satan's plan to destroy as much of humanity as possible in the short time I believe he is aware he has left.

I am convinced that Satan's number-one priority is to convince as much of mankind as possible to do away with one particular Scripture. That's it! Just do away with one Scripture, and the devil's plan will blossom to full bloom...and men, women, and children will be swept into the abyss.

I must give proper credit to whom credit is due. The person who piqued my interest in this fact is Dr. Billy Crone of Sunrise Baptist Church of Las Vegas, Nevada. Noah Hutchings, president of Southwest Radio Ministries, interviewed Dr. Crone, and the programs aired October 2, 3, and 4.[106] Satan's number-one priority is to convince America's Christians that Jesus wanted, above all, unity of belief. Jesus Christ wanted us to accept that unity of all religious systems must be achieved—that His followers must learn to tolerate each other and all other "believers," no matter their "beliefs." If this happens, all wars will be eliminated, because—Satan wants us to believe—all wars are instigated in one way or another by religious intolerance.

Secondly, the devil wants us to believe that the real gospel involves the realization that we must not be judgmental. This, you see, is closely related to intolerance—the basis for all hatred, bigotry—and, well, for wars.

If we just would not be judgmental, the rant goes, we would tolerate all religious belief systems. This would produce unity, which is what Christ taught. He wanted all "believers" to come together in unity. Thus, the "progressives" of the religious world within Christianity exclaim they are correct in saying we must accept all ways to God, ways proposed by each and every religion of the world.

Strangely, it is only Christianity that, in actuality, overtly hangs onto one way only!

Dr. Crone pointed out that John 3:16 has been replaced today in the church, particularly as the most quoted by younger people. He stated the statistics to prove his contention—statistics that I don't recall at the time of this writing. The Scripture that has replaced John 3:16 as the most-quoted Scripture is the following:

Judge not, that ye be not judged.

Matthew 7:1

This is the verse that is thrown in the face of every Christian who witnesses that Jesus is the only way to salvation. We are not to "judge" others, or their religions.

Like all Scripture taken out of context, a case can be made in this instance that convolutes the Word of God. This sounds so pious and condemning of being judgmental—of intolerance. But, the meaning in context of the Scripture is that we must judge rightly, righteously. One does that by first making sure one is in right (righteous) relationship with God through Christ. That is the teaching of God's Word about having good judgment. Unless we have the mind of Christ, and are subject to Holy Spirit guidance, we cannot judge another. In Christ, we are discerning of truth and of the false.

But, the father of lies has convinced an ever-growing number of Christians and, of course, multiplied millions of others, that the new Scripture personifying Christianity is Matthew 7: 1, rather than John 3:16.

However, that replacement attempt does not constitute Satan's number-one priority to which I'm referring here.

What, then, is Satan's number-one priority that supersedes all other priorities in his assault on the world today?

It is this: That one certain verse must be forever done away with in the minds and hearts of those who claim Christianity. To do away with this Scripture means there will one day come acceptance of all other religious systems. An ecumenical system will one day amalgamate into spiritual unity that will give worship to Satan's man, Antichrist.

That verse is this:

I am the way, the truth, and the life.
No man cometh to the father but by me.

John 14:6

Get rid of that truth, and the way will be clear for there to be unity and tolerance. It will forever do away with judgmentalism. We recently heard Pope Francis give lip service to this new "tolerance" by implying there are many pathways to God. Jesus said, however, that He will one day say to those who fall victim to such satanic convolution of God's Word:

> And then will I profess unto them, I never knew you:
> depart from me, ye that work iniquity.
> Matthew 7:23

October 21, 2013
Prepping for Departure

These are times the entertainment industry gleefully uses to take advantage of those they see as nutcases. The supposed nutcases are those whose determination is to prepare for what they envision as the coming meltdown of civilization.

You can see the programs on the various channels during the course of any given week. The producers of such programs, it is obvious from the programming, pick and choose the most conspiratorially prone of the "preppers," as they are called, to film while the producers follow those preppers' every move.

You can sense from the tone of the narration that it is, for the most part, tongue-in-cheek so far as the producers of these programs are concerned. They are simply trying to entertain the viewers by doing case studies on the fringe "kooks" who are out there in the few wildernesses left in America.

Of course, the kooks themselves are clueless. They are dead serious about their prepping, and that makes it all the more entertainment fodder for the hip TV production crews as they send the filmed fruits of their labor into such areas as, particularly, the sophisticated, metropolitan regions of the Northeast and the cool, with-it West Coasters of places like San Francisco.

I think I'm considered in with the "nut jobs," at least until they talk to me, by the producers of such programming. It used to be that I only got emails, followed by phone calls, from the documentary producers who wanted my take on the Rapture. The Rapture is, of course, also fodder for entertaining the hip of the nation. However, now I am included in the producers' search for those who want to make the case for the prepping going on in this nation and elsewhere. In most cases, I never hear from the producers again after the initial pre-interview. When those call, I give them the biblical explanation of these things, with chapter and verse. I don't go into my personal opinion—at least I rarely do so.

They don't seem to like the answers they get. I think it is because I usually end it with the gospel message, weaving it as adroitly as possible into my answers to their inquiries.

By the end of our conversations, they usually say something like, "Thank you so much. This is great. We'll get back shortly." Then they ask: "Do you know anyone we might talk to who says they know the day of the Rapture?" Or, in the case of this prepping question: "Can you give us the names of anyone who believes the world will soon be destroyed?"

I never give them the names they seek. I never hear from most of them again.

I have to say that I'm not a fan of the prepping TV programs. But I think it wise to at least think about having finances in order and some degree of preparations in place, like food and emergency-kit-type things in case of severe economic downturn, not unlike preparations that the wise citizens of places along the coastal areas might make, just to be ready in case of hurricane aftereffects.

But there seems to be a kind of prepping in reverse going on in this country and around the world. This is what I want to address, if I may explain…

The prepping for truly bad times to come is being done, as I see it, by government and its enablers/propagandists in mainstream media, in particular. Forget the masses. They are, for the most part, absorbed into the entertainment and day-to-day ether that obscures all perception of what's really going on around them. They seem blissfully ignorant when it comes to the preparatory activity taking place, readying the hapless masses for fulfillment of Bible prophecy.

Two areas I see as most obvious are those involving economy and religion. Another is preparations being made for setting up the false peace that will bring all nations to Armageddon—but that one will have to take second place for the moment.

Anyone who has carefully examined the financial upheaval since 2006 or so, leading into the 2008 collapse and rise in debt of nations around the world, and particularly in America, will acknowledge that control of finances by individuals has forever been usurped by governments who have mortgaged the futures of the citizenry of those indebted national entities. This is all about prepping for fulfillment of Bible prophecy, although largely not realized by those in governments who have done the usurping.

It is the same in the religious realm. All have been prepping. Congresses and presidents, parliaments and prime ministers in the Western nations have for decades been turning out the light of Christianity by proposing banning God, particularly the name of Jesus Christ, from public places. Many ways to God are embraced within the governance of the people in the name of "tolerance," although total neutrality is preferred by the increasingly agnostic leaders. Jesus Christ is unmentionable, proving the Lord's word as true that the world would hate Him, and eventually, will hate all who claim His Holy Name through belief in Him. This is all prepping by the humanistic, one-world builders who are determined to establish change. They want change that doesn't include God in any fashion except that which will be the god of this world once this false religious system comes to fruition.

We find this religious and economic prepping's prophetic culmination in 2 Thessalonians 2 and Revelation 13. The way is being prepped for worldwide religious worship, as given in Revelation 13: 8:

> And all that dwell upon the earth shall worship him, whose names are not written in the book of life of the Lamb slain from the foundation of the world.

The object of this New-World-Order worship is found in the following prophetic passage given through the apostle Paul:

> Let no man deceive you by any means: for that day shall not come,
> except there come a falling away first,
> and that man of sin be revealed, the son of perdition;
>
> Who opposed and exalteth himself above all that is called God,
> or that is worshipped; so that he as God sitteth in the
> temple of God, shewing himself that he is God.
>
> 2 Thessalonians 2:3–4

Prepping is being carried out at every level of culture and society by Satan-inspired human governments for fulfillment of Bible prophecy. That prophecy involving worldwide economic control is found in the following:

> And he caused all, both small and great, rich and poor, free and
> bond, to receive a mark in their right hand, or in their foreheads:
>
> And that no man might buy or sell, save he that had the mark,
> or the name of the beast, or the number of his name.
>
> Here is wisdom. Let him that hath understanding
> count the number of the beast: for it is the number of a man;
> and his number is Six hundred threescore and six.
>
> Revelation 13:16–18

So, how should the Christian be prepping for the bleak future that is immediately set before us? I think the following scriptural admonitions are the best preparation to be found:

> Lay not up for yourselves treasures upon earth, where moth and
> rust doth corrupt, and where thieves break through and steal:

> But lay up for yourselves treasures in heaven,
> where neither moth nor rust doth corrupt,
> and where thieves do not break through nor steal.
>
> Matthew 6:19–20

The most solid advice of all is given to us by the Word of God as follows:

> Trust in the Lord with all thine heart; and lean
> not unto thine own understanding.
>
> In all thy ways acknowledge him,
> and he shall direct thy paths.
>
> Proverbs 3:5-6

Then we are to do the following:

> And when these things begin to come to pass, then look up,
> and lift up your heads; for your redemption draweth nigh.
>
> Luke 21:28

October 28, 2013
The Pope, the Pen, and Peace

Jorge Mario Bergoglio—Pope Francis, 266th pontiff of the Catholic Church—seems to be taking the world by storm. He is, of course, the 112th pope since twelfth-century Irish Bishop, St. Malachy, "prophesied" that the last pope would be number 112 from the time he made the "prophecies," as we've all learned about by now.

Obviously, he hasn't overtly taken the official name "Petrus Romanus," Peter the Roman, as Malachy predicted would be the moniker of the final pope who would preside over the Catholic Church during an era of the greatest time of trouble in its history. Let's think again briefly upon what Malachy said he foresaw. Malachy's biographer, St. Bernard of Clairvaux, reported in *Life of Saint Malachy* that St. Malachy wrote briefly, in

Latin, on each succeeding pope of the future, and then gave the document to Pope Innocent II, who had it placed in Vatican archives, where it remained for several centuries. It was rediscovered in 1590 and published.

Some scholars who have studied these predictions carefully claim that Malachy was remarkably accurate about succeeding popes right up through Pope Benedict XVI, who abdicated his papal throne in 2013. Others who have looked into these things have found that in most cases regarding the Malachy prophecies, the bishop's predictions were too oblique, too veiled, or couched in esoteric description to be validated as having been fulfilled to any great extent. Our conclusion must be that, while most of Malachy's "prophecies" about the popes are questionable as to absolute proof that the bishop was accurate in every case, there is little doubt that the 112th pope from the time he wrote the predictions is a strange pope to be sure.

The world at large literally loves the guy. His popularity really jumped on a global scale, especially in the view of national and international mainstream media, when he implied that there might be many ways to God and heaven and declared that Christians must be more tolerant of things we don't embrace or understand. At least, that was the gist of his statements.

The pope made it clear in a number of statements in various speaking forums that the Catholic Church and all of Christendom must cease condemning and excluding from God's kingdom homosexuals and those who hold other religious views than those that are Jesus Christ-centered.

That sentiment, even among a growing number within so-called Christian churches, is a visceral part of all of humanism's elite and their mouthpieces. The Christian Bible and its harsh, restrictive, "one way to God" is intolerant, bigoted, homophobic, and bordering on fundamentalist insanity that desires to bring the world to Armageddon. (The pope didn't say that; I did, based upon the pontiff's stance of recent days that has won him great accolades.)

America's current president is perhaps the most recent of the global leaders to express this pope's elevated standing in his opposition to biblical restrictions. Barack Obama said recently: "I have been hugely impressed with the pope's pronouncements." He described Pope Francis as "somebody who lives out the teachings of Christ [who, by the way, claimed He is the only way to God, the Heavenly Father]. Incredible humility—incredible sense of empathy to the least of these, to the poor."

In his interview with the CNBC business news channel, Obama was asked about Francis' recent comment that the Catholic Church has become too "obsessed" with issues like gay rights and abortion. Obama said:

> [Pope Francis is] somebody who is—I think first and foremost—thinking about how to embrace people as opposed to push them away; how to find what's good in them as opposed to condemn them.... And that spirit, that sense of love and unity, seems to manifest itself in not just what he says, but also what he does. And, you know, for any religious leader, that's something—that's a quality I admire.[107]

Sure sounds good, doesn't it? Unity—that's the ticket for the coming Antichrist system. Unity means to embrace all belief systems as acceptable to God's prescription for living on planet earth, according to the globalists elite. This is the route to "peace."

We are to embrace those religionists who behead women for having been raped. We are to accept as brothers those who murder anyone with whom they don't agree.

Pope Francis met a week or so ago with Palestinian president Mahmoud Abbas. He wasn't prepared to give the Israeli prime minister an audience, however. Yet, he is pushing the peace process so Palestine can have its statehood on Israel's tiny land mass.

The pope gave the Palestinian leader a special pen. He said when handing it to him, "Surely, you have a lot of things you have to sign."

Abbas responded, "I hope to sign a peace treaty with Israel with this pen."

My thought was, upon reading about the pope's generosity, the first beast of Revelation chapter 13 will have a sidekick who will—like Mr. Big himself—push the peace that will be the covenant made with death and hell (Isaiah 28:15, 18).

NOVEMBER 2013

November 4, 2013
Anti-Biblical Prophetic Trend

Troubling matters have leaped to the surface of evangelical Christianity in recent days. Movement away from some of the basic tenets of prophetic truth is being expressed by teachers many of us thought were immune to such corruption.

At the outset of this essay, I'll say that I don't intend to mention names, because I don't wish to have what I will write here seen as being personal attacks on individuals. That is not my purpose. My purpose is, rather, to point to egregious error so that readers will be aware of the false premises being foisted in these waning days of this Church Age.

The ones who are bringing the error to the surface of discourse are not neophytes to Bible prophecy. They are among the most respected and noteworthy of such teachers. Therefore, it is doubly necessary that you be aware of what is being proposed by them.

Before getting to the alarming claims by these prophecy teachers, we will look at trends that have perhaps prepared the way for false teaching along this line to emerge. Seeds have long been planted that make fertile the ground for growth of such serious error.

First, we look at the so-called unity movement, which is more an unspoken way of doing business in the modern evangelical church than a specific, official movement. It is nonetheless a concerted, lockstep march in the same direction—a march toward the heresy of inclusiveness. Jesus Christ, as the way, the truth, and the life, and as the only way to God the Father, you see, is too harsh, too...well...exclusive. Did not Jesus, Himself, welcome all sinners? Did He not go into the homes of sinners, and even meet one on one with prostitutes and demon-possessed persons?

To shut out the world as we live in it—in which we must operate every day—is to keep people from coming to Christ. Those outside the fold have to be welcomed into the confines of our organized church activities. To make them comfortable, our services must be tailored to reflect that to which they are accustomed, to some extent.

Our music, in particular, must be instrumentally orchestrated and beat oriented to provide the rhythmic pulsations that make all, especially the youth, feel right at home.

"Old fogey!" I can hear the challenges begin. Yes. I'll admit to probably being a "back number," as Dr. J. Vernon McGee would put it.

But, my concern goes beyond personal musical preference for style of service in the sanctuary. It is the melding of the world in these unity-type churches that is at the heart of this critique. Such melding sets the stage for doctrinal corruption. And, such has already set in, in a major way.

Jesus does indeed embrace all who come to Him—but on His terms, not ours. He told the rich, young ruler to go and sell all he had, and then come follow Him. This was not merely a call for the young man to give all he had to the poor, or to Jesus' church organization, but to divest himself of anything that would encumber the young man's worship of Christ, who would be his Savior.

The unity-type church today is saying "Bring all of the world influences you love into the worship with you. There is little difference in this environment and the one you are so afraid you might lose by accepting Jesus as your Savior."

This movement away from sound Bible doctrine isn't only happening in fringe denominational or other groups within what is known by secular observers as Christendom. It is rampant now within worship bodies that were once spiritually sensitive to the apostle Paul's warning:

> I charge thee therefore before God, and the Lord Jesus Christ,
> who shall judge the quick and the dead
> at his appearing and his kingdom;

> Preach the word; be instant in season, out of season; reprove, rebuke, exhort with all longsuffering and doctrine.
>
> For the time will come when they will not endure sound doctrine; but after their own lusts shall they heap to themselves teachers, having itching ears;
>
> And they shall turn away their ears from the truth, and shall be turned unto fables.
>
> But watch thou in all things, endure afflictions, do the work of an evangelist, make full proof of thy ministry.
>
> 2 Timothy 4:1–5

I intended when beginning this writing to go into a number of other things that have been spawned by movement away from Bible truth in these closing days of the age, things like the "Jesus-only movement," the lie wrapped up in "dual covenant" inculcation, and especially the "many ways to salvation" championed by an exponentially growing number of people within evangelical Christianity and without. But, alas! Those will have to wait another time of examination.

I must get right to the matter of the false teaching that has surfaced in recent days by some Bible prophecy teachers whom I previously thought impervious to such corruption. I'm talking about the proposition—actually, the firmly held belief, apparently—that following the Rapture, those who accept the mark of the beast will still have a chance to be saved—that is, go to heaven. This is their claim, and it has raised quite a furor.

Here is what God's Word plainly says about those who will in that Tribulation time accept the mark of the beast, which means they will agree to worship Antichrist as God:

> And he causeth all, both small and great, rich and poor, free and bond, to receive a mark in their right hand, or in their foreheads:

> And that no man might buy or sell, save he that had the mark,
> or the name of the beast, or the number of his name.
>
> Revelation 13:16-17

That description of the process of taking the mark is followed by a precise overview of the unmistakable consequences that will result:

> And the third angel followed them, saying with a loud voice,
> If any man worship the beast and his image, and receive his mark
> in his forehead, or in his hand,
>
> The same shall drink of the wine of the wrath of God, which is
> poured out without mixture into the cup of his indignation; and he
> shall be tormented with fire and brimstone in the presence of the
> holy angels, and in the presence of the Lamb:
>
> And the smoke of their torment ascendeth up for ever and ever:
> and they have no rest day nor night, who worship the beast and his
> image, and whosoever receiveth the mark of his name.
>
> Revelation 14:9-11

We must hold firm to absolute truth given in God's Word, no matter whether it seems fair or whether considering any other human divergence from what is written by the holy hand of God. Here's what the Creator of all things has to say about His Word—especially His prophetic Word:

> For I testify unto every man that heareth the words of the prophecy
> of this book, If any man shall add unto these things, God shall add
> unto him the plagues that are written in this book:
>
> And if any man shall take away from the words of the book of this
> prophecy, God shall take away his part out of the book of life, and out
> of the holy city, and from the things which are written in this book.
>
> Revelation 22:18-19

November 11, 2013
On Being Rapture Worthy

Lately, emails and articles I've been receiving are trending toward the thought that Christians who are not living exemplary lives as believers will miss being taken in the Rapture of the church, should they not be fully "repented up" and ready to go. These will be "left behind," as the Tim LaHaye and Jerry Jenkins novel title puts it. First, it is perhaps best to consider what is meant by the "exemplary life" in terms of prerequisites for making it to heaven in the Rapture.

Those who insist that one must be living the exemplary life usually frame that as "living a life of holiness" or "living righteously." By this, I presume they mean for the most part that one must be doing "good works" rather than living life in the "broad way" along which the pedestrian world moves. I would, of course, agree that the born-again believer in the Lord Jesus Christ should be doing exactly that every day. There's no question that God's Word calls us to that model for life while upon this fallen planet.

However, the question is now raised—and it is closely akin to the question raised whenever the declaration is made that one can lose one's salvation: At what point does one "lose" his or her salvation? What particular "sin point" is reached that causes the salvation meter in heaven to go TILT, removing the sinner's name from the Lamb's Book of Life? Or, for our purposes here, at what point does one sin enough to be taken off the list of those who hold tickets into heaven, who will be lifted to be with Jesus Christ in that millisecond of time known as the "twinkling of an eye" when Jesus calls "Come up hither!" (Revelation 4:1–2)?

Those who believe that the names of the redeemed can be removed from the Lamb's Book of Life, of course, use the following Scripture as one that prove their position is true:

> He that overcometh, the same shall be clothed in white raiment; and I will not blot out his name out of the book of life, but I will confess his name before my Father, and before his angels.
>
> Revelation 3:5

This is proof, say the "conditional security" proponents, that one's name can be removed from the Book of Life. But, let's have a closer look to examine whether this is true.

Those who hold that believers' names can be erased from this blessed Book of Life insist that the born-again must "overcome" sin. In their belief dictionary, this means we must stay sin-free—that is, either live above sin or stay continually "repented up" in order to keep our names in the Book.

They miss the point entirely as to who actually does the overcoming. It isn't the believer who overcomes all sin, but the Lord Jesus, who died in order to take sin away from those who believe so that we are no longer separated from God the Father in the eternal sense. This is seen, for example, in the following:

> For whatsoever is born of God overcometh the world:
> and this is the victory that overcometh
> the world, even our faith.
>
> Who is he that overcometh the world, but he that
> believeth that Jesus is the Son of God?
>
> 1 John 5:4-5

It is simple belief in the Savior who takes away the sins of the world that makes us overcomers. We still sin and come short of the glory of God, but His precious blood shed at Calvary covers all of our sins—past, present, and future. We overcome the world, the flesh, and the devil—all sin in this earthly sphere—only by belief in the only begotten Son of God (John 3:16). Our overcoming is only through God's great grace, through faith. We can never overcome by our own power.

When we sin, we break fellowship with our Lord, but we never break the eternal, family relationship. We do the following to take steps toward making right the sinful break in fellowship that we have caused. First, we must realize and admit that we are not sinless, because repentance cannot truly be made unless we confess that we have sinned. Upon such confession and repentance there is given blessed remedy:

> If we say that we have no sin, we deceive ourselves,
> and the truth is not in us.
>
> If we confess our sins, he is faithful
> and just to forgive us our sins,
> and to cleanse us from all unrighteousness.
>
> 1 John 1:8-9

God's Word shows us that our salvation and our ability to overcome are totally based on what Christ did for us and our faith in Him alone. This brings us to the matter of the title of this week's article, "On Being Rapture Worthy."

Going to Christ when He calls as Paul outlines in 1 Corinthians 15:51–55 and 1 Thessalonians 4:13–18, and given by John in Revelation 4:1–2, is a salvation matter. We know that from the overall gospel message and from the total context of God's dealing with His family. Remember when Jesus prayed that beautiful prayer to His Father, as the Lord faced the cross (John 17)? Read it again, and you will see that it is absolutely clear that born-again believers are forever secure in the Father's hand, based upon what Jesus did on the cross.

We know with absolute certainty that we are once and forever in God's family because of the words of the One who created all that exists:

> My Father, which gave [them] me, is greater than all;
> and no [man] is able to pluck [them] out of my Father's hand.
>
> John 10:29

Paul confirms that the Rapture is a salvation matter as follows:

> For God hath not appointed us to wrath,
> but to obtain salvation by our Lord Jesus Christ,
>
> Who died for us, that, whether we wake or sleep,
> we should live together with him.

Wherefore comfort yourselves together,
and edify one another, even as also ye do.
1 Thessalonians 5:9–11

The Rapture will be Christ keeping us from the hour of temptation or Tribulation (read Revelation 3:10). The Tribulation is the time of God's wrath, to which Paul tells us we are "not appointed." However, many insist that Christians who haven't properly confessed their sins will go through that time of God's wrath (and the entire seven years of the Tribulation will be God's judgment and wrath). These use the following verse to make their case:

Watch ye therefore, and pray always, that ye may be accounted
worthy to escape all these things that shall come to pass,
and to stand before the Son of man.
Luke 21:36

The key word they hold forth as relevant here is the word "worthy." Does this word not mean that we as born-again believers must be good enough to stand before Jesus in that raptured throng? Does this word not mean, therefore, that if we fail to live up to God's standards while on this earth, we will (at some point in God's holy view of what it takes to fall from being Rapture ready) lose our ticket in that translation moment, thus not be taken when the shout is heard, "Come up hither!"?

Like in examining the issue of salvation, in looking at the term "overcoming," we now look at the word "worthy." What does it mean to be "worthy," as given in this Rapture example? Again, the answer is wrapped up in the same name as before: Jesus. Jesus is the only person worthy, in God's holy eyes, to be in the heavenly realm.

Remember what Jesus said to a man who addressed Him as "Good Master"?

And Jesus said unto him, Why callest thou me good?
none is good, save one, that is, God.
Luke 18:18

Jesus, the second person of the Godhead, was not seeking to chastise the man for addressing Him in this way. The Lord was confirming through this question that He is indeed God, the only good, the only righteousness. Righteousness is the only ticket to heaven, either through the portal of death or through the Rapture. Only through Jesus can a person enter the heavenly realm.

Jesus spoke to this all-important matter by addressing Nicodemus:

> Jesus answered and said unto him,
> Verily, verily, I say unto thee,
> Except a man be born again,
> he cannot see the kingdom of God.
>
> John 3:3

God's Word says about fallen mankind:

> As it is written, There is none righteous no not one.
>
> Romans 8:10

> For all have sinned and come short of the glory of God.
>
> Romans 8:23

So, Jesus is the only person "worthy" to enter heaven. It is through Him that any of us are worthy to stand before Him in that heavenly realm. That is the truth found in the Scripture in question.

On a less magnificent scale, the word "worthy" in this passage means that we should be in a constant mindset of prayerful repentance. We should always want to be found "worthy"—cleansed of all unrighteousness, as stated in 1 John 1: 9 so that we will hear our Lord say to us on that day:

> Well done, good and faithful servant.
>
> Matthew 25:23

November 18, 2013
It's Peace or Else...

Peace is again about to take front and center stage in the ongoing drama of *Israel vs. the world.* There is no other matter so relevant to end-of-the-age prophecy than what is about to unfold.

While Obamacare and its nation-degrading effects are raging in American news headlines, far more significant matters are shaping up for a confrontation of truly monumental consequence. With all of the other signals of the coming Tribulation in view (and having been in view for many months, even years), pressures that attempt to force Israel to accept peace are growing, led by the American presidential administration.

Most mainstream journalists and pundits are wringing their hands over the fear that President Obama is about to lose the supposed key to his presidential legacy, the establishing of socialized medicine in America. The actual quest to forge that legacy, however, rumbles ominously upon the battle front of an ages-long war to bring the false peace that will set in motion man's final conflict, Armageddon. It is on this front that the president really wants to make his mark.

It seems that the leadership of the Islamist Palestinian Liberation Organization (PLO) and other organizations, the leadership of the international community, and Obama administration State Department, diplomatic interlocutors have just realized something I've been pointing out for some time. Israeli Prime Minister Benjamin Netanyahu has been playing them along in exactly the way Yasser Arafat, who has now gone on to his seventy-two virgins in Allahland, used to play the international community and the American government.

The Ringo Starr look-alike Arafat would smile slyly and tell us all that he was willing to sit down and reasonably discuss Israel giving up land for peace. But, even when he was handed everything he wanted with the exception of total ownership of the Temple Mount, he got up and walked out. Of course, if he hadn't done so, he would have forfeited his life as did Anwar Sadat, who made peace with Islam's chief enemy during the Carter administration. To the haters of Israel in the Middle East, nothing short of Netanyahu leading every last Jew into the Mediterranean, preferably with concrete and chains around their necks, would be a good enough "peace plan."

Suddenly, now, with Netanyahu slyly—like Arafat—saying he still is wanting peace, but that he wants to proceed slowly, sitting down to hammer out every nuance of the issues involved in potential peace, everybody on the opposite side of the table is demanding a broad, comprehensive peace. They demand that the Israeli leaders agree to such a non-nuanced plan.

Leading in this charge is American Secretary of State John Kerry, who has gathered with Israel's enemy leaders to forge such a plan. In the process, Mr. Netanyahu was left sitting on the outside, apparently not invited into the cabal to establish the peace that will save the world: save the world, and Israel be hanged!

The goings-on did not sit well with the Israeli leader, and his friend from France, who was privy to the meetings that excluded Israeli input to any extent, warned of dire consequences should a pact of any sort be framed contrary to Israel's well-being.

> A French member of Parliament telephoned French Foreign Minister Laurent Fabius in Geneva at the weekend to warn him that Prime Minister Benjamin Netanyahu would attack Iran's nuclear facilities if the P5+1 nations did not stiffen their terms on a deal with Iran, Israel's Channel 2 News reported Sunday....
>
> "I know [Netanyahu]," the French MP, Meyer Habib, reportedly told Fabius, and predicted that the Israeli prime minister would resort to the use of force if the deal was approved in its form at the time. "If you don't toughen your positions, Netanyahu will attack Iran," the report quoted Habib as saying. "I know this. I know him. You have to toughen your positions in order to prevent war."[108]

The powers that be are tightening the pressure, saying it's peace or else. It seems that Benjamin Netanyahu is countering. It will be a peace that destroys many, if that's the case.

That smacks of a Scripture I've read somewhere…

November 25, 2013
Cry for Peace: Chief Indicator

No sooner had I written the words, "Peace is again about to take front and center stage in the ongoing drama that is Israel versus the world," than we find ourselves arrived at that point. No other matter is so relevant to end-of-the-age prophecy than what is about to unfold. Some of the most recent headlines on our Rapture Ready News pages tell the story of the passion for peace—a flawed attempt to avoid war, I might add:

- Iran's Rouhani Warns West against "Excessive" Nuclear Demands Netanyahu
- Iran Has Enough Low-Grade Uranium for 5 Nuclear Bombs
- Abbas: Regardless of What Happens, Peace Talks to Continue
- Syria Peace Conference Likely in Mid-December
- Ex-IDF Intel Chief: Regional War Unlikely if Israel Strikes Iran
- Mossad Working with Saudis on Plans for an Attack on Iran
- The United States Must not Cease to Be Vigilant about Iran
- Israel and Strategic US Partner Fall Out over Iran

My prediction isn't because of any prescience on my part. The signals should be obvious to even the blind…well… like me, for example. But, the spiritually blind, I'm afraid, continue to miss the truly significant import of this end-times signal.

While the one-world builders of the international community fret over how the threat to world stability will affect their drive to achieve long-sought goals of enslaving the rest of us (for our own good, of course), the prophetic truth slips right past their cognitive awareness capability.

The unrest that is in the process of causing movement toward war, thus the almost frantic call for peace, is set forth in God's Holy Word. In terms of the world's top politicians, it looks like Benjamin Netanyahu might be the only one with an inkling that things going on between Israel and the rest of the world have been prophesied by the only One who knows the end from the beginning. I base this observation on Netanyahu recently bringing Old Testament quotations into his speeches. Even the Israeli prime minister, however, doesn't really recognize why things have come to this portentous point.

It should be obvious to anyone who studies the treatment of the Jewish people over the eons of time that war more often than not revolves around God's chosen people, and they are at the center of the issues of war and peace at this very moment while history bulldozes ahead, pushing all nations toward Armageddon.

With human intellectual curiosity being what it is, having brought forth answers to many questions of life on this planet, there should be a blazing curiosity to know why there has been a hatred for the Jews of such magnitude and in apparent perpetuity. But, there isn't.

"Christ-killers" was the accusation against the Jews by those of the Spanish Inquisition and other such periods. Adolf Hitler's ravings revolved around similar rants, mixed with racial accusatory insanity. They killed God's Son, is the primary scream of accusation. Yet, Hitler and all others of the Jew-hating world denied the very Son of God at every turn, making the whole matter beyond comprehension—that is, unless God's Word is believed by the observer of the long history of hatred of the Jewish race as absolute truth. Then it becomes understandable.

Here is the reason for the hatred: It is a spiritual anger that the world harbors against the Jew. The Bible pinpoints the reason the world, whose constituency—lost humanity—murders and persecutes God's chosen people. It is the inner rage that is the separation from the Creator that foments the insane notion that the Jews killed God's Son, all the while denying that God's Son be given any credence whatsoever.

And I will put enmity between thee and the woman,
and between thy seed and her seed;
it shall bruise thy head,
and thou shalt bruise his heel.
Genesis 3:15

Satan hates the human race and did his dead-level best to forever separate man from God. God provided the way to reestablish that broken, fallen relationship. Eve's offspring would eventually produce the Savior of the world, the Christ, who would bring redemption to those who believe and are born again (John 3:3).

It was through Eve's progeny, Abraham's seed, that Jesus came in the flesh into the world.

True peace can only be re-established when Christ is at the center of the relationship, no matter the relationship. Lucifer, the fallen one, uses the very Son of God in his mind-bending methodology of making the Jew the hated people who caused the death of the Christ, the Redeemer—who, of course, the devil hates with all his perverse heart. He continues to battle against the seed of the woman that eventually produced the Messiah—whom, sadly, that seed (the Jews) rejected. Israel today is at the center of all controversy that is leading to earth's final battle before Christ's return. The prophet Jeremiah gave the reasons this is so. The following Scriptures paint the picture of the rebellious chosen people, the Jews, and of the lack of peace that is prominent today in our headlines.

Why then is this people of Jerusalem slidden back by a perpetual backsliding? they hold fast deceit, they refuse to return.

I hearkened and heard, but they spake not aright:
no man repented him of his wickedness, saying,
What have I done? every one turned to his course,
as the horse rusheth into the battle.

Yea, the stork in the heaven knoweth her appointed times; and the turtle and the crane and the swallow observe the time of their coming; but my people know not the judgment of the Lord....

For they have healed the hurt of the daughter of my people slightly, saying, Peace, peace; when there is no peace.

Jeremiah 8:5–7, 11

Rebellious Israel and the whole world system so filled with satanic hatred for the nation will soon have to undergo God's mighty hand of course correction for Israel, and wrathful judgment for anti-God earth dwellers.

For when they shall say, Peace and safety;
then sudden destruction cometh upon them,
as travail upon a woman with child;
and they shall not escape.

1 Thessalonians 5:3

DECEMBER 2013

December 2, 2013
Big Prophetic Question

The Obama administration has just led the international community in pulling the proverbial rug out from under Israel. In putting the finishing touches on my book, *Cauldron: Supernatural Implications of the Current Middle East*, I wrote the following:

> Sunday, November 24, 2013, the Obama Administration, with Secretary of State John Kerry in the lead, joined with the inter-

national community in making an agreement with the Iranian regime that many view as a betrayal of Israel.

Just as the sanctions against Iran for pursuing development of a nuclear program to produce atomic weaponry was beginning to make an impact, the U.S., in concert with the world powers that constitute the international community, agreed to lift part of those economic sanctions on Iran for six months. The Islamic republic promised to cooperate with the international nuclear observers and to limit its enrichment of uranium.

The Israeli leadership—which wasn't privy to the behind-the scenes-dealings—wasn't deceived by the near jubilation displayed by the cabalist diplomats' actions. The Israelis realize that in Islam, it is not only okay to lie in negotiations with enemies, it's preferred. Ends justify means, just as in the Marxist playbook for dealing with adversaries. The Obama team was apparently not as immune to the venomous deception as Benjamin Netanyahu and his leadership team.

The Israeli Prime Minister said, "What was reached last night in Geneva is not a historic agreement, it is a historic mistake. Today the world became a much more dangerous place because the most dangerous regime in the world made a significant step in obtaining the most dangerous weapons in the world."

Israel's minister of intelligence, Yuval Steinitz, added that the deal was based on "Iranian deception and international self-delusion."

Israel, based upon a long history of dealing with treacherous enemies, is skeptical of Iran's claims that its nuclear program is strictly for peaceful purposes. The Jewish state has threatened a military strike against Iran as a preemptive measure against the acquirement of a nuclear weapon.

Luciferic influence, it is obvious to the observer who is biblically attuned to things prophesied for the end of days, rules the minds of those globalists who want peace at any price. The deception is becoming overwhelming.

Or, perhaps, the American negotiators in this instance are not as deceived as they are in collusion with the Israeli despisers. It certainly seems that this president has been, at almost every juncture, in opposition to Benjamin Netanyahu's vision for Israel and his government's determination to keep the Jewish state secure in these increasingly precipitous times.

Joel Rosenberg, in his blog of Tuesday, November 26, 2013, posted comments by Yossi Klein Halevi, the American-born Israeli author of *Like Dreamers: The Story of the Israeli Paratroopers Who Reunited Jerusalem and Divided a Nation*. Halevi said in an interview:

> If you're going to make a deal, this is the best deal they could make. But there should not have been a deal. The Iranian regime was being cornered. Sanctions might even have brought about the fall of the regime. This is an unthinkable surrender....
>
> Obama has created a condition in which Iran will be gradually reaccepted into the international community, and Israel could well find itself a pariah. That's Obama's gift to the Jewish people.... I think this deal makes an Israeli strike inevitable.

All of this throws some interesting fodder for thought into the matters involved in the Ezekiel 38–39 Gog-Magog assault. A big question mark has always been part of the puzzle in that attack, assuredly one of the most astounding prophecies for the time immediately preceding Christ's Second Advent. The question: With Israel's powerful arsenal of nuclear weapons, and if Iran (Persia) has nuclear weapons at that time, why are none, seemingly, used in the assault? The attack is described as a conventional land war, to my way of thinking. Iran seems to have no "super weapons" that they throw at the tiny nation while they rage with their allies toward Israel's borders.

God Himself is going to employ the "super weapon." It will destroy all but one-sixth of the invading force, the prophecy tells us. Some believe the reason nuclear weapons aren't used is that an EMP (electromagnetic pulse) event of some sort will have rendered most sophisticated weaponry useless at that time. The conventional thinking on the matter seems to be that Israel might have destroyed all facilities or at least damaged Iran's nuclear program enough to prevent its full development.

We can't know for sure, of course, why this war will be conducted as it is, according to Scripture. Nor are we likely to know this side of the Tribulation, which is the era during which I'm convinced the Gog-Magog assault will take place.

However, it is most interesting to conjecture. Might it eventuate that the Iranian mullahs fool everyone and agree to stop the development of their current nuclear program? Not likely, I agree, but they are known as masters of chessboard chicanery. Their friend Vladimir Putin—that great peacemaker—has proven he wants to exert increasing control over things to the south of his domain. Convincing the ayatollahs to temporarily cool their nuclear reactors for awhile while bigger things are afoot in Russia's and Iran's plans for Israel...well, it's legitimate fodder for consideration.

December 9, 2013
Israel Forever!

I am writing this piece this morning, the first day of the Pre-Trib prophecy conference in Dallas—the twenty-third such conference, according to Dr. Tim LaHaye, the founder of the forum. This year's conference is on Israel and that nation's destiny.

We have addressed this subject on a number of occasions, but it is one that never grows stale—at least not with me. And, the insights gained so far while listening to Dr. David Hocking made the trip worthwhile, even if I didn't plan to sit through another session. Israel is the prophetic signal—if one were to choose just one—that should prove to any rationally oriented mind that: 1) God's Word is true; and 2) This generation is very near the end of the dispensation of grace.

Dr. Hocking, one of the most knowledgeable scholars and speakers on Israel, spent forty-five minutes or so laying out the case for Israel being the one nation that is guaranteed to be such forever. In the process of his presentation, he, without having to say so, built the foundation to show that the God of the Bible is the one and only God.

He told how he had opportunity to witness to a cabbie who had driven him from the airport to the hotel. He said the cab driver made the mistake of asking what he was doing in Dallas. Dr. Hocking told him he was speaking at a conference. The cabbie, a Muslim a native of the Middle East, asked him what he was speaking on, and the conversation that followed was one of great interest. The shuttle van's driver said something about Allah being in charge of everything, and Dr. Hocking went into depth—for the brief duration of the ride from DFW to the hotel, how there is only one God and His Name is Yahweh. He didn't say—or I don't remember him reporting that he did so—how the conversation ended. But, David spoke the following morning with his head still attached, so I presume the driver didn't consider the infidel's offense of sufficient magnitude to take jihad action. Or, maybe Dr. Hocking didn't mention Mohammed, which seems to be the red line for employing the scimitar, like in the case we remember involving the writer Salman Rushdie from some years back.

Again, David Hocking's presentation was on Israel and her destiny. That topic is at the heart of what is going on, prophetically, in the world today. One question Hocking addressed was the question of whether Israel today is fulfillment of Bible prophecy. Is the modern state of Israel a literal fulfillment of Bible prophecy?

The more academic of Bible prophecy scholars—the seminarians—mostly hold that Israel being back in the land God gave the descendants of Abraham, Isaac, and Jacob, is "preparation" for fulfillment of prophecy, in their view, but not literal fulfillment of any specific prophecy. I was rather surprised, and pleasantly so, to learn that David Hocking considers it literal fulfillment, not merely preparation for fulfillment of prophecy from the futurist point of view.

Dr. Hocking certainly fits into the fold of academia, but his overwhelming, evidence-laden exposition on modern Israel being prophecy fulfilled in our time proved, to me, at least, that the academic purists within the pretrib view of eschatology camp are out of sync with what God predicts for Israel.

The bottom line is summed up scripturally with the prophetic words:

> He who keepeth Israel neither slumbers nor sleeps.
>
> Psalms 121:4

To put it another way—"Israel forever!"

December 16, 2013
Antichrist-Jordan Foretelling in View

Antichrist is going to rule the whole world at some point before Christ returns—right? That is the thought of many who have studied Bible prophecy throughout the decades. It is not an accurate assessment of what is scheduled, however.

Much of the thinking regarding the all-encompassing rule of the beast of Revelation chapter 13, Antichrist, is based upon the prophetic passage:

> And he causeth all, both small and great,
> rich and poor, free and bond, to receive a
> mark in their right hand, or in their foreheads.
>
> Revelation 13:16

It certainly appears from this portion of Scripture—Revelation 13:12–18—and others that the entire world of earth dwellers comes under Antichrist's beastly rule. But this is not the case.

There is a fancy term that defines why the simple word "all" doesn't necessarily mean "all." The term is "synecdoche," which, according to the *World English Dictionary*, is a figure of speech in which a part is substituted for a whole or a whole for a part, as in fifty head of cattle for fifty cows or the army for a soldier.

This means for our purposes here that the use of the expression "He causeth all" is a synecdoche, or representative of many people throughout the earth, but not necessarily every single individual on earth or every nation. The Bible might include a synecdoche in terms of geography, but never in matters dealing with the soul. In other words, when Paul wrote that "all" will be changed in the twinkling of an eye, he meant that literally everyone who is born again will be changed in that atomos of time that will be the moment of Rapture. When John wrote "He causeth all," he meant "all" in the synecdochical sense.

All of that explanation is to say that Antichrist will have absolute power over much of planet earth, but not all of it. He will not, according to Bible prophecy, be allowed to spread his tyrannical hegemony to the Middle Eastern nation of Jordan, for example. That prophecy is most interesting when considered in light of the news story just reported this past week.

> The Obama Administration and the Hashemite Kingdom of Jordan have both reportedly sided with Israel in its demand to retain control over the Jordan Valley in any future peace agreement with the Palestinians....
>
> Israel has long insisted that, even if it surrenders the bulk of Judea and Samaria (the so-called "West Bank"), it must retain control of the Jordan Valley as a buffer against future external threats, and as a deterrent and protection against Palestinian aggression.
>
> Jordan wants Israel in the Jordan Valley to prevent further influx of Palestinian Arabs into the Hashemite Kingdom. Jordan's Palestinian majority has threatened the Bedouin-backed Hashemite monarchy in the past, including in the 1970–1971 Jordanian Civil War.[109]

There has been over the decades an almost comfortable arrangement between Israel and Jordan. The late Jordanian King Abdullah (and now his son) has always received a degree of protection from Israel, the much-hated Arab enemy.

Of course, the geopolitical reason for the arrangement is that Jordan and surrounding area give Israel a buffer zone against attacks that could otherwise be launched, giving the Jewish state a much shorter warning time. However, the real reason for the peaceful arrangement doubtless derives from heavenly directive. Jordan is scheduled to escape the deadly Antichrist regime's tyrannical grip during the time of Tribulation. There are interesting aspects of this apparently heaven-given arrangement we will examine momentarily.

Let's look first at the prophesied rise of Antichrist in the region and the lead-up to the matter of Jordan escaping his murderous control. Daniel the prophet gives the beast of Revelation 13 the title "the king":

> And in his estate shall stand up a vile person, to whom they shall not give the honour of the kingdom: but he shall come in peaceably, and obtain the kingdom by flatteries.
>
> And with the arms of a flood shall they be overflown from before him, and shall be broken; yea, also the prince of the covenant.
>
> Daniel 11:21-22

> And the king shall do according to his will; and he shall exalt himself, and magnify himself above every god, and shall speak marvelous things against the God of gods, and shall prosper till the indignation be accomplished: for that that is determined shall be done.
>
> Daniel 11: 36

> He shall enter also into the glorious land, and many countries shall be overthrown: but these shall escape out of his hand, even Edom, and Moab, and the chief of the children of Ammon.
>
> Daniel 11:41

Daniel switches from ancient wars and conquest, as recorded in chapter 11 prior to verse 40, to suddenly bring the reader to the end of the age and the Antichrist's appearance and rampage across the pages of end-times history. This vile king overtakes many nations, but Daniel foretells that Edom, Moab, and the chief of the children of Ammon escape his terrible land grab.

Moab, which is in essence modern-day Jordan, it is fascinating to consider, isn't mentioned as part of the coalition in the Gog-Magog war of Ezekiel 38 prophesied to attack Israel. It is also interesting that Edom, part of modern Jordan, is the place the Lord will come from at the Second Advent in great fury. Bozrah was that area's capital. Here is what Isaiah said about that area when Christ returns to do battle with Antichrist and earth's rebels:

> Who is this that cometh from Edom, with dyed
> garments from Bozrah? this that is glorious in his apparel,
> travelling in the greatness of his strength?
> I that speak in righteousness, mighty to save.
>
> Wherefore art thou red in thine apparel,
> and thy garments like him that treadeth in the winefat?
>
> I have trodden the winepress alone; and of the people there was
> none with me: for I will tread them in mine anger, and trample
> them in my fury; and their blood shall be sprinkled upon my
> garments, and I will stain all my raiment.
>
> For the day of vengeance is in mine heart,
> and the year of my redeemed is come.
>
> Isaiah 63:1-4

Another fascinating point of prophecy to consider, seeing as how Jordan and its relationship with Israel is in the headlines, is that nation's apparent treatment of the Jews as Antichrist's full fury storms against them as given in Revelation 12. The remnant of Israel will escape into the wilderness while Satan's forces rage after them. It will be in the middle of Daniel's seventieth week, the last half or three and a half years into the time of "Jacob's trouble" (Jeremiah 30:7). All Jews are told to flee Jerusalem, for Antichrist's full fury will come against them.

The remnant of Israel will flee, many believe to Petra, the ancient, rose-red city. And that is, guess where, in the Jordanian desert area, somewhat south of the place known in ancient times as Bozrah.

Whether the hiding place is Petra or another, it almost will certainly be in the area of the Jordanian valley, and Christ will make a stop there, as we know, to save God's chosen people: the remnant (all) of believing Israel.

Jordan is proving to be one more indicator of this late date on God's prophetic timeline.

December 23, 2013
HeavenVision Revisited

Please indulge me just a bit in my using this week's column as a cathartic exercise, at least in part. I believe you will find my ruminations relevant to our purpose in presenting these articles each week.

Sunday, December 15, I received a phone call. It was Brenda, wife of a life-long friend, and I do mean life-long. Her husband, Howard, and I were born one month apart—Howard in El Dorado, Arkansas, and me in Camden, Arkansas. Each city is about the same distance from Hampton, a very small town in the southern part of the state. El Dorado is thirty miles south and Camden thirty miles west. They had the hospitals; Hampton didn't. Our parents both lived in Hampton, one block apart, when we were born.

I knew the news wasn't something I wanted to hear. Brenda and I, although friends, too, don't talk very much.

"Howard passed away about 12:30 this morning," she said.

Howard had, until about two years ago, been beating men in their forties in tennis, one of his passions in life. He wasn't prideful about it; he just enjoyed quietly—with finesse, not power—beating the tennis shorts off those youngsters, as we viewed them from our lofty perch in our late sixties at the time.

Howard was on his roof one day about two years ago, sweeping pine needles to the ground, when he suddenly got weak and had trouble breathing. His weakness increased and the doctors told him he had heart arrhythmia. They put in a pacemaker, but the problems persisted and increased. Finally, he was diagnosed with a degenerative heart disease that had to be treated with chemotherapy, although, as I take it, it wasn't cancer. The treatments were astronomical in cost and quite taxing on his body.

So, when I heard Brenda's voice, I knew instantly, even before she said so, that my life-long pal had passed into that glorious realm he often talked about during his many, many years of teaching Sunday school at First Baptist Church.

It was a long, painful time of dying, and I was relieved for him, although I will miss him greatly.

I have related in these columns about Good Friday, April 22, 2011, when, following a brisk workout, I suffered a "widow-maker" heart attack. To briefly restate what happened: My heart stopped at least three times and they brought me back from clinical death with defibrillation shocks. Each time, I was in the heavenly presence of a throng of young, cheering people. The last time the heart stopped, I was among that group, and we were running as if in a victory lap—I have since come to believe—toward the very gate that was the entrance to God's eternal abode.

I am totally blind, as many know, but could see perfectly well—even better than that—while with those young people. But then things grew dark again, and, each time, I returned to this earthly existence. On the final trip back, I returned to the catheterization lab, where they had removed the blockage to the affected artery. The interventional cardiologist who removed the blockage told my wife that I had been dead on arrival. He said that 95 percent of all who have this occurrence don't live through it. The cardiologists were so impressed with my case that they made me the Arkansas "Cardiac Patient of the Year." This gave me opportunity to tell the cardiologists in their meetings at Little Rock about how, while I appreciated everything their profession had done for me, it was the Lord

Jesus Christ who determined that I would return to fight another round or two.

My friend Howard and his wife Brenda were among the very first to show up in the cardiac ICU recovery room where I lay for the next several days. I was terribly disturbed because I didn't have an opportunity to visit Howard, except by phone, during his time of dying. He just felt too sick to receive company, and needed constant medical assistance. Visitors would disrupt that care.

Each morning when I have awakened since that time of visitation to the cloud of witnesses of Hebrews 12:1–2, I see them in my mind's eye. They are as clear in the deepest reaches of my spirit as if I were standing before them again.

Now, I constantly wonder if my friend Howard was met by this same group of cheering, jubilant youngsters. I'm a little envious, because I suspect he was escorted, in victory-lap fashion, through that gigantic gate of pearl and into the presence of Jesus Christ. I can see that scene, and I am blessed to have that picture as I cope with my wonderful friend's absence.

I wish I could convey the comfort and even joy that I sense knowing that Howard is in that heavenly realm. I, of course, can only try to paint that scene in word pictures.

December 30, 2013
2014 Prophecy Prospectus

The upcoming year invites a look into its major prophetic potentialities, based upon the way 2013 is ending. If this was a prospectus on any number of the general matters on which a prospectus is normally issued, it would be directed only to those who have invested interests or potential investment interests in the financial possibilities presented.

In other words, the prospectus would be highly limited in scope to but a relatively few people. For example, stockholders of a publicly held company would want to know the potential economic advantages that holding stock in that company offers. The analysis within a prospectus would be to inform potential investors about products and or services, now or in the immediate future, and probable company performance before they determined whether to buy new stock being offered.

Our prophecy prospectus differs in a couple of major ways from that just described: 1) Those investors potentially affected by future performance are neither limited in scope nor in numbers involved. Bible prophecy involves, literally, every person alive on planet earth. 2) The prophecy prospectus literally involves investment potentialities not of meager, earthly dollars and cents, but things that determine future dividends for investors throughout all of eternity.

We will try to analyze some of the primary issues and events at this year's end and project the prophetic trends, based upon that analysis as we move into 2014 and beyond.

Admittedly, this will offer only the very slightest look at these things. We will do so, not with hubris or self-aggrandizement; only the God of heaven knows the future. But, our Lord has indeed given us—and in many cases, in considerable detail—an overview of things to come. We are told by Him to "watch" (Mark 13:37) for those things to come that He promises us we can know, at least in general terms:

> Thus saith the LORD, the Holy One of Israel, and his Maker,
> Ask me of things to come concerning my sons,
> and concerning the work of my hands command ye me.
>
> Isaiah 45:11

> Howbeit when he, the Spirit of truth, is come,
> he will guide you into all truth: for he shall not speak of himself;
> but whatsoever he shall hear, that shall he speak:
> and he will shew you things to come.
>
> John 16:13

The Holy Spirit, God in His omniscience, gives those who are in His family both the ability and the command to watch for prophetic signals in discerning the times in which we live. Therefore, let us look at the prospects for 2014, with the confidence that we can achieve at least a certain degree of understanding about things to come.

The bottom line in considering things to come at this juncture is that the time of Tribulation is no longer just a faint rumble of distant thunder on the prophetic horizon. Every major element of Bible prophecy leading up to Christ's Second Advent can be discerned by anyone with a futurist viewpoint of biblical eschatology—that is, everyone who believes that there are major prophecies yet to be fulfilled. As the year 2013 closes, we very briefly analyze those key elements of prophecy yet future and consider the prospects for 2014 and thereafter.

Israel

Israel is at stage center for the final act of Satan's war against God to play out. The American president has exerted his power and authority, to considerable extent, in putting the Jewish state's prime minister on notice that Israel will be given U.S. support only if Israel complies with the stipulations Secretary of State John Kerry and the so-called Palestinian leadership contrive.

Chief among these matters of compliance is, apparently, the cessation of construction within Israel's sovereign territory. On the other hand, the Palestinians do not have to agree to even recognize Israel as a legitimate national entity. Certainly, for the immediate future, there can be no peace arrangement under this broad area of disagreement.

If the dreadful peace of Isaiah 28 is to be made, there will likely have to develop even more severe potential for war in the region, with the Palestinian leadership perceiving they will lose any chance to achieve statehood, I believe. Then, that leadership—like all good Islamists—will lie to agree to some of Israel's demands. Whether this government, led by Benjamin Netanyahu, will buy those lies is another matter. It seems to me that a much broader peace scheme must be in play for it to come up to the dimension of the Isaiah 28:15, 18 covenant, so look for the current peace efforts to limp along for quite awhile.

Iran

This nation that comprises most of ancient Persia smugly senses a weak U.S. administration, I suspect. It will play the game of Middle East chess until it is right back to doing within its mountainous underground nuclear laboratories what it has been doing since setting its sights on building a weapon that can carry out the mullahs' designs of hegemony over the entire region and the elimination of the hated little Satan—Israel.

Russia

Russia will continue to demonstrate it is resuming superpower status in its climb back from the fall as the U.S.S.R. Prophetically, Russia's ties to Iran can only grow stronger, even though the two nations will likely attempt to show, publicly, a marked independence from each other. I believe that Israel's increasing capabilities in the area of natural gas production and its growing gas industry's inroads into European and other markets greatly disturb Putin. Look for Russia to keep strengthening its military position and influence to the south.

Electronic control technologies: Electronic control technologies in the U.S. and on a global scale look to be growing ominously as the weeks roll on. Despite the National Security Administration and other scandals, with the divulgences by Edward Snowden and other revelations of privacy-destroying snooping by governments, the worldwide system of control is progressing geometrically and, perhaps, is already of sufficient strength and ubiquity to give Antichrist what he needs to subjugate most of the world's populations once he takes the reins of power as indicated in Revelation 13:16–18.

These are the areas of most particular prophetic relevance while we finish this year and look into the next, in my opinion. Other areas, such as economy, religion, and cultural matters are only slightly less critical in considering prospects for 2014. We will continue to look at these aspects of life as well through the prism of God's prophetic Word.

The most profitable investment any of us can make for the upcoming year is to pray, study God's Word, and put our efforts and resources into His kingdom for reaching souls of men, women, and children. We at Rapture Ready solicit your help in investing in that mission in 2014. Your "heavenly bank account" will increase beyond measure.

About the Author

Terry James is author, general editor, and coauthor of more than twenty books on Bible prophecy and geopolitics, hundreds of thousands of which have been sold worldwide. He has also written fiction and nonfiction books on a number of other topics. His most recent releases are:

- *Cauldron: Supernatural Implications of the Middle East*—an in-depth examination of the history of the Middle East struggles that reach back to the beginning of man's existence on planet earth and a look at the whole story—past, present, and future—of the ages-long, satanic conflict centered on that region of the country, a conflict that is pushing the world toward Armageddon.
- *Heaven Vision: Glimpses into Glory*—a collaboration with author Angie Peters in which the authors examine near-death experiences through the lens of what the Bible says about life after death and amazing promises about heaven.
- *Do Our Pets Go to Heaven?*—a collaboration with Thomas Horn and others that explores the comforting and exciting scriptural answers to that compelling, ages-old question.

James is a frequent lecturer on the study of end-time phenomena, and interviews often with national and international media on topics involving world issues and events as they might relate to Bible prophecy. He is partner with Todd Strandberg and general editor in the www.raptureready.com website, which was recently rated as the number-one Bible prophecy website on the Internet.

Notes

1. This excerpt originally appeared on a website entitled 2012endofdays.org, which is no longer operational.
2. Peter Leonard, "Russia's Putin Dreams of Sweeping Eurasian Union," Associated Press, 01/03/12, http://news.yahoo.com/russias-putin-dreams-sweeping-eurasian-union-084122179.html.
3. Sharon Udasin, "Oil Shale: A Sound Way to Achieve Energy Independence," *Jerusalem Post*, 01/03/12, http://www.jpost.com/Enviro-Tech/Oil-shale-A-sound-way-to-achieve-energy-independence.
4. David Blair, Peter Simpson, "Russia 'Worried' Over Iran's Nuclear Ambitions," *Telegraph*, 01/20/10, http://www.telegraph.co.uk/news/worldnews/middleeast/iran/9005134/Irans-Mahmoud-Ahmadinejad-and-Venezuelas-Hugo-Chavez-taunt-US-over-big-atomic-bomb.html. My thanks to Jonathan Stettin.
5. Mary Kay Linge, "Schools 'Spy' on Fat Kids," NYPOST.com, 01/15/12, http://nypost.com/2012/01/15/schools-spy-on-fat-kids/.
6. Ibid.
7. Ibid.
8. Jasmin Melvin, "Congress Puts Brakes on Anti-Piracy Bills," Reuters, 01/21/12, http://www.reuters.com/article/2012/01/20/us-usa-congress-internet-idUSTRE80J10X20120120.
9. Ibid.
10. Department of Homeland Security, "Operation Shield," http://www.dhs.gov/operation-shield.
11. Paul Joseph Watson, "DHS Officers Armed with Semiautomatics Set Up Unannounced ID Checkpoint," 05/05/12, http://www.infowars.com/dhs-officers-armed-with-semiautomatics-set-up-unannounced-id-checkpoint/.
12. *Arkansas Democrat-Gazette,* "In the News," 01/30/12.
13. Associated Press, "Jury Finds Afghan Family Guilty in Honor Killings," Fox News, 01/29/12, http://www.foxnews.com/world/2012/01/29/jury-finds-afghan-family-guilty-in-honor-killings/.
14. Khaled Yacoub, "Russia's Lavrov Seeks Peace in Syria as Forces Bombard Homs, Reuters, 02/07/12, http://www.reuters.com/article/2012/02/07/us-syria-idUSTRE80S08620120207. Thanks to Jonathan Stettin and to Dana Neel for news sources.

15. Alex Spillius and agencies, "Downing St.: Syria UN Vote 'Incomprehensible and Inexcusable,'" Telegraph, 02/06/12, http://www.telegraph.co.uk/news/worldnews/middleeast/syria/9063618/Downing-St-Syria-UN-vote-incomprehensible-and-inexcusable.html.
16. S. Isayev and T. Jafarov, "Russia-Iran Relations Are Fragile, Iran's Former President Says," Trend, 02/12/12, http://en.trend.az/regions/iran/1986722.html.
17. Valentina Pop, "Greek MPs Back Crucial Austerity Deal," EUobserver, 02/13/12, www.euobserver.com.
18. Stephen Bierman, "Striking Iran Would be Truly Catastrophic: Putin," Business Week, 02/26/12, http://www.businessweek.com/news/2012-02-26/striking-iran-would-be-truly-catastrophic-putin.
19. Vladimir Isachenkov, "Putin Warns West over Syria, Iran, Moscow," Associated Press, 02/28/12. Thanks to Jonathan Stettin for news items.
20. Ted Thornhill, "What's Causing the Mysterious Sounds Coming from the Sky That Are So Loud They Set Off Car Alarms?", Mail Online, 03/06/12, http://www.dailymail.co.uk/sciencetech/article-2110523/Whats-causing-mysterious-sounds-coming-sky-loud-set-car-alarms.html.
21. Philip Pullella, "Pope Denounces U.S. Political Push to Legalize Gay Marriage," Reuters, 03/09/12, http://www.reuters.com/article/2012/03/09/us-pope-gays-idUSBRE8280TQ20120309.
22. Michael Snyder, "Saudi Arabia and China Team Up to Build a Gigantic New Oil Refinery—Is This the Beginning of the End for the Petrodollar?" The Economic Collapse, 03/22/12, http://theeconomiccollapseblog.com/archives/saudi-arabia-and-china-team-up-to-build-a-gigantic-new-oil-refinery-is-this-the-beginning-of-the-end-for-the-petrodollar.
23. "Bolton Accuses Administration of Leaking Story on Israeli Planning along Iran Border," Fox News, 03/29/12, http://www.foxnews.com/politics/2012/03/29/bolton-accuses-administration-leaking-story-on-israeli-planning-along-iran/.
24. Sean Hannity, "The Real Obama: Betraying Israel," Fox News, 04/03/12, http://nation.foxnews.com/president-obama/2012/04/03/real-obama-betrayaing-israel.
25. Joel Rosenberg, "War This Summer," Joel C. Rosenberg's Blog, 04/16/12, http://flashtrafficblog.wordpress.com/2012/04/16/war-this-summer-israel-tv-network-reports-the-moment-of-truth-is-near/.
26. Ibid.
27. Greg Tipper, "Israeli TV Report Shows Air Force Gearing Up for Iran Attack," Times of Israel, 04/15/12, http://www.timesofisrael.com/iaf-plans-for-iran-attack/.
28. Rosenberg.
29. Reuters, "China Makes Veiled Warning to North Korea Not to Carry Out Nuclear Test," 04/25/12, http://www.reuters.com/article/2012/04/25/us-korea-north-china-idUSBRE83O09220120425. My thanks for the source to Jonathan Stettin.

30. Ben Shapiro, "Obama White House Fundraises for Anti-Christian Bully Savage," Breitbart.com, 04/29/12, http://www.breitbart.com/Big-Government/2012/04/29/Obama-Administration-Dan-Savage.
31. William T. James, ed., *Prophecy at Ground Zero* (Starburst, 2002).
32. Eric King, "Billionaire Hugo Salinas Price—Elites Plan to Control the World," KingWorld News-Blog, 05/03/12, http://kingworldnews.com/kingworldnews/KWN_DailyWeb/Entries/2012/5/3_Billionaire_Hugo_Salinas_Price_-_Elites_Plan_to_Control_the_World.html.
33. Staff, "PM: Yielding Temple Mount Would Be Fatal Mistake," *Jerusalem Post*, 05/21/12.
34. "13 Bound Bodies Found in Eastern Syria," UPI.com, 05/30/12, http://www.upi.com/Top_News/US/2012/05/30/UPI-NewsTrack-TopNews/UPI-19271338393600/.
35. Ibid.
36. Alan Franklin, "Big Brother Is Watching," in Terry James, ed., *The Departure: God's Next Catastrophic Intervention into Earth's History* (Crane, MO: Defender, 2010).
37. Vanessa Allen, "Software Giants Will Use Military-Grade Cameras to Take Powerful Satellite Images," Campaign for Liberty, 06/11/12, http://www.campaignforliberty.org/members-posts/beware-the-spy-in-the-sky-after-those-street-view-snoopers-google-and-apple-use-planes-that-can-film-you-sunbathing-in-your-back-garden/.
38. Wilfred Hahn, "The Bible on the Next World Leader," *Eternal Value Review*, www.eternalvalue.com; see also, Newest Articles, raptureready.com.
39. Bill Gertz, "U.S. Concerned Israel May Launch Attacks on Syrian WMD Sites," Associated Press, Rapture Ready News 06/24/12.
40. Terry James, "End of Days," Rapture Ready, http://www.raptureready.com/terry/end_of_days.html.
41. Ben Nuckols, "2 Million without Power as East Coats Temperatures Top 100," Associated Press, San Jose Mercury News, 07/02/12, http://www.mercurynews.com/nation-world/ci_20990988/2-million-without-power-east-coast-temperatures-top.
42. Executive Order, "Assignment of National Security and Emergency Preparedness Communications Functions," The White House, 06/06/12, http://www.whitehouse.gov/the-press-office/2012/07/06/executive-order-assignment-national-security-and-emergency-preparedness-.
43. Jaikumar Vijayan, "White House Order on Emergency Communications Riles Privacy Group," Computer World, 07/10/12, http://www.computerworld.com/s/article/9228950/White_House_order_on_emergency_communications_riles_privacy_group.
44. Ibid.
45. Neil Cavuto, "Your World Cavuto," Fox News, 07/23/12, http://www.foxnews.com/on-air/your-world-cavuto/2012/07/23/cavuto-gun-violence-isnt-unique-us.

46. Mark Weiss, "Israel Demands Nuclear Ultimatum for Iran," Telegraph, 08/13/12, http://www.telegraph.co.uk/news/worldnews/middleeast/iran/9471079/Israel-demands-nuclear-ultimatum-for-Iran.html.
47. "Israel Tests SMS Missile Alerts as Iran Chatter Grows," Daily Star, Lebanon, 08/12/12, http://www.dailystar.com.lb/News/Middle-East/2012/Aug-12/184355-israel-tests-sms-missile-alerts-as-iran-chatter-grows.ashx#axzz34wPqIDwA.
48. Yaakov Lappin, "Talk of Military Strike 'Makes Tehran Nervous,'" Post/Reuters, 08/13/12.
49. "Germany Returning to Deutsche Mark?" SilverDoctors, 08/18/12, http://www.silverdoctors.com/germany-returning-to-deutsche-mark-e-sculpture-removed-from-frankfurt-intl-airport/.
50. Ambrose Evans-Pritchard, "Finland Prepares for Break-up of Eurozone," Telegraph, 08/16/12.
51. Ibid.
52. Maj. Gen. Jerry Curry, USA (Ret.), "Who Does the Government Intend to Shoot?" *Daily Caller*, 08/17/12.
53. Ibid.
54. "Iran Commander Warns Israel, U.S. against Attack," *USA Today*, 09/17/12, http://usatoday30.usatoday.com/news/world/story/2012/09/17/iran-commander-warns-israel-us-against-attack/57788776/1. Thanks to Jonathan Stettin for the article.
55. *London Times*.
56. Andrew Carey and Masoud Popalzai, "Suicide Attack Kills 12 in Afghanistan," Dallas Weekly, 09/18/12, http://www.dallasweekly.com/news/international/article_a1104222-01a5-11e2-857b-001a4bcf6878.html.
57. Bruno Waterfield, "Václav Klaus Warns that the Destruction of Europe's Democracy May Be in Its Final Phase," Prague, 09/24/12.
58. Alex Newman, "Swiss, Swedes Shine Amidst European Calamity," WND, 09/29/12, http://www.wnd.com/2012/09/swiss-swedes-shine-amidst-european-calamity/.
59. Doug Book, "Will Obama Betray the U.S. in October Surprise Deal with Iran?" Western Journalism, 10/06/12, http://www.westernjournalism.com/will-obama-betray-the-u-s-in-october-surprise-deal-with-iran/.
60. Ambrose Evans Prichard, "IMF's Epic Plan to Conjure away Debt and Dethrone Bankers," Telegraph, 10/22/12, http://www.telegraph.co.uk/finance/comment/9623863/IMFs-epic-plan-to-conjure-away-debt-and-dethrone-bankers.html.
61. "Franklin's Appeal for Prayer at the Constitutional Convention, 1787." WallBuilders, http://www.wallbuilders.com/libissuesarticles.asp?id=98.
62. CBSDC/AP, "Turkish PM: 'Israel a Terrorist State'" WND, 11/19/12, http://www.wnd.com/2012/11/turkish-pm-israel-a-terrorist-state/.
63. "U.S. Tries Behind Scenes to End Israel-Hamas Warfare as Egypt Hosts Cease-fire Talks," nydailynews.com. My thanks to Jonathan Stettin.

64. "Obama Warns al-Assad against Chemical Weapons, Declares 'the World is Watching,'"CNN, 12/03/12, http://www.cnn.com/2012/12/03/world/meast/syria-civil-war/.
65. 2012endofdays.org.
66. "India Gang-Rape Victim Dies in Singapore," Aljazeera, Reuters, 12/12/12, http://www.aljazeera.com/news/asia/2012/12/20121228215753910399.html.
67. "Planned Parenthood Record Numbers, Taxpayer Funding and Abortions," Inquisitr, 01/08/13, http://www.inquisitr.com/473890/planned-parentohood-record-numbers-taxpayer-funding-and-abortions/#e5UtrxaaeDvk hie3.99.
68. Ibid.
69. Franklin Graham, "Fiscal Cliff? What about Our Spiritual Cliff?"Billy Graham Evangelistic Association, 12/27/12, http://billygraham.org/story/fiscal-cliff-what-about-our-spiritual-cliff/comment-page-6/.
70. Ibid.
71. David Horowitz, "A Different Israel after January 22," Times of Israel, 01/15/13.
72. Jeffrey Goldberg, "Obama: 'Israel Doesn't Know What Its Best Interests Are,'" Bloomberg, 01/14/13, http://www.bloomberg.com/news/2013-01-14/what-obama-thinks-israelis-don-t-understand-.html.
73. Ibid.
74. Wilfred Hahn, "Rebuilding on Weak Foundations," Eternal Value Review, February 2013, http://www.eternalvalue.com/adownload/EVR_02_2013_WEB.pdf.
75. Ibid., "Mephistopheles & the Global Monetary Magician, Eternal Value Review."
76. "Peres: Two States Solution Agreed Beginning for Peace," Israel News, March 12, 2013.
77. Thomas Sowell, "Can It Happen Here?" www.townhall.com, 03/26/13, p. 1.
78. Tom Parfitt, "Russia's Putin in Surprise Support for Cypress Bailout," Telegraph, 03/25/13, http://www.telegraph.co.uk/finance/financialcrisis/9952952/Russias-Putin-in-surprise-support-for-Cyprus-bailout.html#mm_hash.
79. Michael Gryboski,"Fla. University Puts 'Stomp on Jesus' Professor on Administrative Leave," Christian Post, 04/01/13, http://www.christianpost.com/news/fla-university-puts-stomp-on-jesus-professor-on-administrative-leave-93009/#bGGbBz5MwzVTh5fi.99.
80. Jack Minor, "Christians Targeted ahead of Muslim Brotherhood, Al-Qaida, KKK," WND, 04/09/13.
81. Jeannie DeAngelis, "Kermit Gosnell: Secret Hero of the Left," American Thinker, 04/16/13, http://www.americanthinker.com/2013/04/kermit_gosnell_secret_hero_of_the_left.html.
82. "A Day of Terror: Bush's Remarks to the Nation on the Terrorist Attacks," New York Times, 09/12/01, http://www.nytimes.com/2001/09/12/us/a-day-of-terror-bush-s-remarks-to-the-nation-on-the-terrorist-attacks.html.

83. "President Bush on the Middle East," PBS Newshour, 04/04/02, http://www.pbs.org/newshour/updates/white_house-jan-june02-bush_04-04/.
84. Condoleezza Rice, American Jewish Committee's 96th Annual Meeting Highlights, http://www.ajc.org/site/apps/nlnet/content3.aspx?c=ijITI2PHKoG&b=851489&ct=1118851.
85. Merle David Kellerhals Jr., "Clintin: U.S. Remains Engaged in Middle East Peace Efforts," IIP Digital, US Embassy, 12/01/12, http://iipdigital.usembassy.gov/st/english/article/2012/12/20121201139429.html#axzz36LnkLwDn.
86. "Remarks of President Barack Obama to the People of Israel," Jerusalem National Convention Center, Jerusalem, 03/21/13, http://www.whitehouse.gov/the-press-office/2013/03/21/remarks-president-barack-obama-people-israel.
87. Sinem Tezyapar, "New Muslim Vision: Rebuilding Solomon's Temple Together," The Jewish Press, 03/12/13, http://www.jewishpress.com/indepth/opinions/a-new-muslim-vision-rebuilding-solomons-temple-together/2013/03/12/0/?print.
88. Frederik Pleitgen, "Attack on Military Site Was a 'Declaration of War' by Israel," CNN, 05/06/13, http://www.cnn.com/2013/05/05/world/meast/syria-violence/.
89. Reuters, 05/21/13.
90. For those who aren't familiar with what I term my "HeavenVision," I invite you to look into the archives of the "Newest Articles" at www.raptureready.com and read my article of the same title. For an even deeper review of what happened on that day, my book *HeavenVision: Glimpses into Glory* is available at http://www.amazon.com/Heaven-Vision-Glimpses-Into-Glory-ebook/dp/B00B0JBD2Y/ref=sr_1_1?ie=UTF8&qid=1404943697&sr=8-1&keywords=HeavenVision+Glimpses.
91. Sheryl Gay Stolberg, "Obama's Views on Gay Marriage 'Evolving,'" *New York Times,* 06/18/11, http://www.nytimes.com/2011/06/19/us/politics/19marriage.html?_r=3&.
92. Adolf Hitler, from a speech delivered on 6 November 1933.
93. "Clinton Speaks at Shimon Peres' 90th birthday Event, Urges 2-State Plan," UPI, 06/18/13, UPI.com.
94. From Ben Franklin's speech on June 28, 1787, Constitutional Convention, at eighty-one years of age. My thanks to Bill Federer's American Minute, June 28, 2013.
95. Ibid.
96. John Bingham, *Telegraph*.
97. Mandel Ngan, "Kerry Says Israel, Palestinians Laid Groundwork for New Peace Talks," World News, AP/Reuters.
98. "Obama Urges Netanyahu to Resume Peace Talks," www.israelnationalnews.com, Rapture Ready News, 07/19/13.
99. Maayana Miskin, "Feiglin Declares 'Time to Flood the Temple Mount,'" Inside Israel, Israel National News.
100. Maayana Miskin, "Muslim Anger over Virtual 'Third Temple,'" Inside Israel, Israel National News.

101. Colin Flaherty, "Man in Coma after Black Mob of 50 Pummels Him," WND, 08/11/13.
102. Herb Kinon, "PM: Israel's 'Finger on the Pulse' of Syria Developments, if Necessary, Will Also Be 'On the Trigger,'" JPost, Israel News.
103. Shepard Ambellas, "New Police Toy Resembling 'Ray Gun' Can Disable Threatening Vehicles Via EMP," Intellihub News, 09/16/13.
104. Lazar Berman, "Troops Clash with Palestinians on Temple Mount," Times of Israel, 09/25/13.
105. "Iranian FM: We Have Seen Nothing But Lies from Netanyahu," JPost, Israel News, 10/1/13.
106. Access the archived radio programs at www.swrc.com.
107. Http://www.usatoday.com/story/theoval/2013/10/02/obama-pope-francis-cnbc-abortion-gay-rights/2911067/.
108. "'Israel Will Attack Iran if You Sign the Deal,' French MP Told Fabius," Times of Israel, 11/12/13.
109. Ryan Jones, "US, Jordan Agree: Israel Should Control Jordan Valley," Israel Today, 12/09/13.